AMERICAN CAR SPOTTER'S GUIDE
1920-1939

TAD BURNESS

Motorbooks International
Publishers & Wholesalers Inc

Library of Congress Cataloging in Publication Data

Burness, Tad, 1933–
    American car spotter's guide, 1920–1939.

    1. Automobiles, American.   2. Automobiles—Pictorial
works.   I. Title.
TL23.B77   629.22'22'0973   75-22366
ISBN 0-87938-026-8 pbk.

7 8 9 10

PREFACE

In the 1940-1965 edition of *American Car Spotter's Guide,* I refer to automobiles as "four-wheeled friends." One may laugh at this analogy, but in many ways old cars are like old friends. Surely you remember your first car with fondness, even if it was a klunker.

My first car was a 1935 DeSoto Airstream sedan. It was already old and tired when I saw it advertised at the bottom of a newspaper's classified column of low-priced 'transportation specials' — FREE. Even though I was not yet sixteen, I still could hardly believe that any car lot would give away its merchandise. A trip verified the ad. The car was free; but to be awarded to the winner of a straw drawing contest. My straw was a loser but a friend drew the right one — the car was mine. And with a total expenditure of fifteen dollars I was on wheels!

During the years that followed, I bought many other old cars, mostly from the twenties and thirties. These years were, to many, the most fascinating era in automotive history. There are many cars which have been forgotten but now are able to live again in this book.

A considerable amount of information and technical detail has been included with the pictures to help you identify and familiarize yourself with each model. Your personal favorites should be here, along with pictures of many hundreds of cars both well-known and obscure. The book also includes an alphabetical listing of lesser-known marques, some of which were never more than promises to stockholders.

A great deal of this book's pictures are original illustrations or photos from old catalogs or advertisements. Some are original factory photos and others were drawn by me, with just a few photos of restored cars — sometimes even a professionally restored car carries equipment that is not authentic.

Work on this book took more than a year, with much effort made to assure maximum accuracy. The most common problem was the occasional disagreement between reference sources — technical details which could not be verified are omitted. In compiling this material I had a great deal of kind help and cooperation, and it is with much gratitude that I direct the reader's attention to the Acknowledgements.

An update on my Introduction to the 1940-1965 *Car Spotter:* As promised, two-thirds of the book's royalties are being used for the care of orphaned and neglected children, through contributions to two church-sponsored children's group homes.

I welcome any questions or comments from readers of this book. Inquiries accompanied with a self-addressed, stamped envelope sent to me in care of the publisher will be personally answered.

Tad Burness
San Jose, California

ACKNOWLEDGEMENTS

I am very grateful to my wife and daughter for their patience with me while I was involved with this book.

My special thanks go to Keith Marvin for his help in compiling a list of many of the forgotten and unsuccessful cars of the twenties. Rare cars of the twenties are his specialty!

Also, special thanks are due to Walter F. 'Frank' Robinson, Jr., who was kind enough to make many library trips to photocopy pages from early automotive journals. I reimbursed him for a part of his costs, but he wouldn't accept a cent for all his time, effort and postage expenses.

Thanks are due to the following individuals for pictures, catalogs or technical details: Bill Adams, David Allen, Roger Allen, Ray E. Amundsen, Warren Baier, Swen H. Carlson, Will Carter, Mike Concordia, John A. Conde, Howard DeSart, Jim Evans, Fred K. Fox, R. C. Freitag, Norm Frey, Bruce Gilbert, Percy R. Gilbert, Dick Grove, Phil Hall, Stanley Hanenkratt, David Lindsay Heggie, Larry C. Holian, Dr. Earl G. Huwatschek, C. E. Jones, Mike Lamm, June Larson, Dick Laue, Scott Lewandoske, William B. Lewis, Larry W. Mauck, John B. McKean, Carl Mendoza, Al Michaelian, Elsa Montgomery, H. Morrison, Harold C. Nauman, Al Newman, Doug O'Connell, Mark Oppat, Everette J. Payette, Raymond B. Petersen, Isadore Rabinovitz, Evan L. Richards, Fred H. Rust, B. F. Schroeder, Wayne Sisk, Kirk Slater, Paul A. Stover,

Tom Terhune, Walt Thayer, Bruce Thompson, R. J. Walton, Gates Willard, Ken Wilson, Kenneth 'Butch' Wilson, and R. A. Wawrzyniak.

Thanks are due as well to the following corporations and organizations for either making little-known facts public or for making direct contributions of pictures and/or information: Airflow Club of America, American Motors Corp., Antique Automobile Club of America, Chrysler Corp., Contemporary Historical Vehicle Assn., DeSoto Club of America, Automotive History Collection-Detroit Public Library, Ford Motor Company, General Motors Corp., Harrah's Automobile Collection (and Jim Edwards), Horseless Carriage Club, Society of Automotive Historians, Studebaker Driver's Club, Veteran Motor Car Club of America, Willys-Knight Registry and the W.P.C./Chrysler Product Restorer's Club.

CONTENTS

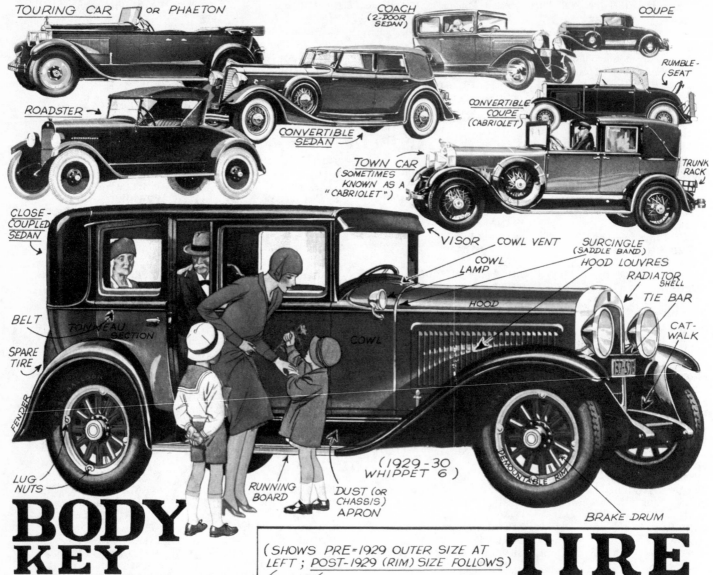

TOURING CAR OR PHAETON

COACH (2-DOOR SEDAN)

COUPE

ROADSTER →

RUMBLE-SEAT

CONVERTIBLE SEDAN

CONVERTIBLE COUPE (CABRIOLET)

TOWN CAR (SOMETIMES KNOWN AS A "CABRIOLET")

TRUNK RACK

CLOSE-COUPLED SEDAN

VISOR   COWL VENT   SURCINGLE (SADDLE BAND)

COWL LAMP   HOOD LOUVRES

RADIATOR SHELL

TIE BAR

HOOD

CAT-WALK

BELT

TONNEAU SECTION

COWL

SPARE TIRE

FENDER

137-571H

LUG NUTS

RUNNING BOARD

DUST (OR CHASSIS) APRON

(1929-30 WHIPPET 6)

DEMOUNTABLE RIM

BRAKE DRUM

BODY KEY

TIRE KEY

(SHOWS PRE=1929 OUTER SIZE AT LEFT ; POST-1929 (RIM) SIZE FOLLOWS)

25 × 3.75	= 3.75 × 18	30 × 4.50	= 4.50 × 21	31 × 7.00	= 7.00 × 17		
28 × 3.00	22"	30 × 4.75	4.75 × 21	31 × 7.50	7.50 × 17		
28 × 4.40	4.75 × 20	30 × 4.95	5.00 × 21	32 × 4	24"		
28 × 4.75	4.75 × 19	30 × 5.00	5.00 × 20	32 × 4½	23"		
28 × 5.25	5.25 × 18	30 × 5.25	5.25 × 20	32 × 5.00	5.00 × 22	33 × 6.75	7.00 × 21
28 × 5.50	5.50 × 18	30 × 5.50	5.50 × 20	32 × 5.77	6.00 × 22	33 × 7.00	7.00 × 19
29 × 4.40	4.40 × 21	30 × 5.77	6.00 × 20	32 × 6.00	6.00 × 20	33 × 7.50	7.50 × 19
29 × 4.50	4.50 × 20	30 × 6.00	6.00 × 18	32 × 6.20	6.50 × 20	34 × 4	26"
29 × 4.75	4.75 × 20	30 × 6.20	6.50 × 18	32 × 6.50	6.50 × 20	34 × 4½	25"
29 × 4.95	5.00 × 20	30 × 6.50	6.50 × 18	32 × 6.75	7.00 × 20	34 × 6.00	6.00 × 22
29 × 5.00	5.00 × 19	30 × 6.75	7.00 × 18	32 × 7.00	7.00 × 18	34 × 7.00	7.00 × 20
29 × 5.25	5.25 × 19	31 × 4.95	5.00 × 22	32 × 7.50	7.50 × 18	35 × 5	25"
29 × 5.50	5.50 × 19	31 × 5.00	5.00 × 21	33 × 4	25"	35 × 6.00	6.00 × 23'
29 × 6.00	6.00 × 17	31 × 5.25	5.25 × 21	33 × 4½	24"	35 × 7.00	7.00 × 21
29 × 6.50	6.50 × 17	31 × 6.00	6.00 × 19	33 × 5.77	6.00 × 23	36 × 4	28"
		31 × 6.20	6.50 × 19	33 × 6.00	6.00 × 21	36 × 4½	27"
30 × 3.00	24"	31 × 6.50	6.50 × 19	33 × 6.20	6.50 × 21	37 × 5	27"
30 × 3½	23"	31 × 6.75	7.00 × 19	33 × 6.50	6.50 × 21	38 × 4½	29"

ACE
(1920-1922)

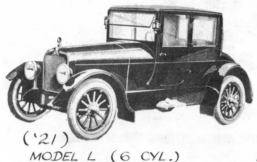

('21)
MODEL L (6 CYL.)

APEX MOTOR CORP., YPSILANTI, MICH.
USED 4-CYL. GRAY-BELL OR
6-CYL. HERSCHELL-SPILLMAN
AND CONTINENTAL ENGINES.

BECAME A PART OF AMERICAN
MOTOR TRUCK CO., NEWARK, OHIO.

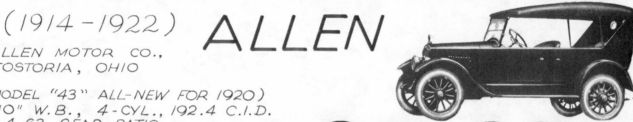

(1914-1922) # ALLEN

ALLEN MOTOR CO.,
FOSTORIA, OHIO

(MODEL "43" ALL-NEW FOR 1920)
110" W.B., 4-CYL., 192.4 C.I.D.
4.63 GEAR RATIO
32 × 4" TIRES

20-22 MODEL "43"

AMCO (1920)

AMERICAN MOTORS, INC., N.Y.C.
with 4 CYL. G.B. and S. ENGINE
DESIGNED FOR EXPORT ONLY
RIGHT HAND DRIVE AVAILABLE
114" wheelbase

AMERICAN

AMERICAN MOTORS CORPORATION
Factory and General Offices: Plainfield, N.J.
AMERICAN SOUTHERN MOTORS CORPORATION,
Greensboro, N. C.

(1916-1924)

20

(DRUM HEADLIGHTS
and NICKEL TRIM IN '23)

WITH HERSCHELL-SPILLMAN
6-CYL. ENGINE

(NO RADICAL
CHANGES FOR 1920,
BUT COLUMBIA
REAR AXLE IS NEW.)

7

AMERICAN STEAMER

22 (ONLY MODEL YEAR)

(1922 -1924) AMERICAN STEAM TRUCK CO., CHICAGO and ELGIN, ILL.

2 - CYLINDER COMPOUND ENGINE

ANDERSON 6
(1916 – 1926)
ANDERSON MOTOR CO., ROCK HILL, S.C.

The Anderson Patented Convertible Roadster

With tonneau open—a roomy touring car for five, with rear door and complete top.
With tonneau closed—a dashing roadster for two, with ample Yale lock luggage space.
Protected by patents granted and pending in the U. S. and foreign countries.

1920 "SERIES 30" HAS A NEW "7-R" CONTINENTAL ENGINE (6 CYLS., 224 C.I.D.) 4.50 GEAR RATIO

('20)

291-371 N Y 1922

120" W.B. (THROUGH '22) 55 H.P. @ 2600 RPM

20

2 SERIES IN 1923 : "41" = 114" W.B. 195.6 C.I.D. "6-Y" CONTINENTAL ENGINE
"50" = 122" W.B. 242.1 C.I.D. CONTINENTAL ENGINE

23

"J" SPT. TOUR.

21 "SERIES 40" (SAME SPECS. AS '20, CONT'D. 1922)

33 x 4

4.62 GEAR RATIO

32 x 4 ← "50"

"41" AND "50" SERIES CONTINUED, WITH 4.75 and 4.50 GEAR RATIOS

"41" WHEELBASE NOW 115" **24**

'25 "41" HAS 49 H.P. @ 2500 RPM

32 x 4

"41" = IMPROVED "7-U" 195.6 C.I.D. CONTINENTAL ENGINE
IN 1924, BALLOON TIRES OPTIONAL AT EXTRA COST

'25 "50" HAS 56 H.P. @ 2300 RPM "8-R" CONT. ENG. **24-26**

8

APPERSON BROS. AUTOMOBILE CO. (1902-1926)
Kokomo, Indiana

APPERSON

THE EIGHT WITH EIGHTY LESS PARTS

331.8 C.I.D. V-8

STANDARD MODEL

130" WHEELBASES
(8-CYL., THROUGH '26)

20

"ANNIVERSARY" MODEL (NOTE DIFFERENT RADIATOR DESIGN)

"ANNIVERSARY"

4.25 GEAR RATIOS

34 x 4 1/2

33 x 4

1922 = FIRST YEAR WITH SQUARE-BACK AND SQUARE-EDGED BODIES. DRUM HEADLIGHTS ON LATER MODELS OF "BEVERLY" SPORTSTER.

GEARSHIFT AND HAND-BRAKE CONTROLS MOVED AWAY FROM FLOOR IN 1923.

THE SELECTOR

EMERGENCY BRAKE CONTROL

APPERSON
Built on Knowledge

'23 INTERIOR

('24) (6)

21

331.8 C.I.D.
V-8 AVAILABLE THROUGH '25;
(REPLACED BY LYCOMING 276 C.I.D., 65-H.P. STRAIGHT-8 FOR '25-26)

23

NEW 207.1 C.I.D.
SIX ALSO AVAIL.

BALLOON TIRES AND 4-WHEEL BRAKES OPTIONAL

'25 CLOSED CARS SIMILAR, BUT HAVE VENTILATING EAVES. 6, 8, V-8 IN '25.)

ARGONNE FOUR

ARGONNE MOTOR CAR CO., JERSEY CITY, N.J.
(1919* – 1920)

*(ALL CARS 1920 MODELS)

128" WHEELBASE, 32 x 4 TIRES, 12-VOLT ELECTRICAL SYSTEM

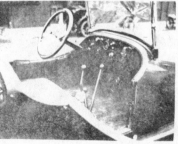

DUESENBERG-DESIGNED "OWN" 4-CYL. ENGINE

(3 3/4" x 5 1/8" BORE + STROKE)

9

AUBURN Beauty·SIX

AUBURN AUTOMOBILE COMPANY, Auburn, Indiana

(1900 – 1937)*

*– 1936 MODEL IS
FINAL AUBURN

"BEAUTY SIX"
DESIGNATION
RETAINED THROUGH
1922.

BLACK HARD-RUBBER (METAL-BOUND)
OUTSIDE DOOR HANDLES REPLACE BRIGHT METAL
TYPE IN 1922.

(DRUM HEADLIGHTS IN 1922)

19-22

33 × 4

"6-39" HAS 120" W.B., 224 C.I.D. 6-CYL. CONTINENTAL ENGINE, 4.66 GEAR RATIO
(1920) "6-51" IS 1922 MODEL WITH 121" W.B., 5.00 GEAR RATIO; "8-R" REPLACES "7-R"
CONTINENTAL ENGINE IN
LATER MODELS.

NEW MODELS ON JAN. 1, 1923, BUT "6-51"
STILL AVAILABLE UNTIL 3-23.

"6-43" HAS 114" W.B.,
195.6 C.I.D. CONTINENTAL "6-Y"
ENGINE   31 × 4 TIRES
SAME SIZE "7-U" CONTINENTAL
ENGINE IN 1924, STARTS
9-1-23.

23-24

"6-43"
AND
"6-63"
(6 CYL.)

"6-63" HAS 122" W.B.,
248.9 C.I.D. AUBURN O.H.V.
ENGINE.* 32 × 4½ TIRES

*- Weidely spec.

EARLIEST 1925 MODELS
(9-24 to 12-24) (8 CYL.)
SIMILAR IN STYLE.
(6 CYL. CONTINUED)

"6-43"

4.63 GEAR RATIO ('24)
"6-43" (1924) FIRST YEAR
WITH CHAIN CHECKS ON
DOORS.

"6-43" "ENGLISH COACH"
OFFERED '24 - EARLY '25.

10

"SPORT CAR" ("6-63")

AUBURN

8-88 ROADSTER

COMPLETELY
RESTYLED
EARLY IN 1925.

25-27

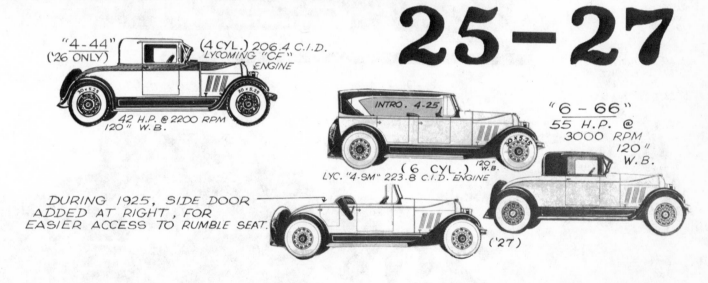

"4-44" (4 CYL.) 206.4 C.I.D.
('26 ONLY) LYCOMING "CF" ENGINE

42 H.P. @ 2200 RPM
120" W.B.

INTRO. 4-25

"6-66"
55 H.P. @
3000 RPM
120"
W.B.

(6 CYL.)
LYC. "4-SM" 223.8 C.I.D. ENGINE
120" W.B.

('27)

DURING 1925, SIDE DOOR
ADDED AT RIGHT, FOR
EASIER ACCESS TO RUMBLE SEAT.

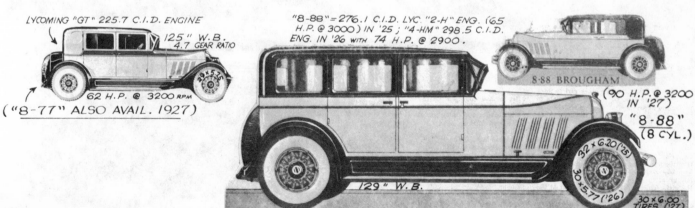

LYCOMING "GT" 225.7 C.I.D. ENGINE

125" W.B.
4.7 GEAR RATIO

62 H.P. @ 3200 RPM

("8-77" ALSO AVAIL. 1927)

"8-88"=276.1 C.I.D. LYC. "2-H" ENG. (65
H.P. @ 3000) IN '25; "4-HM" 298.5 C.I.D.
ENG. IN '26 WITH 74 H.P. @ 2900.

8-88 BROUGHAM

(90 H.P. @ 3200
IN '27)

"8-88"
(8 CYL.)

32 x 6.20 ('25)
30 x 5.77 ('26)
30 x 6.00
TIRES ('27)

129" W.B.

AUBURN

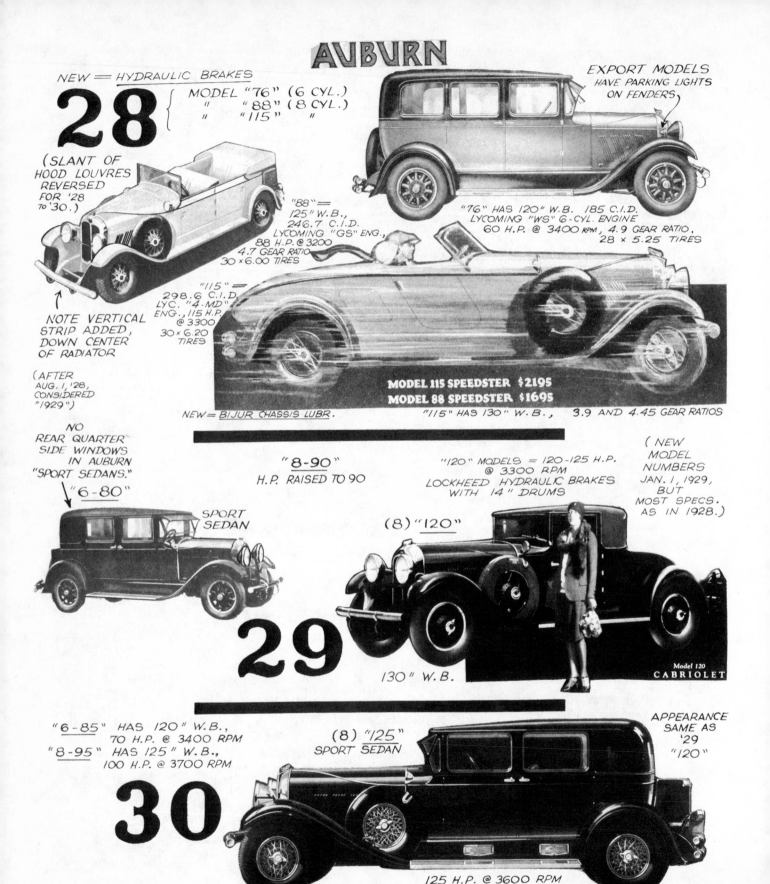

NEW = HYDRAULIC BRAKES

28
MODEL "76" (6 CYL.)
" "88" (8 CYL.)
" "115" "

(SLANT OF HOOD LOUVRES REVERSED FOR '28 TO '30.)

EXPORT MODELS HAVE PARKING LIGHTS ON FENDERS

NOTE VERTICAL STRIP ADDED, DOWN CENTER OF RADIATOR

(AFTER AUG. 1, '28, CONSIDERED "1929")

"88" = 125" W.B., 246.7 C.I.D. LYCOMING "GS" ENG., 88 H.P.@3200 4.7 GEAR RATIO 30 x 6.00 TIRES

"115" = 298.6 C.I.D. LYC. "4-MD" ENG., 115 H.P. @ 3300 30 x 6.20 TIRES

"76" HAS 120" W.B. 185 C.I.D. LYCOMING "WS" 6-CYL. ENGINE 60 H.P. @ 3400 RPM, 4.9 GEAR RATIO, 28 x 5.25 TIRES

MODEL 115 SPEEDSTER $2195
MODEL 88 SPEEDSTER $1695

NEW = BIJUR CHASSIS LUBR.   "115" HAS 130" W.B.,   3.9 AND 4.45 GEAR RATIOS

NO REAR QUARTER SIDE WINDOWS IN AUBURN "SPORT SEDANS."

"6-80"

SPORT SEDAN

"8-90" H.P. RAISED TO 90

"120" MODELS = 120-125 H.P. @ 3300 RPM LOCKHEED HYDRAULIC BRAKES WITH 14" DRUMS

(NEW MODEL NUMBERS JAN. 1, 1929, BUT MOST SPECS. AS IN 1928.)

29
(8) "120"

130" W.B.

Model 120 CABRIOLET

"6-85" HAS 120" W.B., 70 H.P. @ 3400 RPM
"8-95" HAS 125" W.B., 100 H.P. @ 3700 RPM

(8) "125" SPORT SEDAN

APPEARANCE SAME AS '29 "120"

30
125 H.P. @ 3600 RPM

12

COMPLETELY RESTYLED
FOR 1931 !

AUBURN

('31½)   "8-98-A"

4.45
GEAR RATIO

126" W.B.
286.6 C.I.D. LYCOMING "GU"
STRAIGHT-8 ENGINE.
98 H.P. @ 3400 RPM
(THROUGH '32)

2-DOOR
BROUGHAM

31-32

"8-98" ONLY MODEL
AVAILABLE IN 1931.
IN 1932, A CHOICE OF
"8-100" OR "12-160."
"A" AFTER '32 MODEL NO.
DENOTES CUSTOM SERIES
WITH "DUAL RATIO" 2-SPEED
DIFFERENTIAL.

"8-100" HAS 4.7 GEAR RATIO,
127 OR 136"   6.00 × 17 TIRES IN 1932
W.B.

V-12 LYCOMING "BB" 391 C.I.D. ENGINE
160 H.P. @ 3400 RPM   132" W.B.
4 TO 1 GEAR RATIO

V-12 HAS "12"
ON BUMPER

V-12 (1932)

33   8   SPEEDSTER

V-12
"SALON" SERIES

13

AVBVRN

"850"

6-CYL. AUBURNS AVAILABLE AGAIN, FOR FIRST TIME SINCE '30.

119" W.B. "652"
85 H.P. @ 3500
4.60 GEAR RATIO

8

34

THIS NEW STYLING RETAINED JUST 1 YEAR.

1933 SALON-STYLE "12-165" CONTINUED INTO 1934.

COUPE

4.50 G.R. ON '35 "851"

35-36

6 OR 8 CYL.
120"   127"
W.B.   W.B.

4.44 G.R. ON 6

INTERIOR (COUPE)

WITH RIGID TOP FITTED TO OPEN-STYLE BODY.

"851" ('35) AND "852" ('36) HAVE 279.9 C.I.D. LYCOMING "GG" ENGINE, 115 H.P. @ 3600, 6.50 × 16 TIRES

'35 "653" and '36 (FINAL) "654" 6-CYL. MODELS HAVE 85 H.P. @ 3500 RPM, 209.9 C.I.D. LYCOMING "WF" ENGINE, 120" W.B.
5.50 × 17 TIRES ON '35 "653," 6.00 × 16 ON '36 "654"

SUPERCHARGED '36 "SC-852" HAS 150 H.P. @ 4000 RPM 4.08 GEAR RATIO ON '36 8s.

NO 1937 AUBURNS, BUT CORD V-8 and DUESENBERG 8 AVAIL. IN 1937 (FINAL YEAR.)

SPEEDSTER
← (8) →

REAR

14

AUSTIN 4

"BANTAM" CAR

(AFTER 1936, (ALSO KNOWN AS "AMERICAN BANTAM")

(BLT. 1930-1941 AT BUTLER, PA.)

(SLANTING WINDSHIELD and VERTICAL HOOD LOUVRES INTRODUCED FOR '33.)

V-WINDSHIELD ← ON ROADSTER SINCE '31

75" W.B. (THROUGH '41)

33-34

"2-75" SERIES

30-32

12½ H.P. @ 3000 RPM (THROUGH '31)

(1935 HAS SLANTING LOUVRES)

13 H.P. @ 3200 RPM (1932 THROUGH '36)

4 CYLS., 45.6 C.I.D.
5.25 GEAR RATIO (THROUGH '41)
3.75 × 18 TIRES (THROUGH '36)

39

"62"

37

38

"60"

20 H.P. @ 4000 RPM (THROUGH '39)

(DURING '39, HOOD LOUVRES SHORTENED, THEN ELIMINATED.)

By Bantam

BALBOA

BALBOA MOTOR CORP. FULLERTON, CALIF.

(1923 - 1925)

KESSLER STRAIGHT-8 ENGINE   178 C.I.D.
SUPERCHARGED   100 H.P. @ 4000 RPM

BAY STATE

R. H. LONG CO., FRAMINGHAM, MASS.

(1922 -1924)

(CONTINENTAL 6-CYL. ENGINE)

BEGGS

20

BEGGS MOTOR CAR CO., KANSAS CITY, MO.
(1918 -1923)
6-CYL. CONTINENTAL ENGINE

120" WHEELBASE

15

BELL

BELL MOTOR CAR CO., YORK, PA.
(1915 – 1921)

20-21

BIDDLE

BIDDLE MOTOR CAR
CO., PHILADELPHIA, PA.
(1915 – 1923)

121" W.B., 32 × 4" TIRES
4 - CYLINDER DUESENBERG or
BUDA ENGINE

4.5 GEAR RATIO

BIRCH   (1917 – 1923)

BIRCH MOTOR CARS, INC., CHICAGO
(SOLD BY MAIL ORDER, 4 and 6 CYL.)

"SUPER 4"   **20**

BIRMINGHAM

BIRMINGHAM MOTORS, JAMESTOWN, N.Y.
(1920 – 1924)

22
(ONLY YEAR MODEL
IN
PRODUCTION)

6 - CYL. CONTINENTAL "7-R" engine
124" W.B., 32 × 4 TIRES

WILSON BODY, MADE OF "HASKELITE"
PLYWOOD, COVERED WITH DUPONT FABRIKOID

4 - WHEEL
INDEPENDENT
SUSPENSION

BOUR – DAVIS (1915 – 1922)

BUILT AT CHICAGO, ILL.; SHREVEPORT, LA.; also DETROIT
(COMPANY CHANGED LOCATIONS, KNOWN AS BOUR-DAVIS CO.
AND ALSO AS LOUISIANA MOTOR CAR CO.)

125" WHEELBASE

20

NEW FOR 1920:
WESTINGHOUSE STARTING + LIGHTING,
13-DISC CLUTCH, AND NEW CARBURETOR.

224 C.I.D. CONTINENTAL
ENGINE, 4.75 GEAR RATIO

16

BREWSTER

21

(BREWSTER-KNIGHT)

BREWSTER + CO., LONG ISLAND CITY, N.Y.

(1915 - 1925)

"41" TOWN LANDAULETTE

4 - CYL. KNIGHT ENGINE

24

6 - PASS. DOUBLE ENCL. DRIVE

BREWSTER - FORD

(CUSTOM BODY ON FORD V-8 CHASSIS)

SPRINGFIELD MFG. CO., SPRINGFIELD, MASS.

(1934 TO 1936)

BRIGGS AND STRATTON

↙ 1 - CYLINDER AIR COOLED ENGINE

BRIGGS AND STRATTON, MILWAUKEE, WIS.

(1919 - 1923)

BRISCOE

BRISCOE MOTOR CORP., JACKSON, MICH.

(1914 - 1921)   (109" W.B.)

NEW "BEVEL-LINE" STYLING FOR 1920.

20-21

"4-34"

4 CYLS.

LATE '21 = NAME CHANGED TO EARL

4.18 GEAR RATIO, 31 x 4 TIRES

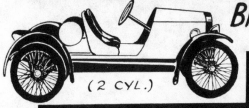

(2 CYL.)

BROOKE-SPACKE

(1920 - 1921)

SPACKE MACHINE and TOOL CO., INDIANAPOLIS, INDIANA

(1921 = MORE COMPLETE BODY)

BROOKS STEAMER

26

MFD. IN CANADA, 1923 - 1926. OPERATIONS MOVED TO BUFFALO, N.Y., 1926.

(FABRIC-COVERED BODY)

17

BRYAN STEAMER

BRYAN STEAM MOTORS, PERU, INDIANA
(1918 – 1923) (TOURING CARS ONLY)

BUICK

BUICK MOTOR COMPANY, FLINT, MICHIGAN
Division of General Motors Corporation
Canadian Factories: McLaughlin-Buick, Oshawa, Ontario

ESTABLISHED 1903; A
G.M. PRODUCT SINCE 1908.

4.0 GEAR RATIO

6 CYLINDERS OVERHEAD VALVES (241.6 C.I.D. THROUGH '23)

19-20

1922 CLOSED CARS HAVE HEATER.

21-22

1922 SIX and NEW FOUR AVAILABLE AUGUST, 1921.

4.08 G.R. ('21)

33 x 4

1922 GEAR RATIOS = 4.66 (4, THROUGH '23) 4.60 ; 4.90 (6)

TRUNK DETAILS

23

NEW COWL VENT

BUICK 4 HAS 170 C.I.D., 35 H.P.

"4-36" COUPE

"4-38" TOURING SEDAN → (2-DOOR COACH)

'23 HAS DRUM-TYPE LAMPS; ALUMINUM HOOD BEADING ON 6. 4

"6-45"

31 x 4

6

32 x 4

4.40 G.R. (6)

18

7 - PASS.

"6-54"

"6-50"

BUICK

4 (FINAL 4-CYL. BUICK)

NEW 4-WHEEL BRAKES

(FRONT BRAKE DETAILS)

"4-37" SEDAN

24

NEW STYLING, NEW RADIATOR DESIGN

"4-34" ROADSTER

"4-35" TOURING

"4-33" 4-PASS. COUPE

PAINTED RADIATOR SHELL ON 4-CYL. MODELS

$\frac{4}{6}$

6

HAS LONGER HOOD AND NICKEL-PLATED RADIATOR

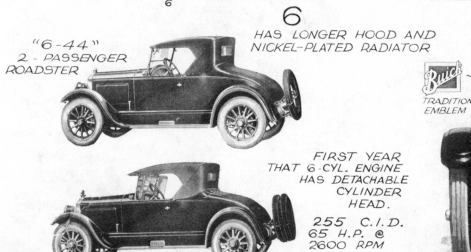

"6-44" 2-PASSENGER ROADSTER

Buick TRADITIONAL EMBLEM

FIRST YEAR THAT 6-CYL. ENGINE HAS DETACHABLE CYLINDER HEAD.

255 C.I.D. 65 H.P. @ 2600 RPM

"6-54" SPORT ROADSTER

BUICK
24
(CONT'D.)

"6-45" 5-PASS. TOURING

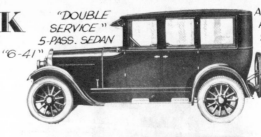
"DOUBLE SERVICE" 5-PASS. SEDAN
"6-41"
A LOW-PRICED SEDAN WITH SQUARE-EDGED REAR PANELS.

"6-49" 7-PASS. TOURING

"6-47" 5-PASS. SEDAN

"6-55" 4-PASS. SPORT TOURING

"6-50" 7-PASS. SEDAN

"6-48" 4-PASS. COUPE

"6-51" BROUGHAM

(EARLIEST '24 BROUGHAM HAS SEMI-RECTANGULAR-STYLE REAR QUARTER WINDOWS INSTEAD OF OVAL AS ILLUSTRATED.)

25

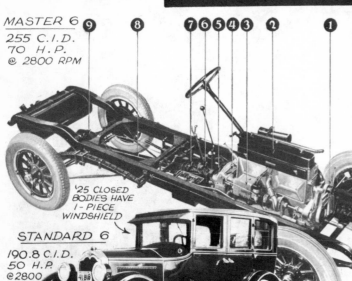

MASTER 6
255 C.I.D.
70 H.P.
@ 2800 RPM

'25 CLOSED BODIES HAVE 1-PIECE WINDSHIELD

STANDARD 6
190.8 C.I.D.
50 H.P.
@ 2800 RPM

ALL MODELS 6-CYLINDERS

WITH "SEALED CHASSIS"

NEW BALLOON TIRES. DUCO FINISH ON ALL MODELS BEGINNING JANUARY, 1925.

2-DOOR COACHES AVAILABLE AFTER NOV., '24.

Here are the vital points at which Buick engineering provides this extra protection:

❶ = FAN HUB
❷ = ENGINE
❸ = STARTER-GENERATOR (IN 1 UNIT)
❹ = FLYWHEEL
❺ = CLUTCH
❻ = TRANSMISSION
❼ = UNIVERSAL JOINT
❽ = TORQUE TUBE (ENCLOSING DRIVESHAFT)
❾ = DIFFERENTIAL

(32 × 5.77 TIRES ON MASTER 6)

"6-48" 4-PASS. COUPE (MASTER 6) WITH NEW OVAL QUARTER WINDOWS)

20

BUICK

STANDARD 6
207.1 C.I.D.
60 H.P. @ 2800 RPM
114 3/8" W.B.

MASTER 6
274.2 C.I.D.
75 H.P. @ 2800 RPM
120" OR 128" W.B.

26

(INTRODUCED AUG. 1, 1925)

CLOSED CARS WITH NEW DOUBLE-BEAD BELT MOLDINGS.

PUROLATOR OIL FILTER ON ALL MODELS.

"54-C" COUNTRY CLUB COUPE

MASTER 6

"27" SEDAN

STANDARD 6

"48" 4-PASS. COUPE

31 x 5.25 TIRES ON STANDARD, 33 x 6.00 " ON MASTER (THROUGH '28)

WHEN BETTER AUTOMOBILES ARE BUILT · BUICK WILL BUILD THEM

"128" HAS INSIDE WATER TEMPERATURE GAUGE AND ORNAMENTAL RADIATOR CAP.

ONE-PIECE WINDSHIELD ON OPEN CARS

SERIES # INDICATES WHEELBASE, EXCEPT "115" HAS 114½" W.B.

(STARTS AUG. 1, 1926)

27

"115" = 63 H.P.

"120," "128" = 77 H.P.

Body by Fisher

21

BUICK

ASSIST CORD

"115," "120" and
"128" SERIES AGAIN

(MINOR RESTYLING)

28

(MODELS AND
SPECS. SIMILAR
TO 1927)

"115" has
31 × 5.25 TIRES, 5.1 G.R.
"120" and "128"
have 33 × 6.00 TIRES, 4.9 G.R.

UPPER RADIATOR
PAN IS DEEPER
FOR 1928.

NEW
BOWL-SHAPED
HEADLIGHTS

IGNITION AND
STEERING LOCK

NEW
RADIATOR
MASCOT

WATER TEMP.
GAUGE ON
ALL 1928
MODELS.

STANDARD
GEARSHIFT
PATTERN
ADOPTED.

LANDAUS WITH
NEW STYLE
QUARTER
WINDOWS

The Silver Anniversary BUICK

29 (COMPLETELY RESTYLED)

(INTRODUCED SATURDAY, JULY 28, 1928)

4.9 GEAR RATIO ("116;") 4.8 ON OTHERS

SILVER ANNIVERSARY BUICK—FIVE PASSENGER SEDAN

29½ MODELS HAVE COLORFUL HUB CAPS OF NEW DESIGN (RED and BLACK, ON SILVER.)

EARLY TYPE HUB CAP (PLAINER STYLE)

"51" CLOSE-COUPLED SEDAN

BECAUSE OF ITS ODD, BULGING SIDE-PANELS, THE 1929 MODEL WAS SOON NICKNAMED "THE PREGNANT BUICK."

239.1 C.I.D., 74 H.P. @ 2800 OR 309.6 C.I.D. WITH 90½ H.P. @ 2800

new FUEL PUMP ON ALL '29 BUICKS.

"26"

"54-CC"

"20" SERIES 116" W.B.
40 " 121 "
50 " 129 "
30 x 5.50 OR
32 x 6.50 TIRES

NEW DASH HAS BLACK CIRCULAR GAUGES IN A ROW.

23

BUICK
(COMPLETELY RESTYLED)
('30 MODEL INTRO. JULY, 1929)

1930 – 6 CYL.
1931 – 8 CYL.

new "ROAD-SHOCK ELIMINATOR"
new NON-GLARE WINDSHIELD (SLANTED 7°)

VALVE·IN·HEAD
Buick
MOTOR·CARS

5.50 OR 6.50 × 19 TIRES

1930 INSTRUMENT PANEL

3 SERIES FOR '30 →	"40"	118" W.B.	80½ H.P.
	50	124	98
	60	132	"

NEW STRAIGHT-8 1931 ENGINES REPLACE ALL 1930 SIXES

30-31

1931 MODEL HAS ALL-NEW INSTRUMENT PANEL. →

FINAL BUICK ROADSTER

4 1931 BASIC MODEL SERIES

"50"	114" W.B.	77 H.P.	220.7 C.I.D.
60	118	90	272.6
80	124	104	344.8
90	132	"	"

TIRES = 5.25 × 18 (50,)
5.50 × 19 (60,)
OR 6.50 × 19 (80 and 90 SERIES)

1931 HAS SYNCHRO-MESH TRANSMISSION.

WINGED "8" → ON RADIATOR CAP OF 1931 MODEL.

24

NEW STYLE
SWEEP-HAND
SPEEDOMETER

32 BUICK
with
WIZARD CONTROL

SPEEDOMETER

DASH GAUGES
MOVED TO *LEFT* SIDE

DETAILS OF
FRONT
END

"50" HAS
230.4 c.i.d.,
78 H.P. @
3200 RPM,
114" W.B.
5.50 × 18 TIRES

"60" HAS
272.5 c.i.d.,
90 H.P. @
3000 RPM,
118" W.B.
6.00 × 18 TIRES

"80" AND "90" HAVE
344.7 c.i.d.,
104 H.P. @ 2900 RPM,
126" AND 134" W.B.
7.00 × 18 TIRES

H. P. INCREASED '33
(@ 3200 RPM)
TO 86 ("50",)
97 ("60",)
113 ("80","90")

NEW 6.00 × 17, 6.50 × 17, 7.00 × 17 TIRE SIZES ('33 ONLY)

WHEELBASES OF 119,127,130,138"

33

25

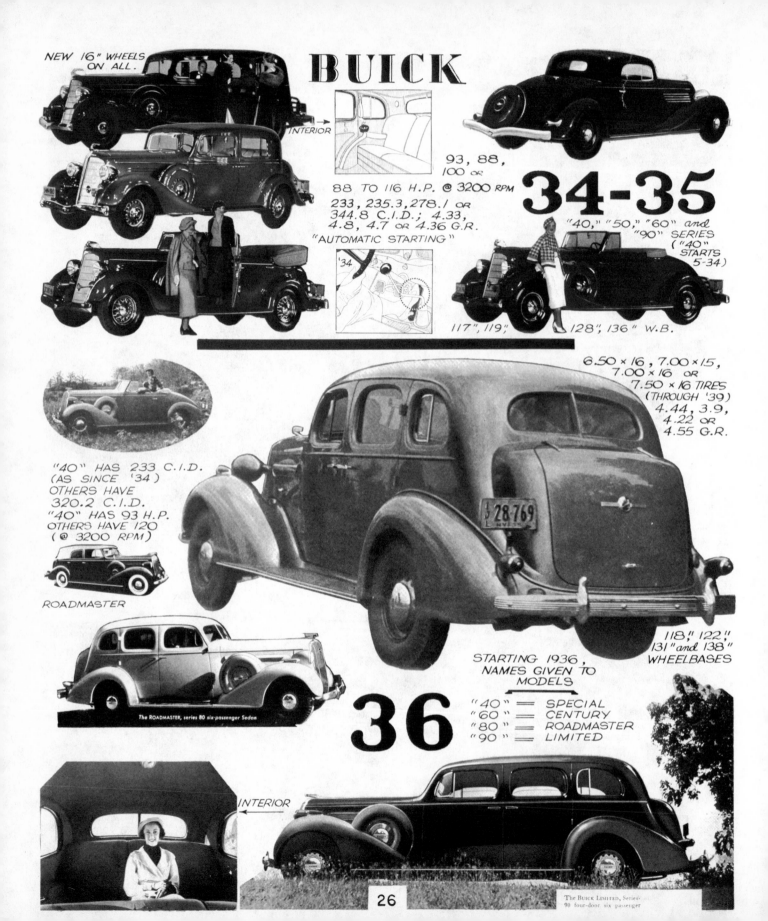

BUICK

NEW 16" WHEELS ON ALL.

INTERIOR →

34-35

93, 88, 100 or

88 TO 116 H.P. @ 3200 RPM

233, 235.3, 278.1 or
344.8 C.I.D.; 4.33,
4.8, 4.7 or 4.36 G.R.

"AUTOMATIC STARTING"

'34

"40," "50," "60" and "90" SERIES ("40" STARTS 5-34)

117", 119", 128", 136" W.B.

6.50 × 16, 7.00 × 15,
7.00 × 16 or
7.50 × 16 TIRES
(THROUGH '39)
4.44, 3.9,
4.22 or
4.55 G.R.

"40" HAS 233 C.I.D.
(AS SINCE '34)
OTHERS HAVE
320.2 C.I.D.
"40" HAS 93 H.P.
OTHERS HAVE 120
(@ 3200 RPM)

ROADMASTER

The ROADMASTER, series 80 six-passenger Sedan

118," 122"
131" and 138"
WHEELBASES

STARTING 1936,
NAMES GIVEN TO
MODELS

36

"40" = SPECIAL
"60" = CENTURY
"80" = ROADMASTER
"90" = LIMITED

INTERIOR →

The BUICK LIMITED, Series 90 four-door six passenger

BUICK

"SPECIAL" has 100 H.P. @ 248 C.I.D. 3200 RPM (THROUGH '49)

320.2 C.I.D. ON OTHERS (TO '52, EXCEPT "SUPER", WHICH STARTS '40.)

37

130 H.P. @ 3400 RPM ON "CENTURY 60" and up.

"LIMITED"

7.50 x 16

4.4, 3.9, 4.22 (1937 WHEELBASES: 122", 126", 131", 138") OR 4.62 G.R.

SPECIAL ══ 122" W.B. 107 H.P. @ 3400 RPM

CENTURY ══ 126" W.B. 141 H.P. @ 3600 RPM, AS ON LARGER MODELS.

ROADMASTER ══ 133" W.B.

LIMITED ══ 140" W.B.

(SAME FIGURES THROUGH '40, EXCEPT "SPECIAL" W.B.)

4.44, 3.9, 4.18 OR 4.56 G.R. (THROUGH '39)

"LIMITED" ←

SINCLAIR

"ROADMASTER"

38

DELCO-REMY IGN. (SINCE '27) FISHER BODIES, AS BEFORE

← DASH

39

DIRECTIONAL SIGNALS

"SPECIAL" WHEELBASE SHORTENED TO 120."

"LIMITEDS" have OLDER STYLE BODIES.

BUICK EIGHT

BUSH
(1916-1924)

BUSH MOTOR CO., CHICAGO

27

4 OR 6 CYLS.

LYCOMING, RUTENBER, OR CONTINENTAL ENGINES

('19-20)

"E.C. 4" has 192.4 C.I.D. LYCOMING ENGINE. "E.C. 6" has 230.1 C.I.D. RUTENBER ENGINE. BOTH have 116" W.B., 33 x 4 TIRES ('21 SPECIFICATIONS)

CADILLAC

DIVISION OF GENERAL MOTORS CORPORATION

(ESTABLISHED 1902; JOINED G.M. 1909)

V-8 ENGINE

20-21
TYPE 59

4-PASS. ('21)

35 x 5" TIRES IN 1920; 34 x 4½", 1921.

314.4 C.I.D. (1915 THROUGH '27)
60 H.P. @ 2700 RPM (TO '23)
125" OR 132" W.B. (THROUGH '21)

4.44 GEAR RATIO

'21 IS FINAL MODEL *with* TILTING STEER. WHEEL.

TRADITIONAL EMBLEM AND MOTTO

Standard of the World

4.5 *and* 2 OTHER GEAR RATIOS

STEERING-COLUMN QUADRANT REPLACED BY SMALLER FINGER-GRIPS FOR SPARK *and* THROTTLE CONTROLS. SUPPLEMENTARY TRANSMISSION LOCK.

22-23
TYPE 61

WITH
AMES CUSTOM BODY ('23)
(MOST BODIES BY FISHER, BUT IN CALIFORNIA, CUSTOM BODIES ARE AVAILABLE BY DON LEE.)

VICTORIA COUPE CONTINUED, *with* DOORS HINGED *at* REAR. NEW FOR 1922 IS 5-PASS. COUPE (ILLUSTRATED,) *with* DOORS HINGED AT FRONT, AND *with* LONGER CAB SECTION.

new '22 TYPE 61 STEERING WHEEL RIM, SPOKES, *and* HORN BUTTON *are* all made of WALNUT.

LARGER COWL VENT.

RADIATOR IS HIGHER FOR 1922.

132" W.B. ONLY
OPTIONAL GEAR RATIOS

33 x 5 TIRES (THROUGH '25)

NEW '22 "61" *has* DELCO SWITCHES AT CENTER OF DASH

33 x 5

new BAUSCH *and* LOMB OPTICAL LENSES

INTERIOR

SPEEDOMETER AND CLOCK

28

CADILLAC

V-63

STANDARD OF THE WORLD

5-PASSENGER SEDAN

NEW 5-PASS. LANDAU →

STANDARD OF THE WORLD

THE NEW V-63 SUBURBAN

DASH

24
NEW "V-63"

AS FITTED WITH DUAL SPARE TIRES

INTERNAL-EXPANDING FRONT-WHEEL BRAKES (EXTERNAL-CONTRACTING ON REAR WHEELS.)

72 H.P. @ 3000 RPM (THROUGH '25)

132" WHEELBASE

C A D I L L A C

25

V 63

COACH INTRO. JAN., 1925

STANDARD W.B. = 132"

* CUSTOM BUILT LINE " = 138"

* - aluminum bodies

4.91 GEAR RATIO

FROM 1926 TO 1935,
MODEL NUMBER
INDICATES DISPL.
OF ENGINE, (EXCEPT
FOR FRACTION-OF-
INCH DIFFERENCES.)

26

33 × 6.75
BALLOON TIRES
(THROUGH '27)

"3I4" (INTRO. 7-30-25)

(3I4.4 C.I.D.)

87 H.P. @ 3000 RPM
(THROUGH '27)

VERTICAL
RADIATOR
SHUTTERS

S T A N D A R D · O F · T H E · W O R L D

(CUSTOM ROADSTER ON 132" W.B.)

HORN IS UNDER LEFT HEADLAMP

SINCE 1-26, CUSTOM
CLOSED MODELS HAVE THIS
TYPE OF WINDSHIELD.

50 BODY STYLES
AND TYPES ;
500 COLOR
AND UPHOLSTERY
COMBINATIONS !

4.91
GEAR
RATIO

27 (STARTS 7-15-26)

NEW 1-PIECE
FRONT FENDERS

"3I4"

BATTERY and
TOOL BOX CONCEALED
BEHIND DUST SHIELD

7-PASS.
CUSTOM SUBURBAN

LIGHT SWITCH ON STEERING QUADRANT

STARTING 1-27, DISTRIBUTOR
MOVED, FROM REAR, TO FRONT, OF ENGINE.

CADILLAC
DIVISION OF GENERAL MOTORS

4.75 GEAR RATIO

28

90 H.P. @ 3000

"341"
(-A)

32 × 6.75 TIRES

SMALL CIRCULAR GAUGES, FRAMED INDIVIDUALLY

140" WHEELBASE

(THROUGH '29)

SYNCHRO-MESH TRANSMISSION (NEW)

New Adjustable Front Seats

FISHER OR FLEETWOOD BODIES

7.00 × 20 TIRES

new FUEL PUMP INTRODUCED

"341-B"

29

H.P. RAISED TO 95 DURING 1929.

PARKING LIGHTS MOVED TO FRONT FENDERS

7-PASSENGER IMPERIAL

'30 has SLANTED, NON-GLARE WINDSHIELD

7.00 × 19 TIRES ON ALL 1930 MODELS.

V-8

7-PASS.

VACUUM TANK RETURNS (SOME MODELS)

30

5.08 GEAR RATIO

"353" (V-8) 95 H.P. @ 3000 RPM (THROUGH '31)

new FULL-LENGTH ROW OF HOOD LOUVRES (V-8)
V-8 CONTINUES 140" W.B. V8

V-16 INTERIOR

"452" (V-16)
452 C.I.D. (THROUGH '37)

SIXTEEN CYLINDERS V16

VACUUM BOOSTER BRAKES

(NEW)

185 H.P. @ 3400 RPM

7.00 × 19

4.39 GEAR RATIO

V-16 has VACUUM FUEL FEED

V-16 HAS 148" WHEELBASE
(THROUGH '31)

1930

31

CADILLAC

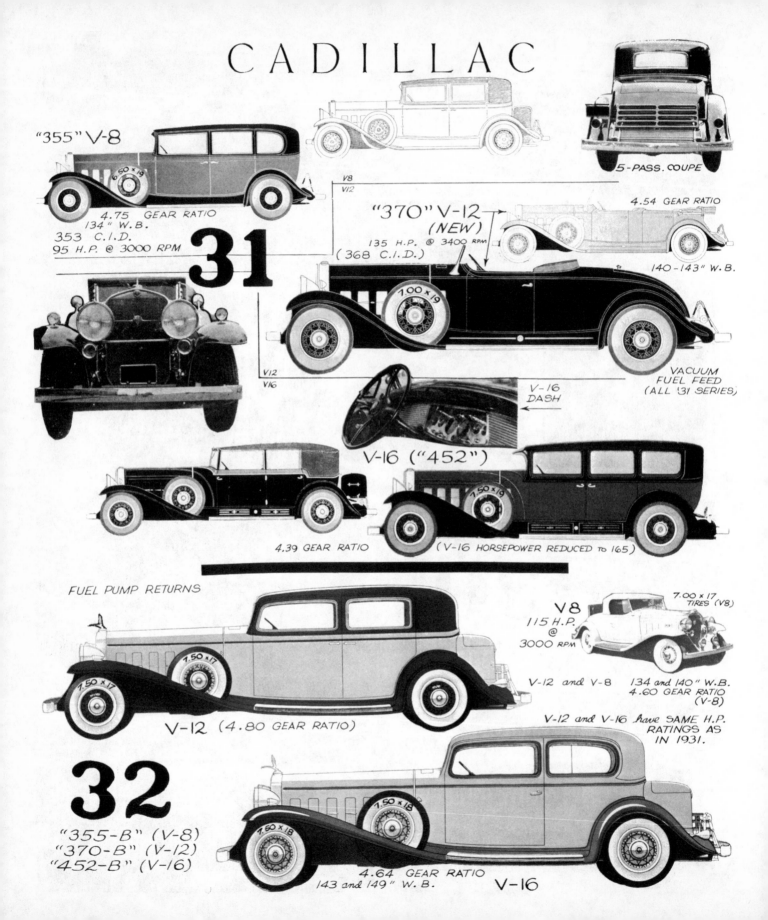

"355" V-8

4.75 GEAR RATIO
134" W.B.
353 C.I.D.
95 H.P. @ 3000 RPM

31

5-PASS. COUPE

V8
V12

"370" V-12
(NEW)
135 H.P. @ 3400 RPM
(368 C.I.D.)

4.54 GEAR RATIO

140 - 143" W.B.

V12
V16

VACUUM
FUEL FEED
(ALL '31 SERIES)

V-16
DASH

V-16 ("452")

4.39 GEAR RATIO

(V-16 HORSEPOWER REDUCED TO 165)

FUEL PUMP RETURNS

V8
115 H.P.
@
3000 RPM

7.00 x 17
TIRES (V8)

V-12 and V-8   134 and 140" W.B.
4.60 GEAR RATIO
(V-8)

V-12 (4.80 GEAR RATIO)

V-12 and V-16 have SAME H.P.
RATINGS AS
IN 1931.

32

"355-B" (V-8)
"370-B" (V-12)
"452-B" (V-16)

4.64 GEAR RATIO
143 and 149" W.B.   V-16

CADILLAC

33

"355-C" (V-8)
"370-C" (V-12)
"452 C" (V-16)

7.00 × 17" TIRES ON V-8
(THROUGH '35)

SAME H.P.
RATINGS AS
IN 1932.

V-12

V-12

7.50 × 17 TIRES
ON V-12 and V-16
(THROUGH '35)

V-16 ENGINE

CHICAGO WORLD'S
FAIR SHOW CAR

V-16

V-16

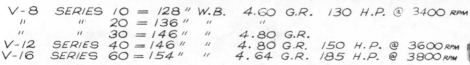

V-8	SERIES 10 =	128" W.B.	4.60 G.R.	130 H.P. @ 3400 RPM
"	" 20 =	136" "	"
"	" 30 =	146" "	4.80 G.R.
V-12	SERIES 40 =	146" "	4.80 G.R.	150 H.P. @ 3600 RPM
V-16	SERIES 60 =	154" "	4.64 G.R.	185 H.P. @ 3800 RPM

(V-8)

34

"355-D" (V-8)
"370-D" (V-12)
"452-D" (V-16)

TEARDROP
HOOD LOUVRES ON V-16

CADILLAC

7.50 x 17
TIRES (V-16)
(ALSO V-12)

(SOLID BUMPERS
MORE TYPICAL DURING '35.)

V-16

V-8

35
(INTRO.
JAN., 1935)

1935 INTERIOR
(PLAIN UPHOLSTERY REPLACES PLAITED)

7.00 x 17
TIRES (V-8)

"355-E" (V-8) "370-E" (V-12)
"16-62" (V-16)

TWO V-8s FOR 1936 : "60" HAS 322 C.I.D. ENGINE
(125 H.P. @ 3400 RPM) (USED IN La SALLE, 1937-1940;)
"70" and "75" HAVE 346 C.I.D. ENGINE
(135 H.P. @ 3400 RPM)

60

85

90

FLEETWOOD V-12

36
(HYDRAULIC
BRAKES ON
V-8 and V-12)

(STARTS OCT., 1935)

"60," "70," "75" (V-8) "80," "85"(V-12) "90"(V-16)

CADILLAC

60 (V-8)

(FINAL V-12 CADILLAC) 85

"60" NOW SHARES 346 C.I.D. V-8 ENGINE WITH "70" and "75".

37
(STARTS OCT., 1936)

FLEETWOOD V 8·12·16

FINAL YEAR FOR OVERHEAD VALVES IN V-16 ENGINE

V-16 HAS HYDRAULIC VACUUM BOOSTER BRAKES, RETAINS TEARDROP HOOD LOUVRES, 154" W.B., 7.50 x 17 TIRES

V-8

V-16 (L-HEAD) 4.31 G.R.

38
(STARTS OCT., 1937)

V-16 HAS NEW ENGINE OF 431 C.I.D., 175 H.P. @ 3600 RPM

35

CADILLAC

38 (CONT'D.)

"75" RATED AT 140 H.P. WHILE OTHER V-8 MODELS RATED AT 135.

"60 - SPECIAL" HAS ITS OWN UNIQUE STYLING. — (WITHOUT RUNNING BOARDS)

127" W.B. ON "60-S" (THROUGH '40)

"SUNSHINE ROOF," NEW TO U.S.A. IN '38, AVAILABLE ON SOME '39 MODELS OF CADILLAC, LA SALLE, BUICK AND OLDSMOBILE.

60-SPECIAL (FRONT DETAILS)

FLEETWOOD V·8 and 16

126" W.B. ON "61," 141" W.B. ON "75" and V-16

V-16

(V-16 DISCONTINUED DURING 1940) 185 H.P. @ 3600 RPM FOR 1939-1940 V-16s.

39 (STARTS OCT., 1938)

36

75

WITH 6-CYL.
CONTINENTAL
ENGINE

CARDWAY
(1923 — 1925)
FREDERICK CARDWAY, N.Y.C.

(REPORTEDLY,
ONLY 6 BUILT)

CASE (1910 TO 1927)
J.I.C. CASE CO.,
RACINE, WIS.

('20)

NEW 126" W.B.

MODEL V

NEW BODIES FOR 1920, AND NEW 1-PIECE
FRONT SEAT IN TOURING. 6 CYL. CONTINENTAL ENGINE
(303.1 C.I.D.) RAYFIELD CARB., DELCO IGNITION,
AND NEW ALEMITE LUBRICATION SYSTEM.

132" W.B.

('24) MODEL "Y"
(REPLACES MODEL "W,"
AUG. 1, '23)
(MODEL "X" ALSO)
(LIKE "JIC") "JAY EYE CEE" 6
(122" W.B.)

SCHEB. CARB. ('26 ON)

32 × 4½

('25)
(HYDRAULIC BRAKES)

'25 "J.I.C."
122" WB 4.9 G.R.
6 CYL. (241.6 CID)
56 H.P. @ 2300
'25 "Y"
132" WB 4.45 G.R.
6 CYL. (234.8 CID;
331.3 IN '26-'27)
70 H.P. @ 2400
34 × 7.30 TIRES ('26-7)
FEW CHANGES THR. '27.

CHALMERS (1908-1924)
CHALMERS MOTOR CAR CO., DETROIT, MICH.
CHALMERS MOTOR CO. OF CANADA, LTD., WINDSOR, ONTARIO
32 × 4 OR 33 × 4½ TIRES

"35-C"
(5-PASS.)

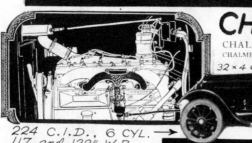

224 C.I.D., 6 CYL.
117 and 122" W.B.

REMY IGN.

20-21
4.75 and
5.18 GEAR RATIOS

22-23
KNOWN AS
"NEW SERIES" ('22)
"IMPROVED" ('23)

32 × 4

5.12 GEAR RATIO
(MOST OTHER
SPECS. SAME
AS 1920)
STROMBERG CARB.
(THROUGH '25)

23½

new
AUTO-
LITE
IGN.

24
(PRODUCED
DURING
LATTER
MONTHS
OF
1923.)

HYDRAULIC BRAKES
AVAILABLE
5.10 GEAR RATIO

REPLACED BY CHRYSLER

NEW
RIBBED WHEELS

THE CHANDLER MOTOR CAR COMPANY
Export Department, 1819 Broadway, New York City

CLEVELAND
Cable Address, "Chanmotor"

(1913-1929)

CHANDLER 20

6 CYLINDERS
288.6 C.I.D.
THROUGH '28

RAYFIELD
CARB.

4.40
GEAR RATIO
THROUGH '22

123" W.B.
(THROUGH
1926)

7-PASS. SEDAN

CHANDLER SIX
Famous For Its Marvelous Motor

21

The Chandler Dispatch

The Royal Dispatch, a new
sport model of utmost dis-
tinction and ultra-smart style

FIRST YEAR
WITH VISOR,
COWL LIGHTS,
COWL VENT,
DRUM-TYPE
HEADLIGHTS.

22
(NEW BODY
LINES)

ROYAL
DISPATCH HAS
34 × 4½ TIRES

CYLINDERS NOW CAST
EN BLOC (1923)

METROPOLITAN
5-PASS. SEDAN (NEW)

STARTS
6-22

NEW 32 × 4 TIRES *
and STROMBERG CARBURETOR
NEW 4.45 GEAR RATIO

23

The New Pike's Peak Motor
Built by Chandler

* = 33 × 4½ ON
CLOSED CARS, ROYAL DISP.

38

CHANDLER

CAR OF THE YEAR

CHANDLER

26

MODEL "SS-35"
55 H.P. @ 2800 RPM

NEW VERTICAL RADIATOR STRIPS →

7-PASS. SEDAN

20TH CENTURY SEDAN

27

STANDARD 6

TILLOTSON CARBURETOR ON STD. 6, SCHEBLER ON OTHERS.

BIG 6

The New Royal Eight BY CHANDLER

27½

314 C.I.D. 80 H.P. @ 3000 RPM
124" W.B.

METROPOLITAN SEDAN
(EARLY '27 TYPE)

STANDARD 6
MODEL "31" (108½" W.B.)
180.2 C.I.D., 45 H.P.
BIG 6 "35" (124" W.B.)
289 C.I.D., 55 H.P. @ 2100 RPM
SPECIAL 6 "43" = 218.6 C.I.D., 60 H.P. @ 2600 RPM
115" W.B.

28
(JOINS HUPMOBILE)

1928

SPECIAL 6
(ALSO "BIG 6")

196 C.I.D.
45 H.P. @ 2600 RPM

EARLY SERIES (DRUM HEADLIGHTS)

ROYAL 8

28½

29

195.5 C.I.D.
"6-65"
55 H.P. @ 3000

"BIG 6" CONT'D. FROM 1928, 331.3 C.I.D. 83 H.P.

CHANDLER'S FINAL CARS

ROYAL 8 "75"

"85" = LARGER 8

CHECKER

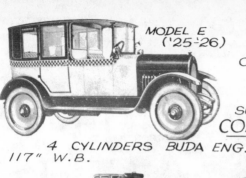

MODEL E ('25-'26)

MODEL F ('26 '27)

CHECKER CAB MFG. CO., KALAMAZOO, MICH. (SINCE 1923)

SUCCEEDS THE COMMONWEALTH CAR

4 CYLINDERS BUDA ENG. 117" W.B.

6-CYL. MODEL G IN '27-'28

MODEL K ('29-'30)

127" W.B., 7.00 x 18 TIRES MANY VARIATIONS ON EACH MODEL!

4.9 G.R. (K)

TAXI

VARIETY OF MODEL M (INTRO. 1931) 122" W.B.

6.50 x 18 TIRES

5.09 G.R.

MODEL M 126" W.B. ('32) (VARIATION)

HAS 228.1 C.I.D. BUDA 6-CYL. "JC-214" ENG.

MODEL T ('33) (NEW PORTHOLES IN HOOD DOORS)

MODEL Y ('36 - '39)

NO PRIVATE CARS AVAIL. UNTIL 1959.

CHEVROLET

(ESTABLISHED NOV., 1911; JOINED G.M. MAY, 1918.)

ASSEMBLY AT FLINT, MICH. (MAIN PLANT)

Chevrolet Motor Co., Detroit, Michigan
Division of General Motors Corporation

"490"

30 x 3½ OR 31 x 4 TIRES
26 H.P. @ 1800 RPM

"490" has 4-CYL. ENGINE 170.9 C.I.D.

102" W.B.

3.63 G.R.

GRAVITY FUEL FEED

"490" SEDAN

20-21

"FB" 110" W.B.

(FB 50)
37 H.P. @ 2000 RPM

"FB" HAS 4-CYL., 224.3 C.I.D. ENGINE
4.62 G.R.

VACUUM FUEL FEED

'22 MODEL IS FIRST "490" WITH HAND-OPERATED EMERGENCY BRAKE

LOWER WINDSHIELD

"490" (32 H.P.)

STEEL FELLOE WHEELS

FRONT SEAT CUSHION LOWERED 4½" TO PROVIDE HIGHER SEAT BACK.

SHORTER STEERING COLUMN.

22

GAS TANK ENLARGED TO 10 GALLONS.

GYPSY-TYPE SIDE CURTAINS

3.66 G.R.

MODEL "FB 42" SEDAN
32 x 4 TIRES ADOPTED DURING '22 (FB)

CHEVROLET

SUPERIOR" (B)

(759 AIR-COOLED SERIES C,M CHEVROLETS ALSO BLT., JAN. '23 TO MAY '23. RECALLED BY FACTORY, JUNE '23. 4 CYL., 134.7 C.I.D., 4.44 G.R.)

WHEELBASE INCREASED TO 103" ON ALL.

23

1923 4-Passenger Sedanette

3.77 G.R.(THROUGH '24)

EARLY "B" TYPE (9-23 TO 1-24)

CURVED FRONT AXLE AND CABLE-OPERATED BRAKES.

24

"SUPERIOR" NAME CONT'D. THROUGH '26.

(24½)

FINAL YEAR WITH CONE CLUTCH 26 H.P. @ 2000 RPM (THROUGH '27)

24½ DE LUXE (NICKEL TRIM)

LATER ("F") TYPE has STRAIGHT FRONT AXLE and BRAKE RODS.

29 x 4.40 BALLOON TIRES (CLOSED MODELS)

8-25: new KLAXON HORN, new STEER. WHEEL WITH CORRUGATED WALNUT FINISH RIM

1-PC. "VV" (VERTICAL VENTILATING) WINDSHIELD (ON CLOSED CARS.)

3.82 G.R.(THROUGH '31)

25

(K)

INTRO. 1-3-25

NEW RADIATOR DESIGN

42

30 x 3½ TIRES ON OPEN MODELS

CHEVROLET

for Economical Transportation

NEW TIE-BAR BETWEEN HEADLIGHTS 29 x 4.40 TIRES (THROUGH '27)

26 (V)

AIR CLEANER INTRODUCED

(INTERIOR)

GENERATOR MOVED FROM RIGHT TO LEFT SIDE OF ENGINE ('26.)

FROM '23 TO '26, CHEVROLET CARS BLT. SEPT. OR LATER ARE SOMETIMES CLASSIFIED AS FOLLOWING YEAR'S MODEL., THOUGH ACTUAL MODEL CHANGE (DURING THESE YEARS) OCCURS IN JANUARY.

COACH HAS GREEN CORDUROY UPHOLSTERY. SEDAN HAS BLUE CORDUROY. BROWN "PLUSH" IN COUPE.

new SPARE TIRE CARRIER

('27½)

TOURING CAR

IMPERIAL LANDAU (INTRODUCED MAY, 1927)

CO-INCIDENTAL STEERING and IGNITION LOCK

new "BULLET" HEADLIGHTS

NEW RADIATOR DESIGN

27 (AA) "CAPITOL"

new AC OIL FILTER, AC AIR CLEANER

ROADSTER

43   new I-PC. FULL-CROWN FENDERS

for Economical Transportation

CHEVROLET

57376

Bigger and Better

HORSEPOWER INCREASED TO 35 @ 2200 RPM

WHEELBASE INCREASED TO 107"

NEW RADIATOR DESIGN AGAIN

(FINAL 4-CYL. MODEL)

28

(AB) "NATIONAL"

4 - WHEEL BRAKES

INTERIOR

for Economical Transportation

CHEVROLET

30 x 4.50 TIRES

NEW CHEVROLET SIX

(6-CYLINDER CHEVROLETS ONLY — 1929 THROUGH 1954.)

ALL-NEW 1929 ENGINE →

193.9 C.I.D.
46 H.P. @ 2600 RPM

29
(AC)
"INTERNATIONAL"
COMPLETELY RESTYLED

new FUEL PUMP

FISHER BODIES, AS BEFORE

'29 DASH HAS 3 UPRIGHT OVALS WITHIN HORIZONTAL OVAL PANEL. ('30 DASH HAS SMALL CIRCULAR INSTRUMENTS.)

CHEVROLET
for Economical Transportation

1929 IS FINAL CHEVROLET WITH FUEL GAUGE LOCATED OUTSIDE, ON TANK.

4.50 × 20" TIRES
3.81 G.R. = (ACCORDING TO CERTAIN SOURCES; 3.82 OTHERWISE.)

45

REAR TOP OF
CONVERTIBLE LANDAU
CAN BE FOLDED

for Economical Transportation

CHEVROLET

30

"UNIVERSAL" (AD)

New Dash Gasoline Gauge

NEW DARK-FACED, CIRCULAR GAUGES

The Chevrolet Special Sedan is a de luxe creation in every sense of the word. Standard equipment includes six wire wheels with fender wells, bumpers front and rear, robe rail, dome light, silk assist cords, etc.

THE ROADSTER

THE SPORT ROADSTER

50 H.P. @ 2600 RPM

THE COUPE

THE SPORT COUPE

(CABRIOLET SUSPENDED FOR 1930; RE-INTRODUCED JANUARY, 1931.)

THE SEDAN

THE PHAETON

THE CLUB SEDAN

4.75 × 19" TIRES (THROUGH '31) AND NEW, SLIGHTLY SLANTED NON-GLARE WINDSHIELD →

(30 ½ MODEL HAS Landau Irons.)

4.75 × 19

47 THE COACH

CHEVROLET

31

NEW 109" WHEELBASE

STANDARD '31s DO NOT HAVE THE NEW RADIATOR STONE GUARD.

(AE) "INDEPENDENCE"

2 NEW BODY TYPES IN '31

THE STANDARD COACH

DASH ('31)

HORN BUTTON — OIL PRESSURE GAUGE / SPEEDOMETER / CHOKE BUTTON — THROTTLE GAUGE / GASOLINE GAUGE

LIGHTING SWITCH / GEARSHIFT LEVER — IGNITION LOCK — AMMETER / WATER TEMPERATURE INDICATOR / SPARK BUTTON

CLUTCH PEDAL — BRAKE PEDAL — HEAD LAMP DIMMER SWITCH — ACCELERATOR / STARTING PEDAL / HAND BRAKE LEVER / ACCELERATOR FOOT REST

'32 HAS NEW SYNCHRO-MESH TRANSMISSION

FREE WHEELING BUTTON — HORN BUTTON — OIL PRESSURE GAUGE / SPEEDOMETER / CHOKE BUTTON — HEAT CONTROL BUTTON / THROTTLE BUTTON / GASOLINE GAUGE / DASH ('32)

LIGHTING SWITCH / GEARSHIFT LEVER — IGNITION LOCK — AMMETER / WATER TEMPERATURE / SPARK BUTTON

CLUTCH PEDAL — BRAKE PEDAL — HEAD LAMP DIMMER SWITCH — ACCELERATOR / STARTING PEDAL / HAND BRAKE / ACCELERATOR FOOT REST

"CONFEDERATE" (BA)

32

60 H.P. @ 3000 RPM

"FREE WHEELING" (New)

4.1 G.R.

48

5.25 x 18" TIRES

THE SPORT ROADSTER

107" W.B.
4.3 GEAR RATIO

5.25 x 17" TIRES

CHEVROLET

33

181 C.I.D.
60 H.P. @ 3000 RPM

MASTER *and* EAGLE "CA"

STARTS 12-32

206.8 C.I.D. 65 H.P. @ 2800 RPM

STANDARD "CC"
(WITH HOOD LOUVRES)
STARTS 3-33

5.25 x 18" TIRES

DASH

(110" W.B.)
ACCELERATOR CONTROLS STARTER

4.11 GEAR RATIO
(THROUGH '36)

NEW "KNEE ACTION" INDEPENDENT FRONT WHEEL SUSPENSION (WITH FRONT COIL SPRINGS) ON "MASTER" (DA) SERIES.

CHEVROLET MASTER SIX COUPE

CHEVROLET MASTER SIX SPORT COUPE

34

"STANDARD" (DC)
SERIES INTRODUCED LATE
(SPRING, 1934) WITH 107" W.B.,
5.25 x 17" TIRES,
181 C.I.D. ENGINE WITH
60 H.P. @ 3000 RPM

"MASTER" HAS 112" W.B.,
5.50 x 17" TIRES,
206.8 C.I.D. ENGINE
WITH 80 H.P. @ 3300 RPM

DASH

49

CHEVROLET

"STANDARD" MODEL (EC) RESEMBLES 1934 BUT HAS PAINTED HEADLIGHT SHELLS. DASH GAUGES MOVED TO CENTER.

"MASTER" (EA and ED)

"ED" SERIES AVAIL. W/O "KNEE ACTION"

35

(ALL MODELS NOW HAVE THE 80-H.P. "BLUE FLAME" ENGINE.)

3-WINDOW SPORT COUPE WITH RUMBLE SEAT

(5-WINDOW BUSINESS COUPE ALSO AVAILABLE)   NEW 113" W.B. (MASTER)   (STD. RETAINS 107" W.B.)

H.P. REDUCED TO 79 @ 3200 RPM, FOR '36

"EXPEDITER" COUPE AVAIL. WITH PICKUP BOX

(FC) STANDARD === 109" W.B. MASTER === 113" W.B. (FA and FD) "KNEE ACTION" OPTIONAL (FA)

36

'36 DASH

NEW 216.5 C.I.D. 1937 ENGINE (85 H.P. @ 3200 RPM)

37

NEW STYLING ALSO

"GB" === MASTER (3.73 G.R.) "GA" === MASTER DE LUXE WITH "KNEE ACTION" (4.22 G.R.)

112¼" W.B. ON ALL (THROUGH 1939)

6.00 x 16" IS NOW THE TIRE SIZE ON ALL MODELS.

'37 DASH

50

(1937 GEAR RATIOS CONTINUED THROUGH '39)

CHEVROLET

"HB" == MASTER
"HA" == MASTER DE LUXE

38

ASH TRAY IN MASTER DE LUXE MODELS

'38 DASH

CHROME TRIM, GRILLE AND OUTSIDE DOOR HANDLES HAVE DECORATIVE VERMILLION-RED STRIPES IN HORIZONTAL GROOVES.

"JB" == MASTER
"JA" == MASTER DE LUXE
85 H.P. @ 3200 RPM, AS BEFORE.

FISHER BODIES, AS BEFORE

NEW STEERING COLUMN GEARSHIFT CONTROL IS OPTIONAL. HAND BRAKE LEVER HUNG AT LEFT, BELOW DASH.

THE MASTER DE LUXE FOUR-PASSENGER COUPE

39

'39 INTERIOR

51

CHRYSLER (DETROIT)

(REPLACES '24 CHALMERS 12-23 INTRO. 1-24)

IMPERIAL SEDAN

NEW HIGH-COMPRESSION (4.6 TO 1) ENGINE

OPEN CARS CAPABLE OF 70 M.P.H.

PHAETON

BROUGHAM

24
(MODEL B)
6 CYL.
201.5 C.I.D.
68 H.P. @ 3200 RPM
112 3/4" W.B.
29 × 4.50 TIRES

Roadster

HYDRAULIC BRAKES

DASH

(CHRYSLER CORP. REPLACES MAXWELL-CHALMERS)

NEW ROYAL COUPE HAS OPENING REAR WINDOW, RUMBLE SEAT

Six (B)
25
(TO 7-25)

GEAR-SHIFT LEVER LONGER FOR 1925.

IMPERIAL

30 × 5.77 TIRES

ROADSTER HAS WIDER DOORS FOR 1925.

COACH

CHRYSLER SALES CORPORATION, DETROIT, MICHIGAN
CHRYSLER CORPORATION OF CANADA, LIMITED, WINDSOR, ONT.

CHRYSLER FOUR

25½

NEW
4 – CYL.
SERIES

(REPLACES
1925 MAXWELL)
"C")

"F – 58"
SERIES
(JUNE, 1925 TO
APRIL, 1926)

HYDRAULIC BRAKES
OPTIONAL ON SOME
4 – CYLINDER CHRYSLERS (ON WHICH
2 – WHEEL MECHANICAL BRAKES WERE
SOMETIMES FEATURED.) HYD. BRAKES
STANDARD ON OTHER CHRYSLERS.

185.8 C.I.D.
38 H.P. @ 2200 RPM
109" W.B.

53

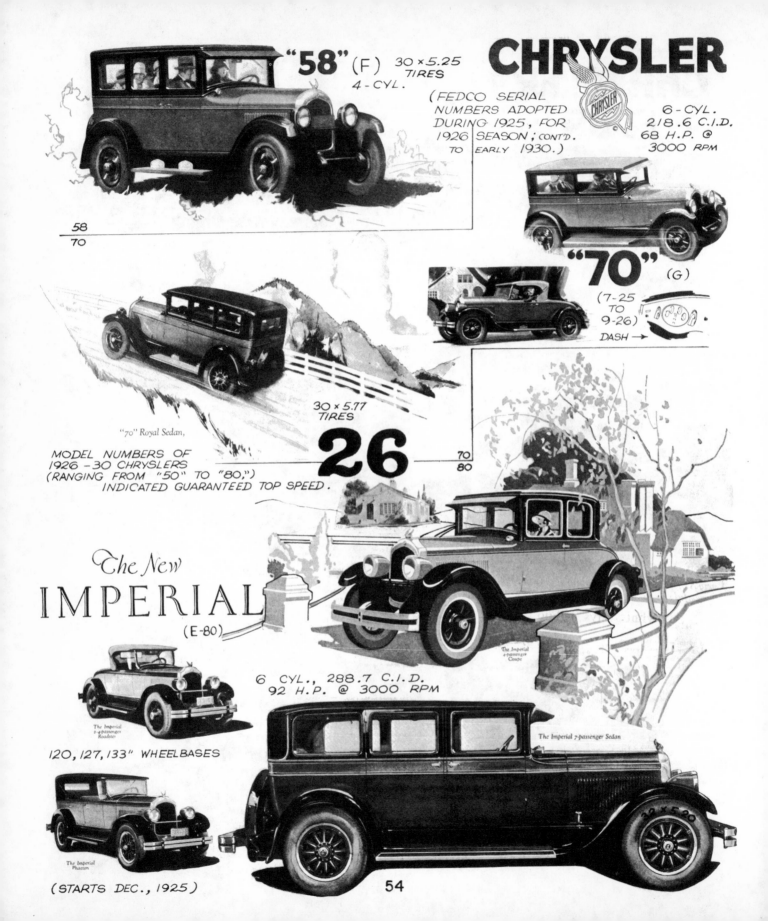

CHRYSLER

"58" (F)   30 × 5.25 TIRES
4-CYL.

(FEDCO SERIAL NUMBERS ADOPTED DURING 1925, FOR 1926 SEASON; CONT'D. TO EARLY 1930.)

6-CYL.
218.6 C.I.D.
68 H.P. @ 3000 RPM

"70" (G)

(7-25 TO 9-26)
DASH →

$\frac{58}{70}$

30 × 5.77 TIRES

26

"70" Royal Sedan,

MODEL NUMBERS OF 1926 –30 CHRYSLERS (RANGING FROM "50" TO "80,") INDICATED GUARANTEED TOP SPEED.

$\frac{70}{80}$

The New
IMPERIAL
(E-80)

The Imperial 4-passenger Coupe

6 CYL., 288.7 C.I.D.
92 H.P. @ 3000 RPM

The Imperial 2-4-passenger Roadster

120, 127, 133" WHEELBASES

The Imperial 7-passenger Sedan

The Imperial Phaeton

(STARTS DEC., 1925)

54

CHRYSLER
"50 - 60 - 70 - 80"
CHRYSLER MODEL NUMBERS MEAN MILES PER HOUR.

LEATHER UPH. IN COUPE →

"50"
(I)
(7-26 TO 7-27)

106" W.B.   4 CYL.
170.3 C.I.D., 38 H.P. @ 2200 RPM

ALL-STEEL Budd BODIES AVAILABLE ON SOME "50" MODELS.

"50" DASH

50

60

"60"
(H)

109" W.B.

↓"60"

(6-26 TO 6-27)
6 CYL., 180.2 C.I.D.
54 H.P. @ 3000 RPM

28 X 5.25   45-100

27

STARTING 8-26 BUDD-MICHELIN DISC WHEELS AVAIL. ON ALL SERIES OF EARLY '27 CHRYSLERS.

60
70

FINER **70**
(G)
(9-26 TO 10-27)

NEW CO-INCIDENTAL LOCK →
68 H.P. @ 3000 RPM

DASH

30 x 6.00 TIRES

112 3/4" W.B.

4-PASS. COUPE (NEW) →

FRANK QUAIL

70

80

IMPERIAL "80"
(E)

NEW 30 x 6.75 TIRES

SAME SPECS. AS 1926

577-900

FRANK QUAIL

55

CHRYSLER

"52" IS FINAL 4-CYL. MODEL WHICH SOMETIMES OFFERS 2-WHEEL MECHANICAL BRAKES.

"52" CHRYSLER BODIES HAVE COMPOSITE WOOD INNER FRAMEWORK, AS ON MOST OTHER PRE-1930 CHRYSLERS.

DASH ("52")

MODEL "52" IS FINAL 4-CYLINDER CHRYSLER, WITH 170.3 C.I.D., 45 H.P. @ 2800 RPM, 106" W.B.

PRODUCED JULY, 1927 TO JUNE, 1928. REPLACED BY THE CHRYSLER-<u>PLYMOUTH</u> CAR. (SEE: "PLYMOUTH")

"52" HAS 4.7 GEAR RATIO

"52" (I) 28 "62" (M)

"62" HAS 4.6 GEAR RATIO
28 × 5.25 TIRES

52
62

CHRYSLER "RED HEAD" ENGINES (WITH HIGH-COMPRESSION CYLINDER HEAD) REQUIRED ETHYL GASOLINE WHEN NEW.)

"52" AND "62" INSTRUMENTS FRAMED SEPERATELY IN INDIVIDUAL PANES.

Great New Chrysler "62" Coupe (with rumble seat), $1245

(108 3/4" W.B.)

"62" GIVES 54 H.P. @ 3200 RPM WITH STANDARD 5.2-COMPRESSION "Silver Dome" HEAD. 6.2-COMPRESSION "Red Head" GIVES 60 H.P.

(JUNE, 1927 TO JUNE, 1928)

DASH (MACHINE-TURNED METAL PANEL)

56

Two-Passenger Coupe

Four-Passenger Coupe

Crown Sedan

CHRYSLER

Royal Sedan, $1595

THE ILLUSTRIOUS NEW "72" (J)

(7-27 TO 6-28)

NEW Close-Coupled Sedan $1695

NEW 248.9 C.I.D. ENGINE

(118¾" W.B.)
30 x 6.00 TIRES

28
(CONT'D.)

"72" GIVES 75 H.P. @ 3200 RPM WITH STD. 5.1-COMPRESSION HEAD. 6.2-COMPRESSION "Red Head" GIVES 85 H.P.

1928 IS FINAL YEAR THAT CHRYSLER USES ANY FISHER BODIES.

(COWL LIGHTS, AFTER JAN., 1928)

"72" and "80" INSTRUMENTS BEHIND LONG GLASS PANEL.

D = DIETRICH BODY
L = LE BARON "

72
80

ILLUSTRIOUS NEW "72"

TOWN CABRIOLET
BODY BY LE BARON

"72" HAS 4.3 GEAR RATIO

EARLY MODEL

LATE MODEL

LATE "72" ROADSTER HAS COWL LIGHTS, NEW WINDSHIELD, NEW SIDE MOULDING.

NEW 309.6 C.I.D. ENGINE
112 H.P. @ 3000 RPM
WITH "Red Head" 6 to 1 COMPR.

(STD. HEAD = 100 H.P.) 4.75 COMPR.

IMPERIAL "80" HAS 4.08 GEAR RATIO

(11-27 TO 6-28) Imperial "80"

L "80" (L-80)

136" W.B.

L

New 112 h.p. Imperial "80" Town Sedan, $2995

D

D

L

RT. DOOR FOR RUMBLE SEAT

INSTRUMENT PANEL

30 x 6.75 TIRES

NO RADIATOR EMBLEM ON '28 "80."

57

Locke Touralette

CHRYSLER

CHRYSLER MOTORS PRODUCT

65 H.P. @ 3200 RPM   195.6 C.I.D.

"65" (P)

5-WINDOW COUPE HAS RUMBLE SEAT

5.2 STD. COMPR.
6.0 - COMPR. "Red Head"
GIVES 70 H.P.

112 3/4" W.B. (6-28 TO 6-29)
5.50 × 18 TIRES
(IGNITION KEY-HOLE REPLACES SWITCH)

(3-WINDOW BUSINESS COUPE ALSO IN "65" SERIES.)

"75" VICTORIA COUPE (RARE!)

"65" INSTRUMENT PANEL ARRANGEMENT GENERALLY SIMILAR TO "62" BUT HAS "WOODGRAIN" TRIM ABOVE.

65
75

6.00 × 18 TIRES

"75" (R)

FEDCO I.D. PLATE

ALL GAUGES BEHIND LONG GLASS PANEL
DARK-FACED GAUGES ON SOME EARLY "75" MODELS; LIGHT-FACED ON LATER MODELS.

ROYAL SEDAN

INTERIOR

(6-28 TO 6-29)
121" W.B.
FIRST CHRYSLER TO FEATURE BUILT-IN RADIATOR SHUTTERS.

(SAME ENGINE SPECS. AS LATE "72")

REAR

29

(HIGH-COMPRESSION "Red Head" OPTIONAL THROUGH 1933, AND OPTIONAL ALUMINUM HEAD FROM 1934 THROUGH 1941.)

75 (TO 1928)

IMPERIAL

(1930 IMPERIAL 6 SIMILAR TO 1929, BUT HAS 4-SPEED "Multi-Range" TRANSMISSION AND SMOOTH, NON-CORRUGATED BUMPERS.)

'29-30 IMPERIAL HAS SAME SPECS. AS '28 MODEL

7.00 × 18 TIRES ('29 and '30)

(SIDE DOOR FOR RUMBLE SEAT)

IMPERIAL CHRYSLER (L)

(STARTS OCTOBER, 1928)

EARLIEST MODEL HAS NO LOWER COWL MOLDING.

Custom Roadster

New Imperial 7-passenger Sedan, illustrated. Also available in 5-passenger Sedan.

CHRYSLER

30

SOME "66" MODELS WITH SPLIT GROUP OF HOOD LOUVRES DURING 1930

3-SPEED TRANS. ON "66"

68 H.P. @ 3000 RPM

5.50 × 18 TIRES

WOOD WHEELS STANDARD. (WIRE WHEELS OPTIONAL)

(ALL 6-CYL. MODELS)

new FUEL PUMP INTRODUCED (ON ALL BUT THE IMPERIAL 6.)

DASH (EXPORT MODEL)

NEW "66" (7-29 TO 5-30)

(CC)

218.6 C.I.D. ("66" AND EARLY "70")

112 3/4" W.B.

66 / 70

CHRYSLER BLDG. (N.Y.) BUILT 1929-30 (77 STORIES)

= HOOD "PENNON" LOUVRES ON 70 (and 77) BLT. BEF. 1-30.

116 9/16" W.B.

"70" DASH

EARLY MODEL

5.50 × 18 TIRES

EARLY 70 (and 77) HAS PARK. LIGHTS HUNG FROM VISOR (CLOSED CARS)

4. The chromium plated sconce-type parking lights, metal cadet visor, tandem windshield cleaner, and the chromium window architraves are new features of design.

5. The concave moulding on the Roadster and Phaeton reflect originality of design.

NEW "70" (V)

75 H.P. @ 3200 RPM

LATE MODEL 11-29 = "77" ENGINE USED

70 / 77

MULTI-RANGE 4-SPEED TRANS.

93 H.P. @ 3200 RPM

268.9 C.I.D.

NEW "77" (W)

70 / 77

LATER "70" AND "77" has VERTICAL HOOD LOUVRES.

124 9/16" W.B.

77 IMPERIAL

1. The Futura Design Instrument Panel, designed by Chrysler, executed by Cartier (Paris-New York.)

1930 "IMPERIAL" RESEMBLES ILLUSTRATED 1929 STYLE. DIFFERENCES LISTED IN '29 IMPERIAL SECTION. (6-CYLINDER IMPERIAL DISCONTINUED IN JUNE, 1930.)

CHRYSLER

NEW 195.6 C.I.D. ENGINE

30½ SIX

MODEL "CJ" (STARTS MARCH, 1930)

UPPER RADIATOR TANK MATCHES CORE ON "CJ" SERIES (LATEST MODEL CJ CONSIDERED "EARLY '31")

ACCESSORY SHAFT IS INCLINED AND THE OIL PUMP IS EXTERNALLY MOUNTED ON THE LEFT SIDE OF THE ENGINE

has FUEL PUMP

FIRST CHRYSLER 6-CYL. ENGINE TO HAVE 4 MAIN BEARINGS INSTEAD OF 7.

(DE SOTO INTRODUCED WITH A 4-BEARING 6 FOR 1929. DODGE OFFERED ONE FOR LATER '30 SEASON.)

BUSINESS COUPE (SIDEMOUNT SPARE TIRES OPTIONAL)

"Royal" RUMBLE-SEAT COUPE ALSO AVAILABLE.

"CJs" BUILT AFTER JULY 20, 1930 SOMETIMES CONSIDERED "EARLY 1931" MODELS.

109" W.B.

62 H.P. @ 3200 RPM
4.7 GEAR RATIO
4.75/5.00 × 19 TIRES

AS ON OTHER PRE-1931 CHRYSLER CORP. CARS, WOOD WHEELS WERE STANDARD EQUIPMENT. (WIRE WHEELS OPTIONAL) STEEL BODY FRAME

CONVERTIBLE COUPE

THE "CJ" SIX WAS THE FIRST CHRYSLER SINCE 1925 WHICH DID NOT BEAR A "TOP SPEED" MODEL NO. (TOP SPEED OF "CJ" = 62.)

ROADSTER, TOURING CAR, ALSO AVAIL. IN THIS "CJ" SERIES.

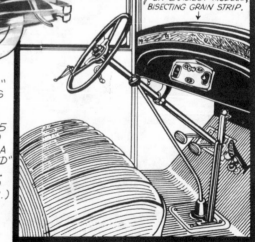

FEDCO I.D. PLATE ON EARLIEST MODELS, BISECTING GRAIN STRIP.

(LATE MODEL "CJ" INTERIOR HAD POSITION OF KEY and SPEEDOMETER REVERSED.)

CHRYSLER

1931 "CM" SIX BEGINS JAN., 1931. 8- CYL. '31 MODELS INTRODUCED JULY, 1930.

SIX (CM)

Six Sedan—$895

217.8 C.I.D. 78 H.P. @ 3400 RPM

116 3/8" W.B.

5.25 × 19 TIRES

(NEW STYLING) V- GRILLE

EARLY 6 SEDAN = (NO VISOR)

WIRE WHEELS STANDARD ON '31 SIX.

31

"70" (6 CYL.)   (TO MAY, 1931)

"70" Business Coupe—$1245

"70" Royal Coupe—$1295

268.9 C.I.D. 93 H.P. @ 3200 RPM

"70" Brougham—$1245

WIRE WHEELS OPTIONAL

"70" Royal Sedan—$1295

116 9/16" W.B.

5.50 × 18 TIRES

EIGHT (CD) (7-30 TO 4-31)

EARLY "CD" HAS 240.3 C.I.D. AND 80 H.P. @ 3400 RPM. (LATER "CD" HAS 260.8 C.I.D. AND 88 H.P. @ 3400 RPM, AS OF JAN., 1931.)

CHRYSLER EIGHT SPORT ROADSTER

CHRYSLER'S FIRST 8s (1930 De SOTO AND DODGE OFFERED A STRAIGHT - 8 ENGINE PRIOR TO CHRYSLER.)

SEDAN

124" W.B. 5.50 × 18 TIRES

(REPLACED BY DE LUXE 8s, SPRING, '31)

EIGHT COUPE $1495 F. O. B. FACTORY

Roadster—$1545

De Luxe Eight

(CD DELUXE) (4-31 TO 11-31)

282.1 C.I.D. 100 H.P. @ 3400 RPM

Convertible Coupe—$1585

124" W.B.

DLX. 8

Eight De Luxe Five-Passenger Coupe—$1565

(INTERIOR)

61

CHRYSLER

DUAL-COWL PHAETON
(BODY BY LE BARON)

(7-30 TO 10-31)

IMPERIAL EIGHT (CG)

VICTORIA
(CUSTOM BODY BY WATERHOUSE)

145" WHEELBASES ON 1931 IMPERIALS

(BODY BY LE BARON)

SEDAN

ROADSTER

31 (CONT'D.)

CLOSE-COUPLED SEDAN

384.8 C.I.D., 125 H.P. @ 3200 RPM (THROUGH '32)

7.50 x 17

FUEL PUMP ON ALL MODELS.

'32 MODELS HAVE "FLOATING POWER" FLEXIBLE ENGINE MOUNTS, AUTOMATIC CLUTCH, FREE-WHEELING.

5.50 x 18 TIRES
224 C.I.D.
82 H.P. @ 3400

Chrysler Six Sedan

116 3/8" W.B. (CI)

(12-31 TO 11-32)

$\frac{6}{8}$ SIX

32

DASH

100 H.P. @ 3400 RPM (CP)

298.7 C.I.D.
125" W.B.

EIGHT (CP)
(12-31 TO 11-32)
298.7 C.I.D., 100 H.P. @ 3400 RPM

6.50 x 17 TIRES

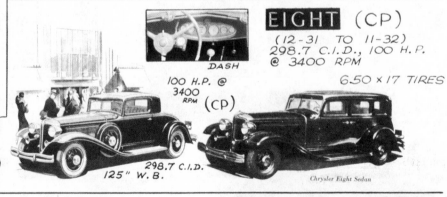

Chrysler Eight Sedan

IMPERIAL EIGHT.

135" W.B. (CH)
Imperial Eight Sedan

7.00 x 17 TIRES

7.50 x 17 TIRES

LENGTHENED HOOD WITH VENT DOORS

146" W.B. (CL)
Imperial Custom Eight Close-Coupled Sedan

CHRYSLER SIX SEDAN $785 (CO)

Chrysler

CHRYSLER ROADSTERS DISCONTINUED IN 1933.

6

SIX (CO) HAS 116½" W.B., →
224 C.I.D., 83 OR 89 H.P. @ 3400 RPM

(CT)
ROYAL 8 (12-32 TO 12-33)
273.8 C.I.D.
90 H.P. @ 3400 RPM

119½" W.B.

126" W.B.

IMPERIAL 8 (CQ)
298.7 C.I.D.
100 OR 108 H.P. @ 3400 RPM, WITH 5.2-COMPRESSION "SILVER DOME" OR 6.2-COMPRESSION "RED HEAD"

33

HIGH-COMPRESSION "RED HEAD" ENGINES AVAILABLE ON CHRYSLERS OF 1928 THROUGH 1933.

(CUSTOM IMPERIAL "CL" SERIES RUNS FROM 2-33 TO 12-33.)
146" W.B.
384.8 C.I.D.
125 OR 135 H.P. @ 3200

Custom IMPERIAL 8 (CL)

(CL) INTERIOR

FOR 1934, "AIRFLOW" BODIES ON ALL 8s

122 H.P. @ 3400 RPM

34

130 H.P. @ 3400 RPM

128" W.B.
AIRFLOW IMPERIAL (CV)   323.5 C.I.D.

241.6 C.I.D.
93 H.P. @ 3400 RPM   6 (CA, CB)
117" W.B., 121" WB

AIRFLOW 8 (CU)
298.7 C.I.D.

122 13/16" W.B.

CW = 150 H.P., 146½" W.B.

(CX, 1934 CHRYSLER AIRFLOW CUSTOM IMPERIAL CW)

63

(C-6)=6
(CZ)=8

AIRSTREAM *Chrysler*

35

AIRFLOW 8 (C-1, C-2, C-3, CW)

H. P. RANGE = 93 (6) TO 150 (CW IMPERIAL AIRFLOW)

(C-7 REAR)

36

(C-8)

(C-10)

INTERIORS

BEAUTIFUL NEW AIRFLOWS

NEW SIX (C-7)
DeLUXE EIGHT (C-8)

NOTE DIFFERENCES IN HOOD LOUVRE DESIGNS

8 CYL. AIRFLOWS (C-9, C-10, C-11, CW)

ROYAL 6 (C-16)

37

Chrysler

AIRFLOW 8 (C-17)

IMPERIAL 8 (C-14)↗

C-15 CUSTOM IMPERIAL NO LONGER AN "AIRFLOW"

ROYAL 6 (C-18)
119" W.B. (THROUGH '39)
241.5 C.I.D. (THROUGH '41)
95 H.P. @ 3600 RPM

38

RICH NEW INTERIORS!

110 - H.P.
NEW YORK SPECIAL
and IMPERIAL (C-19)
8

Custom
130-H.P. IMPERIAL 8
(C-20)
323.5 C.I.D.
('34-50)

144" W.B.
(THROUGH '39)

LIGHT-COLORED
STEERING
WHEEL

NEW V-WINDSHIELD, "WATERFALL" LOWER GRILLE, SUNKEN HEADLIGHTS FOR 1939

ROYAL 6 (and Windsor)
(C-22)

100 H.P.
@ 3600

39

NEW YORKER 8
and Saratoga 8 (C-23)
" Imperial 8

(C-24)   Custom Imperial 8

CLEVELAND SIX

(INTRODUCED JULY, 1919)
112" W.B. and 190.8 C.I.D. (THROUGH '22)

MODEL 40 ("41" = '22)

Cleveland Automobile Company
Cleveland, Ohio

BUILT BY   CLEVELAND

CHANDLER

19 - 22

FOR '21, GRAY AND DAVIS IGNITION IS REPLACED BY **BOSCH** (THROUGH '26) 4.45 GEAR RATIO (THROUGH '22)

1921 = OUTSIDE DOOR HANDLES ON OPEN CARS
1922 = DRUM HEADLIGHTS &

5-PASS. 2-DR. SEDAN (INTRO. 1923)

FISHER BODY

31 × 4

112½" W.B., 4.9 GEAR RATIO

23-24

MODEL 42
'24 HAS CHASSIS APRON PLATES (ALUMINUM KICK PADS,) BOSCH AUTOMATIC SPARK CONTROL, AND THIS NEW RADIATOR DESIGN →
('24 ONLY)

"ONE-SHOT" CHASSIS LUBRICATION

25-26

MODEL 31 (STANDARD)

"31"	"43"
108½" W.B.	115" W.B.
30 × 4.75 TIRES	31 × 5.25 TIRES
165.5 C.I.D. ('25)	218.6 C.I.D.
180.1 " ('26)	60 H.P. @
45 H.P. @ 2800 ('26)	2800 RPM

MODEL 43 (SPECIAL 6) HAS ALUMINUM KICK PADS AND NICKEL TRIM

1926 MODEL HAS INTAKE MANIFOLD <u>ABOVE</u> EXHAUST MANIFOLD.

AUGUST, 1926 = BECAME CHANDLER STANDARD and SPECIAL SERIES.

CLIMBER

(K) = 4 CYLS., 192.4 C.I.D., 4.0 G.R., 33 × 4 TIRES, 117" W.B.
(S) = 6 CYLS., 248.9 C.I.D., 4.75 G.R. (THROUGH '22)
32 × 4½ TIRES, 125½" W.B. (230.1 C.I.D., 4.0 G.R. IN '23)

('20)
(1919 - 1923)
CLIMBER MOTOR CORP.,
LITTLE ROCK, ARK.
4 OR 6 - CYL.
HERSCHELL-SPILLMAN ENG.

('23)

COATS
(1922 - 1923)
COATS STEAM MOTORS, SANDUSKY, OHIO

COLE MOTOR CAR CO., INDIANAPOLIS (1909 - 1925)

Cole Aero-EIGHT

Tourster

NORTHWAY V-8 (346.3 C.I.D.) ENGINES (THROUGH '25)

NEW FOR 1920: 1-PIECE REAR AXLE HOUSING, JOHNSON CARB., ADJUSTABLE STORM-PROOF WINDSHIELDS ON MODELS "884" + "885."
('20)

127" W.B. and 4.45 G.R. (TO '22) 33 × 5 TIRES (THROUGH '24)

NEW BRAKE ADJUSTER

20
"870" SERIES

21

"884" TOUROSINE (7-PASS.)

'22 IS 1ST YEAR WITH SPLIT FRAME ENDS, 4.1 G.R.

22
NEW "890" SERIES IN '22.

"SPORTOSINE"

'23 MODELS have DRUM-TYPE HEADLIGHTS, COWL VENT, and STATIONARY LOWER HALF of WINDSHIELD.

23
DISC WHEELS ALSO AVAILABLE.

SOME '23 COLES have 3/4 RUNNING BOARDS and SIDEMOUNTS.

"897" BROUETTE

127¼" W.B. (DURING '22, and THROUGH '25.)

"MASTER" SERIES

24
FULL-LENGTH RUNNING BOARDS FOUND ON ALL COLES AGAIN, IN 1924.

1925 MODEL SIMILAR TO '24, BUT BALLOON TIRES STANDARD INSTEAD OF OPTIONAL (34 × 7.30)

76 - 80 H.P. @ 2600 RPM (3.5 TO 3.6 COMPR.)

"892-A" 5 - PASSENGER AERO-VOLANTE

'25 has 2-PC. REAR "BUMPERETTES"

COLE INDIANAPOLIS

67

(1916-1924)
RADIATOR SHUTTERS WERE CONTROLLED BY A THERMOSTAT.

Columbia Six
COLUMBIA MOTORS COMPANY, DETROIT, U.S.A.

19-22   115" W.B. (THROUGH '24)

COLUMBIA SIX

The Columbia Six
Five Passenger Touring Car

2-PASS. ROADSTER AND 4 PASS. COUPE ARE NEW MODELS FOR 1920. CHASSIS SPECS. GENERALLY SIMILAR TO 1919. 6 CYL., 224-C.I.D. CONTINENTAL ENGINE. (TO '22)

50 H.P. LIGHT 6 HAS 7-U CONTINENTAL 195.6 C.I.D. ENGINE. BIG 6 HAS 8-R CONT. 241.6 C.I.D. ENGINE

22½-24

1924

125" W.B.

6-CYL. CONTINENTAL ENGINE 303.1 C.I.D. (THROUGH '22) 4.66 GEAR RATIO

COMET
(1917—1922)

COMET AUTOMOBILE CO., DECATUR, ILL.

33 x 4½ TIRES ON '21 "C-53" MODEL AND '22 "C-53-2" MODEL.

20

"4-40"

COMMONWEALTH
COMMONWEALTH MOTORS CO., JOLIET, ILLINOIS (1917-1922)

REPLACES PARTIN-PALMER CAR, 1917.

"4-45" ('21)

EVOLVED INTO THE CHECKER TAXI.

117" W.B.

32 x 4

'20 HAS 4-CYL. LYCOMING 192.4 C.I.D. ENGINE INSTEAD OF 6-CYL. AS IN 1919.

MODEL "41" ('34) 4.33 G.R.

143.1 C.I.D. 4-CYL. 38 H.P. @ 2600 RPM

CONTINENTAL
(1933 — 1934)

CONT. AUTO. CO., DETROIT 1933 MODELS: "BEACON" 4, "FLYER" 6, and "ACE" 6 (V-WINDSHIELD ON "ACE")

CONTINENTAL ENGINES

101½" W.B.

68

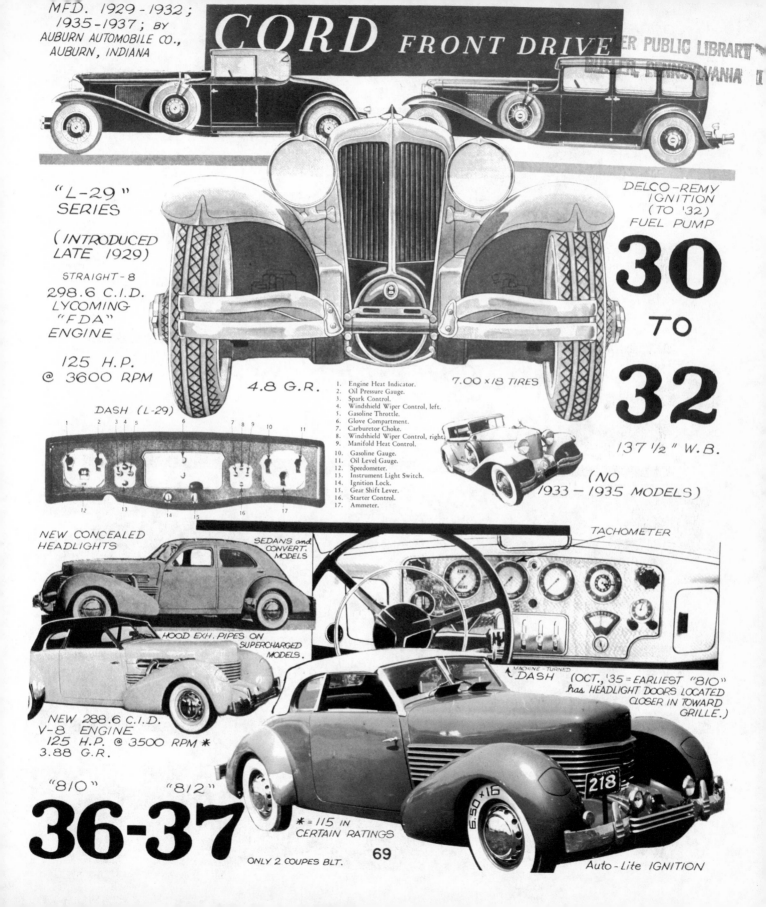

MFD. 1929-1932; 1935-1937; BY AUBURN AUTOMOBILE CO., AUBURN, INDIANA

CORD FRONT DRIVE

"L-29" SERIES

(INTRODUCED LATE 1929)

STRAIGHT-8 298.6 C.I.D. LYCOMING "FDA" ENGINE

125 H.P. @ 3600 RPM

4.8 G.R.

DELCO-REMY IGNITION (TO '32) FUEL PUMP

30 TO 32

137½" W.B.

(NO 1933-1935 MODELS)

7.00 x 18 TIRES

DASH (L-29)

1. Engine Heat Indicator.
2. Oil Pressure Gauge.
3. Spark Control.
4. Windshield Wiper Control, left.
5. Gasoline Throttle.
6. Glove Compartment.
7. Carburetor Choke.
8. Windshield Wiper Control, right.
9. Manifold Heat Control.
10. Gasoline Gauge.
11. Oil Level Gauge.
12. Speedometer.
13. Instrument Light Switch.
14. Ignition Lock.
15. Gear Shift Lever.
16. Starter Control.
17. Ammeter.

NEW CONCEALED HEADLIGHTS

SEDANS and CONVERT. MODELS

HOOD EXH. PIPES ON SUPERCHARGED MODELS.

NEW 288.6 C.I.D. V-8 ENGINE 125 H.P. @ 3500 RPM * 3.88 G.R.

"810"   "812"

36-37

* = 115 IN CERTAIN RATINGS

ONLY 2 COUPES BLT.

TACHOMETER

MACHINE-TURNED DASH

(OCT., '35 = EARLIEST "810" has HEADLIGHT DOORS LOCATED CLOSER IN TOWARD GRILLE.)

218

6.50 x 16

Auto-Lite IGNITION

69

COURIER

COURIER MOTOR CO.,
SANDUSKY, OHIO

(1922-1924)

(REPLACES MAIBOHM)

116" W.B.   6-CYL., OVERHEAD-VALVE
5 TO 1 G.R.   195.6 C.I.D. FALLS ENGINE
32 × 4 TIRES   ATWATER-KENT IGNITION

CRANE-SIMPLEX (1915-1924)

('22)

6 CYL.

SIMPLEX AUTOMOBILE CO.,
NEW BRUNSWICK, N.J.,
L.I. CITY, N.Y.

CRAWFORD

('20)

MINOR CHANGES ONLY FOR '20.
6 CYL. CONTINENTAL ENG.
122½" W.B.

(CRAWFORD AUTOMOBILE CO., HAGERSTOWN, MD.)
(1905-1923)

SEE ALSO "DAGMAR"

CROSLEY (1939-1952)

39

2 CYLINDERS

WEIGHT= ONLY 925 LBS.!
MECH. BRAKES
4.25 × 12" TIRES

5.14 GEAR RATIO

CROW-ELKHART

117" W.B.

(1909-1924)
CROW ELKHART
MOTOR CAR CO.

21

4.25 G.R.

"L-55" ('19-20)
4 CYL. 192.4 C.I.D.
LYCOMING OR
HERSCHELL-SPILLMAN ENGINE

6 CYL. RUTENB. ENGINE ALSO (H SERIES)

19-20

248.9 C.I.D.
HERSCH.-SP.
6-CYL.
ENGINE
ADOPTED
DURING '21
ON "S."

"S-67" 6 CYL. 7-PASS.

"L" CONT'D. AS 4-CYL. MODEL.

CUNNINGHAM

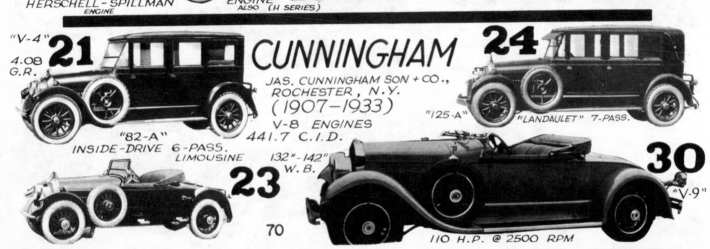

"V-4"
21
4.08 G.R.

"82-A"
INSIDE-DRIVE 6-PASS.
LIMOUSINE

JAS. CUNNINGHAM SON + CO.,
ROCHESTER, N.Y.
(1907-1933)
V-8 ENGINES
441.7 C.I.D.
132"-142" W.B.

24

"125-A"

"LANDAULET" 7-PASS.

23

30
"V-9"

110 H.P. @ 2500 RPM

CRAWFORD AUTOMOBILE CO.;
M.P. MÖLLER CAR CO.,
HAGERSTOWN, MD.
(EARLY "CRAWFORD-DAGMAR"
has 138" W.B.)
6-CYL. CONTINENTAL OR LYCOMING ENGINES

DAGMAR
(1922-1927)
LATER MODEL has
120" W.B.

DANIELS (1915-1924)

NEW FOR 1920: DANIELS-BUILT V-8
(404.1 C.I.D.) ENGINE, IN MODEL "D-19"
DANIELS EIGHT.

DANIELS MOTOR CAR CO., READING, PA.

34 x 4½
TIRES
(THROUGH '21)

"SUBMARINE SPEEDSTER"

132" W.B.

TOURING

6-PASS. TOURING SEDAN

33 x 5
TIRES,
1922-1924

NO SIGNIFICANT MODEL CHANGES
1920-1924, EXC.
"23-28" SERIES
STARTS '23.

DASH

21

HEXAGON KNOB IN CENTER OF DASH
IS VENT CONTROL. NEXT TO IT AT
RIGHT IS HAND AIR PUMP.
(138" W.B. ALSO AVAIL. IN '24)

TOWN CAR

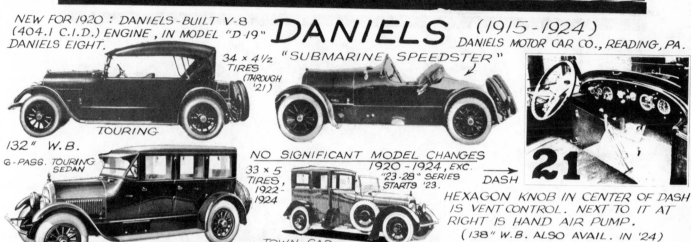

DAVIS (1908-1929)

"Built of the Best"

FEW CHANGES ON "51"
FOR 1920. HAS
224 C.I.D. "7-R"
CONTINENTAL
6 CYL. ENGINE, (THROUGH '22)
STROMBERG CARB.,
120" W.B. (THROUGH '23)

"71" SERIES ADDED
DURING '22, with
115" W.B., 6-CYL.
195.6 C.I.D. "7U"
CONTINENTAL ENG.
(THROUGH '24,
KNOWN AS "90" IN '25)
5.1 G.R. (THROUGH '25)

GEORGE W. DAVIS
MOTOR CAR CO.
RICHMOND, IND., U.S.A.

"60"
SERIES
23
(63-65)
120" W.B.
241.5 C.I.D.
5.09 G.R.

"60", "70"
SERIES
('23 SIMILAR)

The
COUPÉ ("67")

22

24
"71"

(ALL 6 CYLS.,
1916-1927)

"71" PHAETON

HYDR. BRAKES
STARTING
1925

'25 "MOUNTAINEER 91"
has 6-CYL. CONT. "8-R" (241.6)
ENGINE (56
H.P. @ 2300)

26

(LARGER "92" has 115" W.B., 230.1 C.I.D. "11-U"
CONT. ENG., 54 H.P. ('26) 68 H.P. ('27) 4.9 G.R.

"93" (W.B. lowered
to 109") 169.2
C.I.D. "20-L"
ENG. (185 C.I.D.
48 H.P. IN '27)

25 "90" (115" W.B.)
49 H.P. @ 2500

1927="92-97" SIMILAR
TO '26 "92." "SILVER ANNIVERSARY 94" REPLACES "93"
1928="99" has STR.-8 CONT. "14-S" ENGINE, 119" W.B., 84 H.P.
1929="69" (6) and "89" (8)

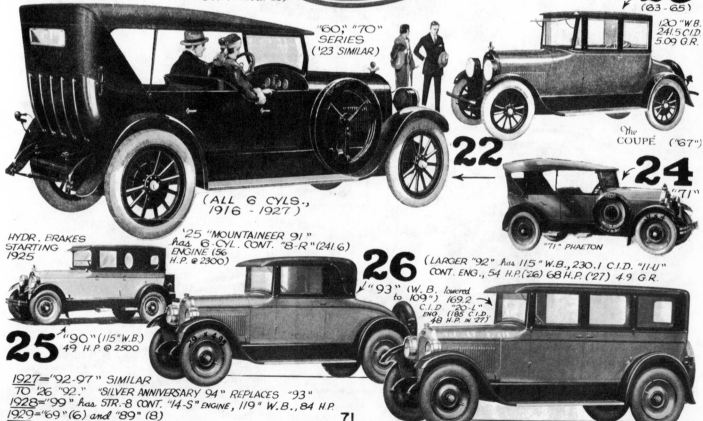

132" W.B.
2.0
G.R.

DELLING STEAM CAR
(1923 – 1927) DELLING STEAM MOTOR CO.,
W. COLLINGWOOD,
N.J. and
PHILADELPHIA

2 CYLINDERS "126" has HYDR. BRKS., ALUM.
BODY, 32 × 6.20 TIRES ('26 SPECS.)

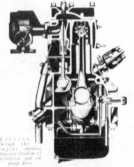

IGNITION :
DELCO : TO 2-1-29
NORTHEAST : AFTER
2-1-29

174.9 C.I.D.
6 CYLINDERS

Section through the engine showing diagonal location of distributor and oil pump drive.

55 H.P. @ 3000 RPM
5.2 COMPR.

(1928 – 1961)

DE SOTO SIX
A CHRYSLER MOTORS PRODUCT

109"
WHEELBASE
STROM. CARB.

29 MODEL K
JULY, 1928
TO
MAY, 1930

Business coupe with rear deck for luggage

Four-door, five-passenger de luxe sedan

(DE SOTO CARS
PRODUCED FROM
7-28 TO 12-60
FINAL CAR :
1961 V-8)

(ALL DE SOTOS HAVE HYDRAULIC BRAKES,
'28 – '61)

HAYES BODIES
ON SOME
"K" MODELS

has
VACUUM
TANK

SOME "K" MODELS HAVE
"De Soto Six" IN
CHROME - PLATED
SCRIPT, FASTENED
TO RADIATOR
CORE . (ALSO
IN '30)

De luxe coupe with rumble seat

Five - passenger, two-door sedan

EARLY '30 "K" LIKE '29, BUT HAS A FEW FALSE HOOD LOUVRES.

DE SOTO SIX

5.00 x 19

(DETAILS OF ROADSTER)

CARTER CARB. REPLACES STROMBERG.

Front Compartment

1—Windshield regulator handle
2—Ignition switch and lock
3—Throttle control hand lever
4—Horn push-button
5—Light control hand lever
6—Door remote control handle
7—Door window regulator handle
8—Windshield wiper control valve
9—Gearshift lever
10—Clutch pedal
11—Brake pedal
12—Rear view mirror

13—Fuel gauge
14—Choke control button
15—Oil gauge
16—Ammeter
17—Speedometer
18—Steering post support bracket
19—Release button
20—Transmission brake hand lever
21—Starter pedal
22—Accelerator pedal
23—Accelerator foot rest

Finer De Soto Six

(CK) STARTS 5-30
(AVAIL. TO 11-30)

NEW DISPL. OF 189.6 CU. IN.
60 H.P. @ 3400 RPM

$\frac{6}{8}$ **30** $\frac{6}{8}$

DeSoto STRAIGHT EIGHT

AFTER 11-30, "CF" has "NARROW PROFILE" RADIATOR SHELL. (SEE 1931)

5.25 x 19

(CF) INTRO. 1-30

STYLE OF '30, with THICK RADIATOR SHELL.

207.7 C.I.D.

114" W.B.
STROMBERG CARB. ON "CF"

70 H.P. @ 3400 RPM
FUEL PUMP ADDED

DASH

EIGHT SEDAN

EIGHT CONVERTIBLE COUPE

73

DE SOTO

NEW DASH (SA) HAS GAUGES BEHIND OVAL GLASS PANEL.

RUMBLE-SEAT DETAILS (8)

6 "SA"

109 3/8" W.B.

205.3 C.I.D. 72 H.P. @ 3400 RPM (6)

8 "CF"

6
8

31
(STARTS 12-30)

(8) 114" W.B. 220.7 C.I.D. 77 H.P. @ 3400 RPM

FUEL PUMP

"CF" AVAIL. TO 2-32

31½ — EARLY **32**

("SA" and "CF" BLT. 7-23-31 and AFTER ARE SOMETIMES KNOWN AS "EARLY 1932.")

(SA)

"SA" OUTER VISOR RESTORED "Free-Wheeling" AVAIL., and "EASY-SHIFT" TRANSMISSION (SA or CF)

"SA" AVAIL. TO 3-32

B+B CARB. (THROUGH '35)

(12-31 TO 10-32)

112 3/8" W.B.

CHROMED RADIATOR SHELL ON EARLY MODELS.

211.4 C.I.D. 75 H.P. @ 3400 RPM NEW 5.25 x 18 AND OTHER TIRES.

Custom 5 Passenger Sedan De Luxe

32 "SC" 6 CYL. ONLY

Custom Convertible Sedan De Luxe

Custom Roadster De Luxe

Standard Coupe

Standard 2 Door Sedan

DE SOTO

(11-32 to 10-33)

33 ("SD") 6

114 3/8" W.B. 86 H.P. @ 3400 RPM

NEW 6 TO 1 COMPR. NEW 5.50 x 17 AND OTHER TIRES.
217.8 C.I.D.

WHAT—NO HAND-STRAPS! "WALK RIGHT IN" THESE DOORS

34 (SE) (1-34 to 10-34)

THE WHEEL IS WHERE YOU WANT IT RIDE INSIDE THE FRAME... NOT ON IT

ALL-NEW, STREAMLINED "AIRFLOW" (2 or 4-DOOR) IS ONLY MODEL OF DE SOTO AVAILABLE FOR 1934.

115 1/2" W.B.

NEW 6.50 x 16 TIRES (ON 1934 THROUGH 1936 "AIRFLOW")

241.5 C.I.D. 100 H.P. @ 3400 RPM 6.2 COMPR.

AIRSTREAM 6 (SF)

116" W.B.
6 TO 1 COMPR.
93 H.P. @ 3400 RPM

AIRFLOW 6 (SG)

6.5 COMP.
100 H.P. @ 3400

35 (STARTS 11-34)

115 1/2" W.B.

6.25 x 16 TIRES (ON 1935 and 1936 "AIRSTREAM")

AIRFLOW 6 (S-2)

115 1/2 WB

(new CARTER CARB.) (BOTH SERIES) 118" W.B.

AIRSTREAM CUSTOM 6 (S-1)

AIRSTREAM ALSO AVAIL. WITH 1-PC. WINDSHIELD

36 (STARTS 9-35)

75

SAME ENGINES AS 1935

DE SOTO

116" W.B.

All Seat Edges Padded.   Safety-height Instrument Panel.   All Panel Controls are Flush.

DISPLACEMENT REDUCED TO 228.1 CU. IN.
6.5 COMPR.   93 H.P. @ 3600 RPM
CARTER B+B CARBURETOR
(THROUGH '38)

37
(S-3)
(9-36 TO 8-37)

DASH

38 (S-5)
(9-37 TO 7-38)

6.00 × 16 OR
6.50 × 16 TIRES
(THROUGH '40)

CARTER CARB.

('38 - 39 SPECIFICATIONS
SAME AS 1937)

39 (S-6)
(8-38 TO 7-39)

SPEED INDICATOR
CHANGES COLORS

COLUMN SHIFT

76

DETROIT AIR-COOLED (1923)

DETROIT AIR-COOLED CAR CO., DETROIT, MICH.
(ALSO KNOWN AS "D.A.C" CAR, 1922-1923)
V-6 AIR-COOLED ENGINE

DETROIT ELECTRIC
(1907-1938)
DETROIT ELECTRIC CAR CO., DETROIT

FALSE "RADIATOR" TRIED BRIEFLY

20

MOST LATER MODELS BUILT TO ORDER, AS IS THIS 1931 MODEL "99" →

"88" 5-PASS. BROUGHAM

32 × 4½

21 100" W.B.

ORIGINAL NAME: TRASK-DETROIT

DETROIT STEAM
(1922-1923)
DETROIT STEAM MOTORS CORP., DETROIT

31

"6-75" 65 H.P. @ 3400 RPM 4.4 G.R.

113" W.B. 5.00 × 19 TIRES

DE VAUX **32**
DE VAUX-HALL MOTOR CORP., GRAND RAPIDS, MICH. and OAKLAND, CALIF.
(1931-1932)
6-CYL. 214.7 C.I.D. CONTINENTAL-HALL *engine*

"80"

70 H.P. and 3.9 G.R. IN '32

DIANA ('26)

SUBSIDIARY OF MOON MOTOR CAR CO., ST. LOUIS, MO.

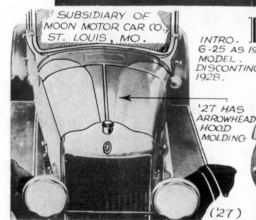

INTRO. 6-25 AS 1926 MODEL. DISCONTINUED 1928.

'27 HAS ARROWHEAD HOOD MOLDING

STRAIGHT-8. CONTINENTAL ENGINE 12-Z

HYDRAULIC BRAKES

32 × 6.00

('27) 5.1 G.R.

240.2 C.I.D. 72 H.P. @ 2950 RPM

125½" W.B.

"H-S-60" 50

Kentucky Wagon Mfg. Co. Louisville Kentucky

20-21 DIXIE FLYER
(1916-1922)

4-CYL. HERS.-SPLMN. ENGINE (165.9 C.I.D. IN '20)

IN 1922, DIXIE FLYER ABSORBED BY NATIONAL

22 4.75 G.R.

4.72 G.R. (THROUGH '21) 32 × 4 TIRES

192.4 C.I.D. (SINCE '21)

112" W.B. ("HS-70" STARTS '21)

DOBLE STEAM

('25)

FORMERLY "DOBLE-DETROIT"

('29-32)

('31-32)

EST. 1914,
DOBLE STEAM MOTORS
MOVED TO EMERYVILLE,
CALIF. IN 1924; IN
BUSINESS UNTIL 1932.

MURPHY BODY

DODGE BROTHERS

(SINCE NOV., 1914)
DODGE BROS., DETROIT
(A PRODUCT OF
CHRYSLER CORP. SINCE MID-1928.)

20

4-DOOR SEDAN
(2-19 TO 7-21)

4 CYLINDER,
212.3 C.I.D.
ENGINE
(1915 TO 1927)

35 H.P. @ 2000 RPM

(4 TO 1 COMPRESSION
(THROUGH 1926)

7-19 TO 6-20

114" WHEELBASE (1916-1923)

32 × 3½ TIRES (THROUGH 1921)

21-22

7-1-20 TO 5-23-22

JULY, 1921
BUDD-MICHELIN
STEEL DISC WHEELS
INTRODUCED ON
SOME DODGES;
SEDAN 4" LOWER.
32 × 4" TIRES
(1922 THROUGH 1925)

DODGE BROTHERS

32 X 4 STEEL DISC
BUDD - MICHELIN
WHEELS AVAIL.

22 ½

5-24-22
TO
6-28-23

TO

BUSINESS
SEDAN
(ANNOUNCED 9-22)

SPEC.
SUBURB.
SEDAN

BUSINESS
COUPE
(AVAILABLE
SUMMER , 1922)

23

CANTRELL
BODY

BABCOCK
BODY

2-PASS.
BUSINESS
CPE.

(4 - PASS.
CPE. ALSO
AVAILABLE)

7-1-23 TO
← 11-1-24

24

NEW 116"
WHEELBASE

BUSINESS SEDAN

1924 Model Cantrell Suburban Body for Latest Type Dodge Brothers Chassis

TYPE A

DODGE BROTHERS

TYPE-A SEDAN

25

NEW
COACH

JAN., '25

HAS NICKEL RADIATOR
SHELL

SPECIAL=

26

SPECIAL
TYPE-B SEDAN

(EARLY '26)
SEDANS

SPECIAL
TYPE-A SEDAN

I-PIECE WINDSHIELD
ON LATER MODELS.

SPECIAL

26½

80

DODGE BROTHERS

EARLY MODEL (TO FEB., '27)
MODEL 126

31 x 5.25 TIRES

27

FEB., '27 ROOF-VISOR
MODEL 124
NEW 4.1 TO 1 COMPR.

4 CYL.

IN 1927, DODGE BROS. CARS ABANDON 12-VOLT ELECTRICAL SYSTEM IN FAVOR OF CONVENTIONAL 6-VOLT SYSTEM. ELECTRICAL SYSTEM CHANGED FROM ONE-UNIT TO 2-UNIT (STARTER + GENERATOR SEPERATED.)

"126"

SPARK and THROTTLE LEVERS MOVED TO TOP OF STEERING WHEEL.

40 H.P. @ 2400 RPM

MODEL 2249
SENIOR 6
224 C.I.D. 6 CYL. 60 H.P. @ 2800 RPM 5.3 COMPR. (FIRST 6-CYL. DODGE)
INTRO. 6-27

27½
(108" W.B.)

FAST 4 "128"
INTRO. 7-27, CONT'D. TO 1928 SEASON
29 x 5.00 TIRES

6 - CYLINDER DODGES FOR 1928

The VICTORY SIX
BY DODGE BROTHERS

(INTRO. 1-5-28) MODEL 130, 131

STD. 6 and VICTORY 6 HAVE 208 C.I.D., 5.2 COMPR. and 58 H.P. @ 3000 RPM with 29 x 5.00 TIRES

(MECHANICAL BRAKES)
STANDARD 6
MODEL 140, 141

110" W.B.

112" W.B. 4.45 GEAR RATIO

HYDRAULIC BRAKES

VICTORY 6

The DeLuxe Sedan

RT. HAND DRIVE - EXPORT MODEL

SENIOR 6 MODEL 2251

28
78 H.P. @ 3000 RPM
241.5 C.I.D.
5.2 COMPR.

31 x 6.00 TIRES
NEW 120" W.B.

DODGE BROTHERS

CHRYSLER MOTORS PRODUCT

6 (DA)

"DA" HAS SAME SPECS.
AS VICTORY 6. BUILT
1-29 TO 3-30

BUDD BODIES,
AS BEFORE

29

DA
VIC.

('29 MODEL STARTS
8-28)

HYDRAULIC BRAKES, INTRODUCED TO DODGE
ON '27-8 "SENIOR" and '28 "VICTORY 6," ARE
STANDARD ON ALL DODGES FROM 1929 ON.

DA
SR.

MURRAY
BODIES
ON
"SENIOR
6"
ONLY.

NEW VICTORY SIX

'29 "VICTORY 6" HAS HIGHER, LONGER BODY
THAN '28. SEDAN DOORS WIDENED 3".
SEAT CUSHIONS AND BACKS ARE DEEPER.

"FROSTED SILVER"
INST. PANEL

SENIOR
6

MODEL 2252 SR. 6
BUILT 7-28 TO 6-29

(CONT'D. TO 6-30,
AS "DB" series)
COMPRESSION INCREASED TO 5.5

CHRYSLER PURCHASED
DODGE BROS. IN SPRING,
1928. 1929 AND LATER
DODGES ARE CHRYSLER PRODUCTS.

6.00 x 19" TIRES

82

DODGE   BROTHERS

SIX

(DA) TO 3-30

VACUUM TANK RETAINED ON "DA" SIX, AS ON LEFTOVER MODELS OF "SENIOR SIX."

NAME SHORTENED TO <u>DODGE</u> DURING 1930.

NOTE NEW POSITION OF COWL LAMPS ON ABOVE MODEL.

30

NEW 8 (DC) HAS 114" W.B., 220.7 C.I.D., 5.4 COMPR., 75 H.P. @ 3400 RPM
4.6 GEAR RATIO
new FUEL PUMP

(DC)

EIGHT

60 H.P. @ 3400 RPM   189.8 C.I.D.   **DODGE SIX** (PRODUCTION STARTS 12-29)

109" W.B.

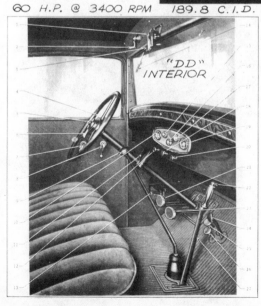

"DD" INTERIOR

new RADIATOR DESIGN

30½ TO MAY, 31 (DD)

HAS FUEL PUMP

4.9 GEAR RATIO   83

224·928
MICHIGAN 1930

DODGE SIX AND EIGHT

5.00 x 19 TIRES ON SIXES

6 (DH)

211.5 C.I.D. 5.35 COMPR.
113 5/8" W.B. 4.66 G.R.
74 H.P. @ 3400 RPM

NEW DODGE SIX SEDAN 1931

31

"Standard" MODELS ARE CONTINUATIONS OF 1930 "DD" 6 AND "DC" 8.

THE LAST DODGE ROADSTER UNTIL 1949 →

8 (DG)
118" W.B.
240.3 C.I.D.
5.4 COMPR.
84 H.P. @ 3400 RPM
5.50 x 18 TIRES
4.60 GEAR RATIO

5.50 x 18 TIRES
4.6 GEAR RATIO (DL) 6

217.8 C.I.D.
79 H.P. @ 3400 RPM
6.35 COMPR. OPTIONAL

114 3/8" W.B.

6 and 8 COUPES and CVT. CPES. HAVE 4.3 (6) and 3.91 (8) GEAR RATIOS

32

4.1 GEAR RATIO
6.00 x 18 TIRES

282.1 C.I.D.
5.2 OR 6.2 COMPR.
90 OR 100 H.P. @ 3400 RPM

8 (DK)

CONVERTIBLE SEDAN (NEW)

122 3/8" W.B.

84

33 **DODGE**

REDUCED TO 201.3 C.I.D. 5.5 OR 6.2 COMPR. 75 OR 81 H.P. @ 3600 RPM

6 (DP)

REAR DETAILS

115" W.B.

The big, new Dodge "6" Sedan—$675 f. o. b. factory, Detroit, special equipment extra

'33 DASH GAUGES IN CENTER

6 / 8

HOOD ON "8" DOES NOT CONCEAL COWL AS IT DOES ON "6"

"8" HAS COWL LAMPS

DODGE "8"
WITH FLOATING POWER

An Aristocrat From Bumper to Bumper

Dodge "8" 122" w.b.

OPTIONAL "RED HEAD" ON 8 GIVES 6.5 COMPRESSION.

'34 DASH GAUGES AT LEFT

92 OR 100 H.P. @ 3400 RPM (8)

(DO) = (*Final Dodge straight-8*)

217.8 C.I.D. 5.6 OR 6.5 COMPR.

82 OR 87 H.P. @ 3600 RPM

117" W.B.

34 (DR)

LUGGAGE CARRIED BEHIND REAR SEAT-BACK.

85

6.5 COMPRESSION
ALUMINUM HEAD
STANDARD ON
"DS"

DODGE

(DS) SPECIAL
121" WHEELBASE

6.25 x 16 TIRES

34½

(FEWER HOOD LOUVRES)

34
(CONT'D.)

"DRXX"
MODEL WAS
LOW-PRICED
1934½ SERIES,
WITHOUT
BUILT-IN VENT
WINDOWS.

217.8 C.I.D. CONTINUED
THROUGH 1941

REAR
DETAILS

The New Dodge Touring Sedan
Four-Door—with Trunk

Convertible Coupe

WITHOUT
TRUNK

Sedan

DASH

35
(DU)

SEDAN INTERIOR

NEW
HORN GRILLES
BELOW LIGHTS

87 H.P. @ 3600 RPM
(THROUGH 1940)

The New Dodge Touring Sedan
Two-Door—with Trunk

WHEELBASE NOW
116" (AS ALSO
IN 1936)

Coupe with Rumble Seat

6.5
COMPRESSION
(THROUGH
1941)

6.00 x 16 IS
STANDARD TIRE SIZE
UNTIL LATE 1940s.

Coupe

DODGE

Two-Door Sedan

STEEL
TIRE-COVER
AVAILABLE

DASH

DODGE (D-2)

36

WESTCHESTER
SUBURBAN WAGON

37 (D-5)

NEW "HIGH-SAFETY" INTERIOR

PULL-DRAWER RECESSED
KNOBS ON
EARLY
MODELS.

NEW
HORIZONTAL
GRILLE
MOTIF

115" WHEELBASE IN
1937 and 1938

WINDSHIELDS DO NOT OPEN ON '38 CHRYSLER-BUILT CARS.

38

(D-8)

'39
ENGINE

INTERIOR

LIGHTED SPEED INDICATOR

FAST
BACK

117"
WHEELBASE

87 ## 39 (D-11)

DORRIS
(1905–1926)

DORRIS MOTOR CAR CO.
ST. LOUIS, MO.

OWN 377 C.I.D., O.H.V.
6-CYL. ENG.

21 132" W.B. WESTINGHOUSE IGNITION (THROUGH '21)

"6-80" 7-PASS.

33 × 5

22 NEW BOSCH IGNITION "6-80"

(NO NEW PRODUCTION AFTER 1923.)

DORT (1915–1924)

Quality Goes Clear Through

Dort Motor Car Company
Flint, Mich.

21 "17-A" OR "17-12" MODELS

NEW, ANGULAR STYLING FOR 1921, NEW 108" W.B.

Top and curtains up
When the storm beats down

20

(4)

4 CYL. 192.4 C.I.D. LYCOMING ENGINE

STOP GO

105½" W.B.

1922 "19-14" MODEL LIKE 1921.

MODEL "15" TOURING
FEW CHANGES FROM 1919.

23 "HARVARD SEDAN"

(6)

31 × 4 TIRES

"27-C" "3-DOOR COUPE" IS A SEDAN WITH JUST ONE DOOR ON LEFT SIDE.

FALLS ENGINE (6 CYL., O.H.V.) 207.1 C.I.D.

24

MODEL 27 NEW RADIATOR DESIGN (THE FINAL DORT)

NEW 1923
MODEL 18-23 HAS 108" W.B., LYCOMING ENGINE AS BEFORE, 4.60 GEAR RATIO

MODEL 25-20 HAS 115" W.B., NEW 195.6 C.I.D.,
6-CYL. FALLS ENGINE, 4.66 GEAR RATIO
45 HORSEPOWER   (INTRO. 11-22)

21 (97.4 CID) 4 CYLS.
104" W.B.
4.75 G.R.

DRIGGS (1921–1923)

DRIGGS ORDNANCE AND
MANUFACTURING CO.,
NEW HAVEN, CONN. AND N.Y.C.

22-23

OWN ENG.   30 × 3½ TIRES

88

DUESENBERG STRAIGHT 8

(1920–1937)
DUESENBERG MOTOR CO., INDIANAPOLIS, IND.

DASH

"A" SERIES
259.7 C.I.D.
STRAIGHT-8 ENGINE
100 H.P. @ 3600 RPM ('26 RATING)

HYDRAULIC BRAKES
STANDARD EQUIPMENT
90 MILES PER HOUR

PRESSURE FUEL FEED IN '26

134" W.B.

21-28

(JOINED AUBURN IN 1926)

('27-'28 MODEL "X")

29-37

AVAIL. WITH PRESSURE FUEL FEED ('32)

"J" SERIES
STRAIGHT-8
420 C.I.D.
265 H.P. @ 4200 RPM

HAS FUEL PUMP ('29)

MURPHY BODY

"SJ"
(SUPERCHARGED)
(NOTE THE EXHAUST PIPES THROUGH HOOD.)

BARKER BODY

142½" – 153½" WHEELBASES

DASH

RENOWNED COACHBUILDERS SUPPLIED MANY VARIETIES OF CUSTOM BODIES.

"J"
(UN-SUPERCHARGED)

89

20 "A" MODEL

DU PONT

DUPONT MOTORS, INC.
WILMINGTON, DEL.
(1920 – 1932)

(ALSO MOORE, PA.)

124" W.B. (THROUGH '26)

16" BRAKE DRUMS, WATER TEMP. GAUGE ON DASH, CONCAVE BODY SIDES.
OWN 4-CYL., 249.6 C.I.D. ENGINE (TO '23) 2-WH. MECH. BRAKES and 4.45 G.R. (THROUGH '24)

21

← 5-PASS. TOURING CAR

23

24 (6-CYL.)

MODEL C 57 H.P.

('24 HAS 6-CYL. HERSCHELL-SPILLMAN "90" ENGINE) (288.6 C.I.D.)

5-PASS. TOURING SEDAN

25 MODEL D (1925 – 1926) HAS NEW O.H.V. WISCONSIN 6-CYL. "Y" ENGINE (268.3 C.I.D. 75 H.P. @ 3000 RPM NEW HYDRAULIC BRAKES

28 MODEL E →

MODEL E RUNS FROM 1927 TO 1929. (MODEL F ALSO, IN '28)

4.7 GEAR RATIO
32 × 6.20 BALLOON TIRES (THROUGH '29)

6-CYL. WISC. "Y" ENGINE 268.3 C.I.D., 75 H.P. @ 3000 RPM 32 × 6.20 TIRES
MODEL E = 125" W.B., 4.7 GEAR RATIO
MODEL F = 136" " 4.45 " "

140-H.P. SPEEDSTER

29-30 MODEL G

125" W.B.

NARROW "WOOD-LITES"

30-32 MODEL G (MERRIMAC BODY)

141" W.B.

MODEL G HAS STRAIGHT-8 CONTINENTAL "12-K" ENGINE (322 C.I.D.) WITH 114 H.P. @ 3200 RPM (GETS FUEL PUMP, '29)

LEFTOVER CARS STILL AVAIL. IN 1933.

MODEL H ('31-32) HAS 146" W.B.

H.P. INCREASED IN 1932, TO 130 @ 3200 RPM

dP DUPONT

90

The DU PONT

DURANT
(1921-1932)
DURANT MOTORS, INC.
(OFFICES IN N.Y.C.)

6 - CYL. "B-22" HAS SQUARE-EDGED HOOD. 6 DISCONTINUED MID-1924. (PHOTO AT UPPER RIGHT.)

('24)

"B-22" 6 CYL. ('22)

ANSTED ENG.

FOUR

"A-22"

21-25

('21-22 HAS WOOD WHEELS. DISC WHEELS ALSO, STARTING 1923.)

('25)

LATE '25 SOMETIMES CALLED "1926."

28
4 and 6 CYLS.

(EARLY '28 4-CYL.= "DURANT-STAR")

CONTINENTAL ENGINES USED (THROUGH '32) DURANT PRODUCTION SUSPENDED 1926-7, BUT STAR CAR CONTINUED.

HAYES-HUNT BODIES

"4-40" ("M")

29
OTHER 6-CYL. MODELS: "55," "60," "65," "6-60," "6-66"

("6-63" CONSIDERED AN EARLY '30 MODEL.)

(M SERIES (REPLACES STAR)

"6-70" DE LUXE SEDAN

119" W.B.

(65 H.P., 4-SPEED TRANS.)

BUDD ALL-STEEL BODIES ON SOME '30 DURANTS.
NOTE NEW EMBLEM

30

DURANT

EARLY '32 IS "619"

'30 "6-14" has NEW FUEL PUMP.

"6-17" GETS IT IN '31

"621," "622" also, IN '32 (71 H.P.)

31
"610," "612"
(4)   (6)
VERTICAL HOOD LOUVRES; SOME MODELS HAVE RADIATOR SHUTTERS and SEATS THAT CONVERT TO A BED.

32
FINAL DURANT

5.00 or 5.50 x 19

"6-14" = 58 H.P., 199 C.I.D.
"6-17" = 70 H.P., 248 C.I.D.
SOME '30s HAVE VERTICAL HOOD LOUVRES.

('31)

91

DYMAXION

(ONLY 3 PILOT MODELS)
DESIGNED BY
BUCKMINSTER FULLER

33-34

SINGLE REAR WHEEL!

FORD V-8 REAR ENGINE

TOURING CARS ONLY

EAGLE

23-24

WITH 6-CYLINDER, 195.6 C.I.D. CONTINENTAL ENGINE (Auto-Lite IGN.)

BUILT, BRIEFLY, BY DURANT MOTORS

115" W.B.   4-WHEEL BRAKES
30 × 3½ TIRES   4.77 G.R.

REPLACES BRISCOE

The EARL
EARL MOTORS, INC.
JACKSON   MICHIGAN

21-24

"Cabriole"

4 CYL. 112" W.B.
('22 MODEL INTRO. 1921)

KNOWN AS "BROUGHAM" UNTIL MID-'22

ELCAR

(1915-1931)

ELCAR MOTOR CO.,
ELKHART, INDIANA

116" W.B. IN '20

NEW STYLING FOR 1921
LYCOMING 4 CYL.
(192.4 CID) ('21)

(NEW STRAIGHT-LINE ROOF)

(6 CYL. MODELS W. 224 CID CONT. ENG. ALSO)
117" W.B. IN '21 (4+6)

DRUM HEADLIGHTS ON 1922 MODELS, 118" W.B.

"4-40" ('23-24) 112" W.B.

"6-60" IS 6-CYL., 118" W.B.

Three-Door Four Cylinder

NEW PEAKED RADIATOR FEATURED, MID-1924.

ELCAR
A WELL BUILT CAR

EMBLEM

'26 INTRODUCES LIGHT CONTROL ON STEERING WHEEL

26

MODEL "8-81"

FROM 1926 ON, LYCOMING ENGINES USED IN 6-CYL. MODELS also.

25

"8-80" 7-PASS.   127" W.B.

FIRST YEAR FOR ELCAR STRAIGHT-8 (254.4 LYCOMING "H" ENG.)

63 H.P. @ 3000

27

"8-90"

(4 CYL. MODEL DISCONTINUED JAN., 1927)

28

29

"PRINCESS"
NEW ROUNDED EDGE ON '29 RADIATOR

ELCAR-LEVER WAS AN ELCAR ENTRY IN 1930 AUTOMOBILE SHOW. IT HAD A POWELL-LEVER ENGINE WITH JOINTED CONNECTING RODS.

92

MODEL K
('20-21)

(1916-1924)

ELGIN MOTOR
CAR CORP.,
ELGIN and
ARGO,
ILL.

(195.6 CID,
1922 ON)

4-WH.
BRKS.
ON
SOME
'24s

118" W.B.
(THROUGH '24)
(DISC WHEELS ON SPT. TOURING)

NEW FOR 1920:
COLUMBIA AXLES. 10"
BORG + BECK CLUTCH REPLACES 8" TYPE.
6-CYL., O.H.V.
FALLS ENGINE

('24)
(NEW STYLING)

ERSKINE 6

CONTINENTAL "8-F" 6-CYL., L-HEAD
ENGINE

27

The Little
Aristocrat
40 H.P.
@ 3200

5.13
G.R.

107" W.B. (THROUGH '28)

(1927 TO 1930)
PRODUCT OF STUDEBAKER

146.1
C.I.D.
IN
1927

28 x 4.40

4-WHEEL
BRAKES

STROM.
CARB.

'27 DASH

"AMERICAN 6"
SERIES
107" W.B.

new
SCHEBLER
CARB. (THROUGH
'30)

MODEL "51"
(STARTS
1-1-28)

28

CONT. "9-F" ENG.
(THROUGH '29)
DOES NOT HAVE FENDER BOXES,
AS SEEN ON '27 ERSKINE.

(160.37 C.I.D.)
42 H.P.

4.78 G.R.

29 x 4.75
TIRES

'28
(DASH GAUGES
GROUPED BEHIND
GLASS PANEL.)

20 x 4.75
TIRES

29

SOME SEDANS HAVE
BUDD BODIES.

DELCO-REMY IGNITION
(1927 THROUGH '30)

MODEL "52"   43 H.P. @ 3000 RPM

109" W.B.
new 109" W.B.

(STARTS 7-9-28. CARS
BUILT AFTER 8-5-29 CONSIDERED "EARLY 1930.")

"DYNAMIC NEW" SERIES
"53"

30

(STARTS
12-26-29)
70 H.P.

(OWN
ENGINE)

30½ STUDEBAKER 6
LOOKS THE
SAME
AS
THIS
MODEL.

HAS FUEL PUMP
(NEW ENGINE
SIZE:
205.3 C.I.D.)

NAME
CHANGED TO
STUDEBAKER 6

ERSKINE

STUDEBAKER BUILT

5.25 x 19

93

4.78 G.R. (SINCE '28)
new 114" W.B., 5.25 x 19 TIRES

ESSEX
INTRODUCED 1919, BUILT BY HUDSON

1919-21

108½" WHEELBASE (THROUGH '23)

4 CYLINDERS
178.9 C.I.D.
55 H.P.
5.09 GEAR RATIO (THROUGH '20)
4.66 GEAR RATIO (THROUGH '23)

OIL CUPS INSTEAD OF GREASE CUPS

Coach (NEW)

new DRUM HEADLIGHTS and FLANGED CROWN FENDERS IN 1922.

22-23
(FINAL 4 CYLINDER ESSEX IN 1923)

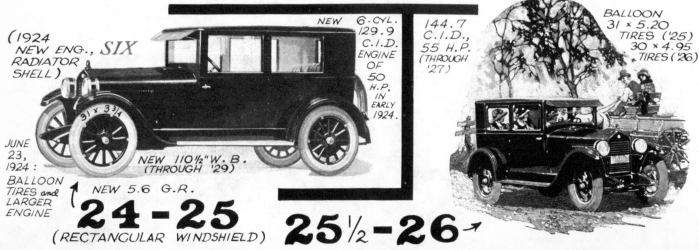

(1924 NEW ENG., SIX RADIATOR SHELL)

NEW 6-CYL. 129.9 C.I.D. ENGINE OF 50 H.P. IN EARLY 1924.

144.7 C.I.D., 55 H.P. (THROUGH '27)

BALLOON 31 × 5.20 TIRES ('25) 30 × 4.95 TIRES ('26)

JUNE 23, 1924: BALLOON TIRES and LARGER ENGINE

NEW 110½" W.B. (THROUGH '29)

NEW 5.6 G.R.

24-25
(RECTANGULAR WINDSHIELD)

25½-26 →

ESSEX 26½

NEW STEEL BODIES WITH CURVED UPPER BACK.
LONG PIANO-TYPE DOOR HINGES = JULY, 1926

NICKEL-PLATED
RADIATOR = JULY, 1926

Speedabout

27

"SUPER 6"
(RESTYLED)

STARTER
CONTROL
ON DASH

JULY,
1927 =

ENGINE STROKE 1/4"
LONGER. NEW 30 × 5
TIRES. REAR TIRE
CARRIER CHANGED FROM
BUCKET TYPE TO HOOP
TYPE (LIKE HUDSON.)

5.4 G.R.

ALUMINUM
BODY PANELS OVER
HARDWOOD
FRAME

"POLISHED EBONY"
INSTRUMENT BOARD

28

153.2 C.I.D.

BENDIX 4-WHEEL
MECHANICAL BRAKES

160.4 C.I.D.   55 H.P. @
3600 RPM

29

"THE
CHALLENGER"

"CHASE SILVERED"
INSTRUMENT PANEL

95

ESSEX

A uniform modernistic design has been carried into the details of Essex door handles, window lifts, lights and other appointments.

ESSEX
SUPER
SIX

5.40
GEAR RATIO

30

*NEW 113" WHEELBASE
(THROUGH '32)*

60 H.P. @ 3600 RPM

31

60 H.P. @ 3300 RPM

*(NEW ENGINE SIZE
OF 175.3 C.I.D.)*

5.1 OR 5.4
GEAR RATIOS

96

ESSEX

FREE-WHEELING CONTROL
IN CENTER OF
GEARSHIFT LEVER KNOB

Now triple sealed in a new-type
housing that retains the oil intact
over thousands of miles, the famous Hudson-Essex oil cushion
clutch adds a new standard of
saving and trouble free operating
to its long-established standard
of durability and efficiency

1932 ESSEX SUPER-SIX COACH
Five Passengers . . . 113" Wheelbase

WINDSHIELD
OPENER

DIAMOND
UPHOLSTERY
PATTERN

NOTE NEW WARNING LIGHTS ON DASH

32

NEW "RIDE CONTROL" ADJUSTS SHOCK ABSORBERS
FROM INSIDE THE CAR.

5.25 x 18" TIRES
5.10 and 4.64 GEAR RATIOS

ESSEX 32 (CONT'D.)

REAR VIEW OF 1932 ESSEX

FOR 1932, ENGINE SIZE AGAIN INCREASED (TO 193.1 C.I.D.) 70 H.P. @ 3200 RPM

IN SUMMER OF 1932, THE ESSEX WAS REPLACED BY THE ESSEX-TERRAPLANE.

6 CYL. 106" W.B.
NEW 8 CYL. 113" W.B.

6

8

The New SEVENTY HORSEPOWER ENGINE *of the* 1932 ESSEX SUPER-SIX

TO

32½ TO 33

SEE ALSO "TERRAPLANE"

FALCON

115" W.B., 4.88 G.R.
32 × 4 TIRES
OWN 4 OR 6-CYL.
ENGINES ═
LIGHT 4
192.4 C.I.D.
SIX
230.1 C.I.D.
(NOT IN FULL PROD.)

22

BODY BY
HEALEY and CO.

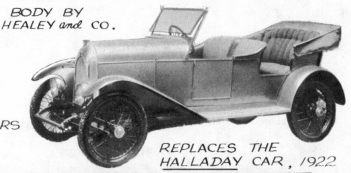

HALLADAY MOTORS
CORP.,
NEWARK, OHIO

REPLACES THE
HALLADAY CAR, 1922

ROOF-VISOR
ON 1927
CLOSED
MODELS

Falcon-Knight
(1927 - 1928)

27

6-CYL. SLEEVE-VALVE ENGINE

FALCON MOTORS CORP., ELYRIA, O.; DETROIT
(WILLYS-KNIGHT AFFILIATE)

1927 ═ 109½" W.B. (MODEL "10")
30 × 5.00 TIRES
5.11 GEAR RATIO ('28 ALSO)
156.6 C.I.D.   4.6 COMPRESSION
45 H.P. @ 3000 RPM ('28 ALSO)
DASH GAUGES UNDER SINGLE GLASS PANE

1928 ═ 109½" W.B. (MODEL "12")
29 × 5.50 TIRES
"FUMER" WARMS CARBURETOR
HARD-RUBBER-COVERED STEERING WHEEL
INDIVIDUAL DASH GAUGES (INCL. GAS
GAUGE)

28

FARGO

(1929 ON, BUILT BY
CHRYSLER CORP.)

29

(PRIMARILY COMMERCIAL
VEHICLES)

(6 CYL.)
HYDRAULIC BRAKES

FERRIS

20-22

OHIO MOTOR VEHICLE CO., CLEVELAND
(1920 - 1922)
130" W.B.
6-CYL. 303.1 C.I.D. CONTINENTAL ENG.
4.08 G.R.   32 × 4½ TIRES
BECOMES MODEL "60" IN 1922;
1922 MODEL "70" ALSO, with 325.1
C.I.D., 6-CYL. CONTINENTAL ENGINE.

BUILDERS OF HIGH GRADE MOTOR CARS

FLINT SIX

120"
W.B.

CONTINENTAL
ENGINES
6 CYLS.

FLINT MOTOR COMPANY
FLINT, MICHIGAN
(1923 - 1927)
AFFILIATED WITH
DURANT AND
LOCOMOBILE

23

268.4 C.I.D.

32
×
4½
TIRES

70 H.P. @ 2500 RPM
4.7 GEAR RATIO

FLINT SIX

24

4.78 G.R.
MODEL E

120" W.B.

(E) 55

MODEL "FIFTY-FIVE" 268.4 C.I.D., 64½ H.P. @ 2400 RPM

120" W.B.

(E) 55

BROUGHAM

FLINT

25

32 x 6.20

Model "55" Five Passenger Sedan

(MODEL "40" ALSO AVAIL.) '24-5
WITH 115" W.B., 196 C.I.D., 49 H.P. @ 2500)

"60" COUPE - ROADSTER
('27)

'27 "60" MODELS
BEGIN AT
18776

The New Flint
"SIXTY"
5-Passenger Sedan

60

FLINT

"60" HAS 230 C.I.D.,
56 H.P. @
2600

The New Flint
"EIGHTY" 268.4 C.I.D.
5-Passenger Sedan
65 H.P.
@ 2400
120" W.B.

80

30 x 5.77

115" W.B.

"Z-18"
"FLINT JUNIOR" COACH ('26-7) 110" W.B.

JR.

HAS 6-CYL.
169.3 C.I.D. ENGINE
40 H.P. @ 2300 RPM
2-WHEEL BRAKES
'26 = #100-1911
'27 = #1912 and up

'27 "80" MODELS BEGIN
AT # 20103

26-27

30 x 5.25

4.875 TO 1 GEAR RATIO

NOTE DIFFERENCES IN HOOD LOUVRE PANEL
AND PLACEMENT OF HOOD LATCH ON
'26 and '27 "60" MODELS ILLUSTRATED.

CENTER-DOOR SEDAN

Ford
THE UNIVERSAL CAR

FORD MOTOR CO.,
DEARBORN, MICH.
(PRODUCTION
BEGINS 1903)

MODEL "T"

(FIRST INTRODUCED LATE 1908, REPLACING MODEL "S.")

17-22

MINOR IMPROVEMENTS DURING COURSE OF PRODUCTION

OWN IGN. SYSTEM

4 CYLINDERS, 176.7 C.I.D. ENGINE
20 HORSEPOWER (THROUGH '27)

100" WHEELBASE
30 x 3½" tires

23-25

FORD USES OWN BRAND OF BATTERY, BUT EXIDE ALSO USED ON SOME 1924 MODELS (ACC. TO *Automotive Industries*, 2-21-24.)

RESTYLED '23 MODELS START AUGUST, 1922. CHOICE OF 2-DOOR OR 4-DOOR SEDANS.*
CLOSED CARS HAVE RECTANGULAR REAR WINDOWS.

(BALLOON TIRES ON '25 MODELS.)

* = OTHER BODY TYPES ALSO.

Ford

IMPROVED '26 MODEL T HAS FUEL TANK IN COWL.

PLANETARY TRANSMISSION A MODEL T CHARACTERISTIC.

THE RUNABOUT

TOURING

26-27

WIRE WHEELS AVAILABLE ON 1927 MODEL T.

COUPE

29 x 4.40 BALLOON TIRES STANDARD EQUIPMENT IN 1927; BALLOON TIRES OPTIONAL DURING 1926.

1927 = FINAL MODEL T

102

MODEL "A" 28-29

(INTRO. 12-2-27)

Ford

NEW 200.4 CUBIC-IN. DISPL., 4-CYL. ENGINE 40 H.P. @ 2200 RPM

EARLY '28 OPEN MODEL As HAVE NO OUTSIDE DOOR HANDLES.

MODEL "A" AN ALL-NEW CAR FOR 1928.

STANDARD TYPE SLIDING-GEAR TRANSMISSION ADOPTED.

new 4-WHEEL MECHANICAL BRAKES (THROUGH '38)

SPORT COUPE (RIGID FABRIC TOP)

STATION WAGON ('29)

TAXI ('29)

103½" W.B.

'28 HAS REDDISH-COLORED STEERING WHEEL.

21" (4.50 x 30) TIRES IN '28-29 3.7 GEAR RATIO

BRIGGS OR MURRAY BODIES

"Ford" IN SCRIPT ON NEW BLUE-AND-WHITE OVAL RADIATOR EMBL.

TUDOR SEDAN

EARLIEST MODELS HAVE BRAKE LEVER AT LEFT.

"LINCOLN" STYLING

TOWN CAR ('29)

103

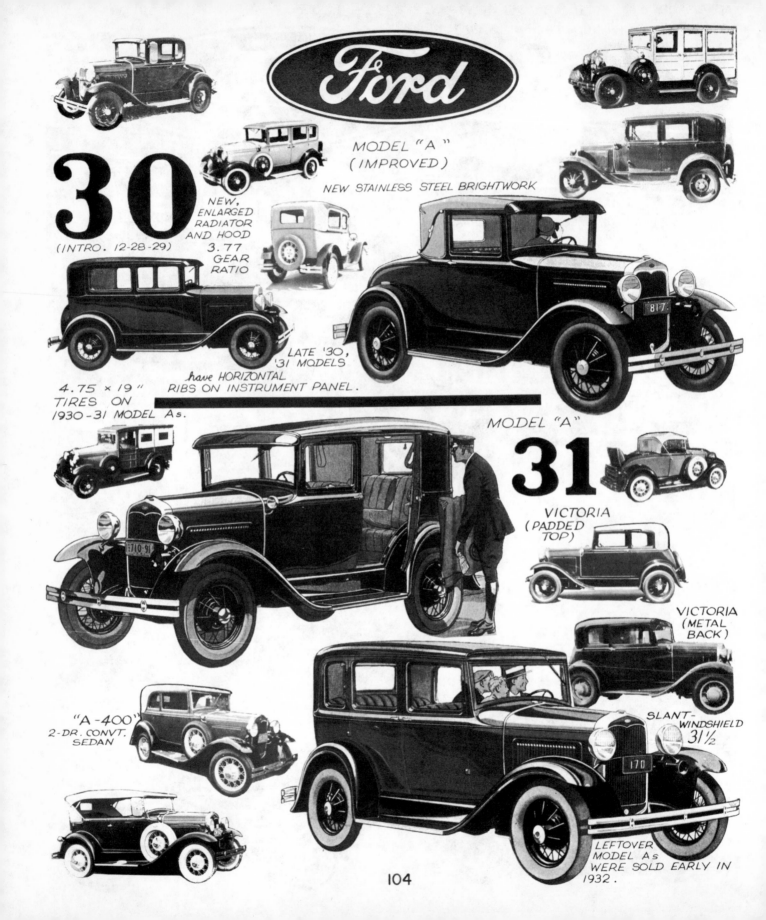

Ford

30

(INTRO. 12-28-29)

MODEL "A" (IMPROVED)

NEW STAINLESS STEEL BRIGHTWORK

NEW, ENLARGED RADIATOR AND HOOD
3.77 GEAR RATIO

LATE '30, '31 MODELS *have* HORIZONTAL RIBS ON INSTRUMENT PANEL.

4.75 × 19" TIRES ON 1930-31 MODEL As.

MODEL "A"

31

VICTORIA (PADDED TOP)

VICTORIA (METAL BACK)

"A-400" 2-DR. CONVT. SEDAN

SLANT-WINDSHIELD 31½

LEFTOVER MODEL As WERE SOLD EARLY IN 1932.

MODEL B- 4 CYL. **FORD**
V8 - 8 CYL. (221 C.I.D.)
106" W.B.

new DASH WITH 3 CIRCULAR GAUGES SET ON AN OVAL PANEL.

HENRY FORD I *with the* FIRST FORD V-8 ENGINE

32 "18" SERIES

V-8 HAS EMBLEM ON TIE-BAR.

BOTH 3-WINDOW AND 5-WINDOW COUPES AVAILABLE FROM 1932 TO 1936.

(FIRST FORD V-8 ASSEMBLED MARCH 9, 1932.)

STARTING '32, BOTH 3-WINDOW (*new*) and 5-WINDOW COUPES ARE AVAILABLE (THROUGH '36)

"40" SERIES **33** (4 and V-8) 3.77 G.R. (4) 4.33 (V-8)

(STARTS 2-33)

112" W.B.

5.50 × 17 TIRES (THR. '34)

WIRE WHEELS STD. (THROUGH '35)

OPTIONAL-STYLE SM. WHEELS

(.50-H.P. (MODEL "4-40" IS RARE 4-CYL. SERIES.)*

* = OFFICIALLY, A CONTINUATION OF MODEL B, BUT WITH 1933 STYLING.

3-WINDOW COUPE

DASH

HEAVIER GRILLE FOR 1934

5-WINDOW COUPE

PHAETON (AVAIL. THROUGH '36)

1934 MODEL HAS 2 HANDLES ON EACH SIDE OF HOOD.

CONT'D. 112" W.B. (THROUGH '40) 4.11 G.R.

34 "40" SERIES (STARTS 12-33)

(V-8s EXCLUSIVELY)

Ford

FINAL YEAR WITH
WIRE WHEELS.
4.11 G.R.

6.00 × 16

35

'35 DASH
RESEMBLES
ILLUSTRATED '36 VIEW,
BUT CENTER VERTICAL
CHROME STRIPS ON
'35 ARE FARTHER APART.

"48"
SERIES
(STARTS 12-34)

"68" SERIES (STARTS OCT., 1935) new POINTED GRILLE
and STEEL ARTILLERY WHEELS. 4.11 OR 3.54 G.R.

NOW 3 HORIZ.
STRIPS ACROSS
HOOD LOUVRES,
(INSTEAD OF 4
AS IN '35.)

36

FORD'S
FINAL
ROADSTER

5-PASS.
CLUB
CABRIOLET
(NEW)

new "60"
KNOWN AS
MODEL 74,
has 4.44
G.R.

85-H.P. 221-C.I.D. V-8 CONT'D.
AND A NEW ECONOMY "60" SERIES
ADDED (WITH 135.9 C.I.D. 60-H.P.
SMALL V-8 ENGINE.)

new ALL-
STEEL
TOP

37 (STARTS
NOV.,
1936)

DAD and
ME (AGE 4)
and OUR
'37 FORD

"85" KNOWN AS MODEL 78,
has 3.78 G.R.

FORD

60 H.P. = "82-A"
85 H.P. = "81-A"

STD.

STANDARD 85 and 60-H.P.

DLX.

DE LUXE 85 H.P.

38

(STARTS NOV., 1937)

FROM 1938 THROUGH 1940, FORD'S STANDARD MODELS SOMEWHAT RESEMBLED (BUT WERE NOT IDENTICAL WITH) THE PREVIOUS YEAR'S DE LUXE MODEL.

STD. 85 and 60 H.P.

112" W.B. (SINCE '33)
SAME GEAR RATIOS SINCE '37.

DASH

60 H.P. = "92-A"

85 H.P. = "91-A"

DE LUXE 85 H.P.

FORD BATTERIES and IGNITION ARE CHARACTERISTIC.

new HYDRAULIC BRAKES

39

(STARTS OCT., 1938)

FOX (1921-1923)

FOX MOTOR CO., PHILADELPHIA, PA.

"1924" MODEL (BUILT 1923)

6 CYLINDER, 50 H.P. AIR-COOLED, OVERHEAD VALVE, OVERHEAD CAM ENGINE

132" wheelbase
32 × 4½ TIRES
4.9 G.R.

DISPLACEMENT INCREASED FROM 248.9 TO 268.3 FOR 1923.

107

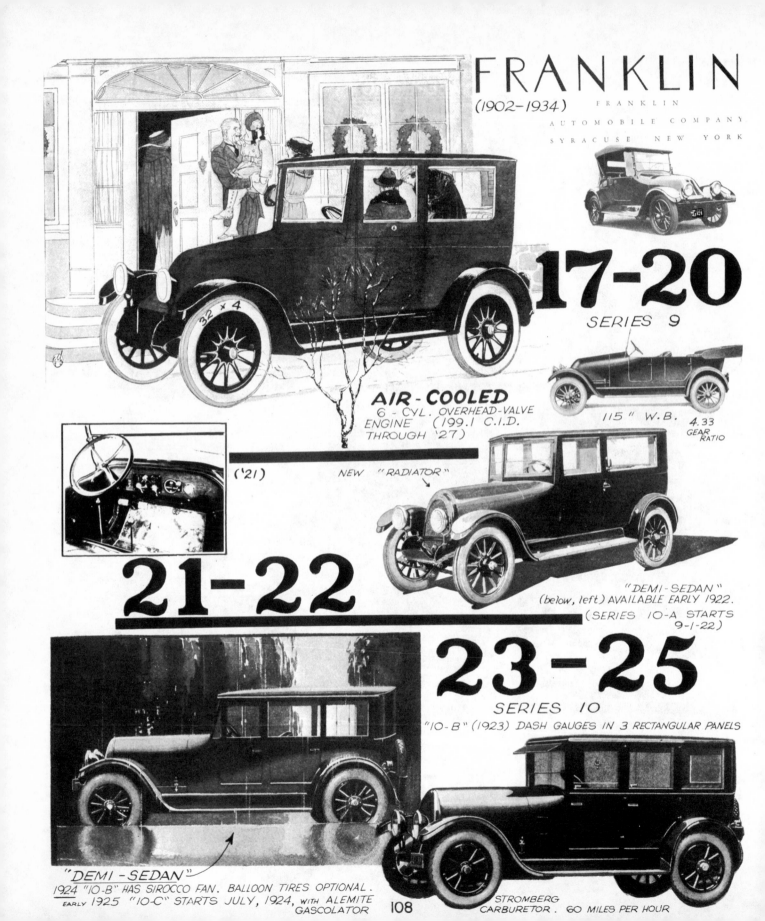

FRANKLIN
(1902–1934)

FRANKLIN
AUTOMOBILE COMPANY
SYRACUSE NEW YORK

32 x 4

17-20
SERIES 9

AIR-COOLED
6 - CYL. OVERHEAD-VALVE
ENGINE (199.1 C.I.D.
THROUGH '27)

115" W.B.   4.33
GEAR
RATIO

('21)   NEW "RADIATOR"

21-22

"DEMI-SEDAN"
(below, left) AVAILABLE EARLY 1922.

(SERIES 10-A STARTS
9-1-22)

23-25
SERIES 10

"10-B" (1923) DASH GAUGES IN 3 RECTANGULAR PANELS

"DEMI-SEDAN"
1924 "10-B" HAS SIROCCO FAN. BALLOON TIRES OPTIONAL.
EARLY 1925 "10-C" STARTS JULY, 1924, WITH ALEMITE
GASCOLATOR

STROMBERG
CARBURETOR. 60 MILES PER HOUR

108

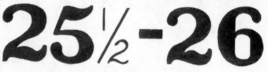

25½-26

SERIES 11
(INTRODUCED MARCH, 1925)

COUPÉ

'25½ TO '28 MODELS
FREQUENTLY KNOWN AS
"DE CAUSSE" FRANKLINS.

STARTING LATE 1926, CLOSED
FRANKLINS HAVE NARROW FRONT
CORNER POSTS WITH "CLEAR VISION"
WINDSHIELD.

VICTORIA
COUPE

26-STYLE
COUPÉ CONTINUED ALSO

27

SERIES 11-B

TIRE SIZE CHANGED
FROM 31 x 5.25 TO
32 x 6.
NEW SWAN
MANIFOLD WITH SQUARE CORNERS.

(INTRODUCED JANUARY, 1927)

SPORT SEDAN

*The 25th
Anniversary
Franklin*

FRANKLIN

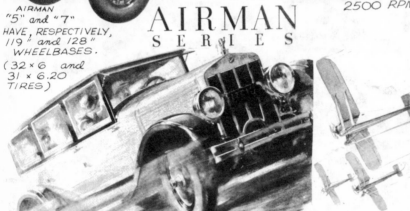

AIRMAN
"5" and "7"
HAVE, RESPECTIVELY,
119" and 128"
WHEELBASES.
(32 × 6 and
31 × 6.20
TIRES)

AIRMAN SERIES

4-WHEEL
LOCKHEED
HYDRAULIC BRAKES
WITH 14" DRUMS.

new 236.4 C.I.D.
46 H.P. @
2500 RPM

28 SERIES 12-A (INTRODUCED OCT., 1927)

The new Franklin

AIRMAN LIMITED

SERIES 12-B

28½

WITH FENDER MIRRORS AND HEADLIGHT FOOT CONTROL

(INTRODUCED JULY, 1928)

WALKER BODIES,
AS
BEFORE

AC FUEL PUMP

FENDER
PARKING
LAMPS

29

"130," "135,"
"137"
(120, 125 and
132-INCH
WHEELBASES)

1929 has SMALLER
CIRCLE ON
"RADIATOR"
TRIM

50 OR 60-H.P. ENGINES

PRESSED STEEL CHASSIS FRAME

31 × 6.50

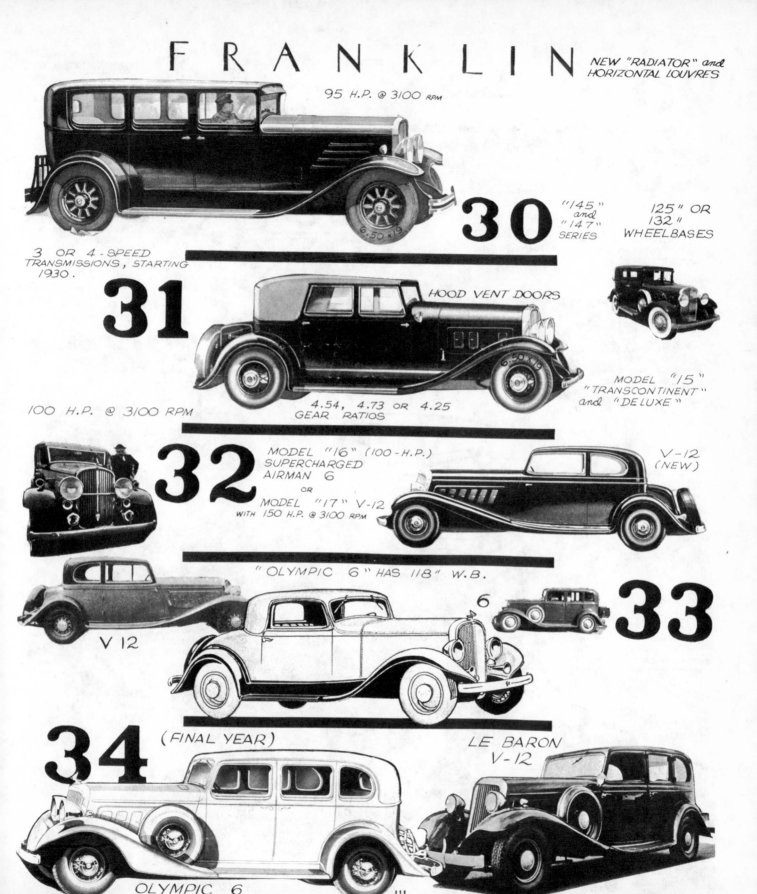

FRANKLIN

NEW "RADIATOR" and HORIZONTAL LOUVRES

95 H.P. @ 3100 RPM

30 "145" and "147" SERIES

125" OR 132" WHEELBASES

3 OR 4-SPEED TRANSMISSIONS, STARTING 1930.

31 HOOD VENT DOORS

100 H.P. @ 3100 RPM

4.54, 4.73 OR 4.25 GEAR RATIOS

MODEL "15" "TRANSCONTINENT" and "DE LUXE"

32 MODEL "16" (100-H.P.) SUPERCHARGED AIRMAN 6

OR

MODEL "17" V-12 WITH 150 H.P. @ 3100 RPM

V-12 (NEW)

"OLYMPIC 6" HAS 118" W.B.

V 12

33

6

34 (FINAL YEAR)

LE BARON V-12

OLYMPIC 6

III

GARDNER MOTOR CO., INC., ST. LOUIS, U.S.A.

GARDNER
(1919-1931)

20 TO 23

112" W.B. "LIGHT 4"

32 x 3½

192.4 C.I.D.
35 H.P. @ 1800 RPM
4-CYLINDER LYCOMING ENGINE

NEW STYLE OF TOP BRACING IN '22, and 4.44 GEAR RATIO

32 x 4 TIRES AND 4.8 GEAR RATIO ON 1923 MODEL "5."

NEW 213.6 C.I.D. LYCOMING 4-CYL. '23 ENGINE HAS 5 (INSTEAD OF 2) MAIN BEARINGS. HAND BRAKE NOW CONTRACTS ON DRIVESHAFT. 43 H.P. @ 2150 RPM

"5-C" (4 CYL.)

24

"RADIO SPECIAL" SEDAN (RADIO SPECIAL IN '23 WAS SPORT TOURING CAR.)

25

"8-A"

2-DOOR BROUGHAM

254.4 C.I.D.
63 H.P. @ 3000 RPM
NEW STRAIGHT-8 MODELS FOR 1925 (ILLUSTRATED)
NEW 6-CYL. "6-A" ALSO (57 H.P.)
4-CYL. "5-C" CONTINUED WITH 44 H.P. @ 2200 RPM.

27

"8-80"

"8-90"

CARS BUILT 8-25 OR LATER ARE CONSIDERED "1926" MODELS, AND HAVE HOOD SUPPORT ROD.

6-CYL. LYCOMING ENG. HAS 207.1 C.I.D. ('25)
223.8 C.I.D. ('26-27)

26

'26 COUPE WINDSHIELD

NO MORE 6-CYL. GARDNERS UNTIL 1930 "136" MODEL.

"6-B" and "8-B" MODELS BEGIN JAN., '26 THESE MODELS, IF BUILT BETWEEN 8-26 AND 12-26, ARE "EARLY '27s."

WESTINGHOUSE IGNITION THROUGH 1924 (DELCO) REMY IGNITION 1925 and on

RADIATOR CAP MASCOT

28

(ALL 8-CYL.) LYCOMING ENG.

29

(INTRO. 9-28)

"120," "125," "130" HAVE 65, 85, 115 H.P.

"75" 225.7 C.I.D., 65 H.P.
"85" 246.7 " , 74 "
"95" 298.6 C.I.D. 115 H.P.

GARDNERS BUILT DURING LATTER MONTHS OF A YEAR ARE USUALLY CONSIDERED TO BE EARLY SERIES OF FOLLOWING YEAR'S MODELS.

'29 RADIATOR HIGHER, NARROWER THAN '28. BODIES BY CENTRAL

GARDNER

6-CYL. 80 H.P.

← FRONT-WHEEL-DRIVE MODEL ('30) WITH SLOPING FRONT END

"136" = 6 CYL., 185 C.I.D. 70 H.P. @ 3500 RPM
"140" = 8 CYL., 246.6 C.I.D. 90 H.P. @ 3300 RPM
"150" = 8 CYL., 298.6 C.I.D. 126 H.P. @ 3300 RPM

30

31

"136" = 122" W.B.
"140" = 125 "
"150" = 130 "

MODELS "136" "148" and "158"

ONLY THE FRONT-WHEEL-DRIVE MODEL HAS THE ABOVE UNIQUE RADIATOR DESIGN.

6 CYL. CONTINENTAL "11-E" ENGINE (248 C.I.D.) USED. LYCOMING "WR," "GR," "MDG" ENGINES IN 3 OTHER MODELS.

MECHANICAL SPECIFICATIONS AS BEFORE

"148" HAS 100 H.P.

MESH-TYPE CHROMED STONE GUARD IN FRONT OF RADIATOR.

GEARLESS STEAM CAR

(1921 - 1923)

GEARLESS MOTOR CORP., PITTSBURGH, PA.

GERONIMO

122" W.B. (1917 - 1921)
GERONIMO MOTOR CO., ENID, OKLA.
(LYCOMING ENGINE) ('18)
(230.1 C.I.D. RUTENBER ENGINE ALSO) DELCO IGN.

TOURING CAR ("6-A-45") ('20)
'20 MODEL BASICALLY UNCHANGED. GERONIMO BUILT OWN BODIES STARTING 1919.
(6)

GLOBE

with "SUPREME" ENGINE
4 CYL., 178.9 C.I.D.
DELCO IGNITION

MODEL "B-10"
115" W.B., 4.9 G.R.
32 × 4 TIRES

(1921 - 1922)
GLOBE MOTORS CO., CLEVELAND, OHIO

GRAHAM-PAIGE (1928 TO 1941, INCLUDING GRAHAM)

THE 3 GRAHAM BROTHERS PICTURED ON EMBLEM.

"614" →

REPLACES PAIGE, JANUARY, 1928   HYDR. BRAKES
NORTHEAST IGNITION SYSTEM

"610" IS LOWEST-PRICED SERIES, has 110½" W.B.,
29 x 5.00 TIRES, 4.45 GEAR RATIO,
6 CYLS., 175 C.I.D., 52 H.P.
@ 3100 RPM

"614" has 114" W.B.,
29 x 5.25 TIRES,
3.9 G.R.,
6 CYLS., 207 C.I.D.,
71 H.P. @
3200 RPM

"619" →

"619" has 119" W.B., 29 x 5.50 TIRES,
6 CYLS., 288 C.I.D., 97 H.P.
@ 3200 RPM

28

(AUG., 1928 = "EARLY 1929s"
SIMILAR, BUT NO LONGER
HAVE VERTICAL SEAMS ON
BACKS OF
BODIES.)

← "629" →

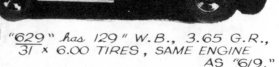

"629" has 129" W.B., 3.65 G.R.,
31 x 6.00 TIRES, SAME ENGINE
AS "619."

"835" has
135" W.B., 31 x 6.20
TIRES, 3.65 G.R.,
STRAIGHT-8 ENGINE, 322 C.I.D.

ALL BUT "610" have
4-SPEED TRANSMISSION;
(AVAIL. ON ALL BUT SMALL
MODELS THROUGH '31.)

ALL MODELS HAVE
FUEL PUMP.

"835"

114

GRAHAM-PAIGE

"612" has
29 x 5.00 TIRES, 4.7
G.R., 190.8 C.I.D.,
62 H.P. @ 3200 RPM

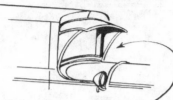

VISOR BRACKETS
ON "612" and "615"

"615" has 5.50 x 19
TIRES, 3.9 G.R., 224 C.I.D.,
76 H.P. @
3200 RPM

BRIGGS
BODY

"621"

"621" has 6.00 x 19 TIRES,
3.6 G.R., 288.6 C.I.D.,
97 H.P. @ 3200 RPM

BODIES BY
GRAHAM-PAIGE
BRIGGS
ROBBINS
LE BARON (SPECIAL PHAETON)

BEGINNING 1929,
DELCO-REMY
IGNITION ON ALL
GRAHAM-PAIGE
and GRAHAM CARS
TO FOLLOW.

AS IN '28,
MODEL NUMBERS
INDICATE NO. OF
CYLINDERS, and
WHEELBASE.

29

new THINNER
HOOD LOUVRES

"827" has
3.6 G.R.

"837" has
3.9 G.R.

"827" and "837"
have 6.50 x 19 TIRES,
STRAIGHT-8 ENGINES OF
322 C.I.D., 120 H.P. @ 3200
RPM

ROBBINS BODIES

"827"

(JULY 29, 1929, TO JANUARY, 1930)

EARLY **30** 3-SPOKE STEERING
WHEEL
NEW GLASS SUN VISOR

JAN., 1930 = 115, 122, 127, 137" W.B.,
66, 76, 96 (8-CYL.) OR 120 H.P. (8-CYL.)

AFTER EARLY 1930,
"PAIGE" NAME RETAINED
ONLY FOR TAXIS AND
COMMERCIAL CARS.
JAN., 1930 = NEW STD. OR
SPEC. 6, STD. OR SPEC. 8, CUSTOM 8s

GRAAM **30½**

QUALITY IS THE BEST POLICY

GRAHAM

STD. 6 (VISOR ON '31 MODEL)

8 HAS DOOR-TYPE
HOOD VENTS, FENDER
PARKING LIGHTS.

31

GRAHAM 6

(CHROME - PLATED
WIRE WHEELS
AVAILABLE ON 6 and 8 - CYL.
'31½ MODELS EXCEPT
"PROSPERITY 6," THE
'31½ ECONOMY MODEL OF
113" W.B., 207 C.I.D., 70 H.P.
(EARLY '32 MODELS
BEGIN JULY, 1931, RESEMBLE
'31 - 31½ GRAHAMS, BUT
have OPTIONAL
FREE - WHEELING.)

1932 SIX
has 113" W.B.
5.50 × 17
TIRES,
207.1 C.I.D.
70 H.P. @
3200 RPM,
4.45 G.R.

DASH
(1932
Blue Streak)

32-33

'32 STD. and DLX. 8 SPECS. ALSO

'32 "BLUE STREAK" 8 (123" W.B.)
HAS 1-PIECE BUMPER, 245.4 C.I.D.,
90 H.P. @ 3400 RPM, 4.3 G.R.,
6.00 × 17 TIRES

The car is WIDER than it is high
('33)

224 C.I.D., 85-H.P. 6 IN 1933 ; 8-CYL. SPECS. LIKE '32.

4.27 GEAR RATIO
ON 1933 TO 1935
GRAHAMS.

8

34

6

6=116" W.B.,
6.25 × 16 TIRES,
224 C.I.D., 85 H.P.
@ 3400 RPM

8=
123" W.B.,
6.50 × 16 TIRES, 245.4 C.I.D.,
95 H.P. @ 3400 RPM
CUSTOM 8=123" W.B., 7.00 × 16 TIRES,
265.4 C.I.D., 135 H.P. @ 4000 RPM (Supercharger avail.)

STD. 6 "74"= 111" W.B., 5.25 × 17 TIRES, 169.6 C.I.D., 70 H.P. @ 3500 RPM
SPECIAL 6 "73"= 116" W.B., 6.00 × 17 TIRES, 224 C.I.D., 85 H.P. @ 3400 RPM

35

6

(GRAHAM 8 HAS
2-PIECE
REAR WINDOW.)

8 "72"= 123" W.B.,
6.50 × 16 TIRES,
245.4 C.I.D., 95 H.P. @
3400 RPM
Supercharged 8 "75"=
123" W.B., 7.00 × 16 TIRES,
265.4 C.I.D., 140 H.P.
@ 4000 RPM

NO MORE
8-CYL. GRAHAMS
AFTER 1935.

ALL 1935 GRAHAMS HAVE
HORIZONTAL HOOD LOUVRES.

116

GRAHAM

6-CYLINDER MODELS ONLY (THROUGH '41)

36

"CRUSADER"

"80" CRUSADER" 111" W.B., 6.00 × 16 TIRES 4.55 G.R., 169.6 C.I.D., 70 H.P. @ 3500 RPM

"90 CAVALIER" 115" W.B., 6.00 × 16 TIRES, 4.2 G.R., 217.8 C.I.D., 85 H.P. @ 3300 RPM
("90-A" STARTS 3-36, has 4.45 G.R., 199.1 C.I.D.)

"110" Supercharged 115" W.B., 6.25 × 16 TIRES, 4.2 G.R., 217.8 C.I.D. 112 H.P. @ 4000 RPM

"85 CRUSADER" 111" W.B., 5.25 × 17 or 6.00 × 16 TIRES, 4.55 G.R., 169.6 C.I.D., 70 H.P. @ 3500 RPM (INDIVIDUAL HOOD PORTS with TRIANGLE CHROME GRILLES)*

(1936 - 1937 "CRUSADERS" RETAIN 1935 BODY STYLING.)

"95 CAVALIER" 116" W.B., 6.00 × 16 TIRES, 4.45 G.R., 199.1 C.I.D., 85 H.P. @ 3800 RPM

37

* '37 "CRUSADER" HOOD LOUVRES DO NOT EXTEND INTO GRILLE AS ON '36.

"116 SUPERCHARGER" 116" W.B., 6.25 × 16 TIRES, 4.27 G.R., 199.1 C.I.D., 106 H.P. @ 4000 RPM

"120 CUSTOM SUPERCHARGER" 120" W.B. (COUPES - 116") 4.27 G.R., 217.8 C.I.D. 116 H.P. @ 4000

6.25 × 16 TIRES (6.00 × 16 ON '39 "96" SERIES)

38-39

FLOOR OR STEERING-COLUMN GEARSHIFT CONTROL IN '39.

STD. and SPEC. "96" have 90 H.P. @ 3600 RPM

SUPERCHARGED CLUB SEDAN ('39)

RUNNING-BOARDS NOT FEATURED ON 1939 GRAHAMS.

('38)

6 CYLS., 217.8 C.I.D. 120" W.B., 4.27 G.R. (ALL '38s - 39s)

"SPIRIT OF MOTION" STYLING

SPEC. and CUSTOM "97" SUPERCHARGER have 116 H.P. @ 4000 RPM

GRANT 6

(OWN 6-CYL. O.H.V. ENG. (198.9 C.I.D., IMPROVED FOR '20.)

GRANT MOTOR CAR CORP., FINDLAY, OHIO (1913-1922)

21

22

('20 MODEL MECH. RE-DESIGNED FROM '19. '20 SEDAN DOES NOT HAVE COWL LIGHTS AS ON '21 MODEL SHOWN.)

(1922-1926)

GRAY MOTOR CORP., DETROIT

4 CYLINDERS (OWN ENGINE) 165.1 C.I.D. 21 H.P. @ 1500 RPM ('25 RATING)

Gray Motor Corporation Detroit

22

SAN FRANCISCO TO NEW YORK OFFICIAL ECONOMY TEST SANCTION AMERICAN AUTOMOBILE ASSOCIATION Gray

100" WHEELBASE (THROUGH '23)

30 x 3½ TIRES (THROUGH '25)

3.9 GEAR RATIO WESTINGHOUSE IGNITION (THROUGH '25)

23

100" OR 103½" W.B. IN '24 TOP SPEED ONLY 46 MILES PER HOUR

24

"N" OR "O" MODELS

'25 AND '26 SIMILAR-LOOKING TO '24, BUT LATE '24 GRAY HAS FUEL TANK AT REAR. BALLOON TIRES AVAIL. ON '25 MODEL, AND 104" W.B. (MODEL "O")

(105" WHEELBASE, 29 x 4.40 BALLOON TIRES, 4-WHEEL BRAKES ON '26 GRAY (MODEL "S" WITH Auto Lite IGN.)

GRAY LIGHT CAR

(NOT AFFILIATED WITH GRAY CAR ILLUSTRATED ABOVE.)

LONGMONT, COLO. (1920)

ONLY 2 CARS COMPLETED.

1 AND 2-CYL. HARLEY-DAVIDSON MOTORCYCLE ENGINES

HALLADAY

1921 = 116" W.B., 6 CYL. RUT. ENG.

1922 = 115" W.B., 4 + 6 CYLINDERS

HALLADAY MOTORS CORPORATION
NEWARK, OHIO, U.S.A.

(1918 – 1922)

Handley-Knight

4.9 G.R.,
32 × 4½
TIRES
ON ALL
'21-'23
MODELS

'23 "6-60" HAS 125" W.B., 268.4 MIDWEST ENG.

6
CYL.
O.H.V.
('23)

EARLY '23
7-PASS.

HANDLEY MOTORS, INC.,
KALAMAZOO, MICH.
(1921 – 1923)

NAME
SHORTENED TO
HANDLEY
DURING '23.

NEW MODEL →

125"
W.B.

('22 = ALUMINUM REPL.
LINOLEUM ON RUNNING BOARDS)

240.6 C.I.D., 4-CYL.
KNIGHT ENG. (THROUGH '22 "B" SERIES)

21-23

'23 "6-40" HAS
195.6 FALLS ENG.,
115" W.B.

23½

HANSON 6

1920 MODEL "54" has 119" W.B.

121" W.B., 1921-1924

EMBLEM →

('20)

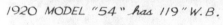

('21)

HANSON MOTOR CO.,
ATLANTA, GA.
(1917-1923)

MODEL "60"
(1921-1922)
HAS 224 C.I.D.,
6-CYL. CONTINENTAL
ENGINE.

(32 × 4 TIRES, 4.66 G.R.)

MODEL "66" (1923-1924) HAS
CONTINENTAL "8-R"
ENGINE
(241.6 C.I.D.)

FINAL '24 MODEL
(INTRO. 1923)

HARRIS 6

23 ONLY

WISCONSIN
AUTOMOTIVE
CORP.,
MENASHA,
WIS.

HAYNES **20**

THE HAYNES
AUTOMOBILE COMPANY,
Kokomo, Indiana

IN PRODUCTION
1904 – 1925

ORIGINALLY
"HAYNES-
APPERSON"

1920 GEAR RATIOS:
4.42 ("45")   4.06 ("46")

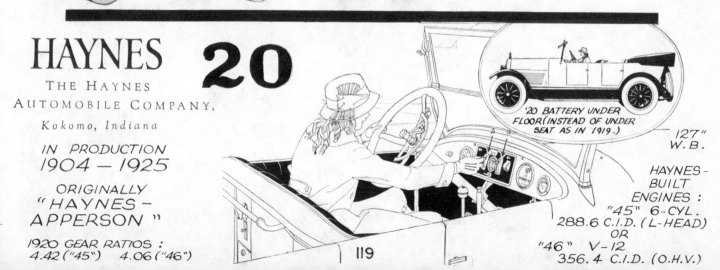

'20 BATTERY UNDER
FLOOR (INSTEAD OF UNDER
SEAT AS IN 1919.)

127"
W.B.

HAYNES-
BUILT
ENGINES:
"45" 6-CYL.
288.6 C.I.D. (L-HEAD)
OR
"46" V-12
356.4 C.I.D. (O.H.V.)

119

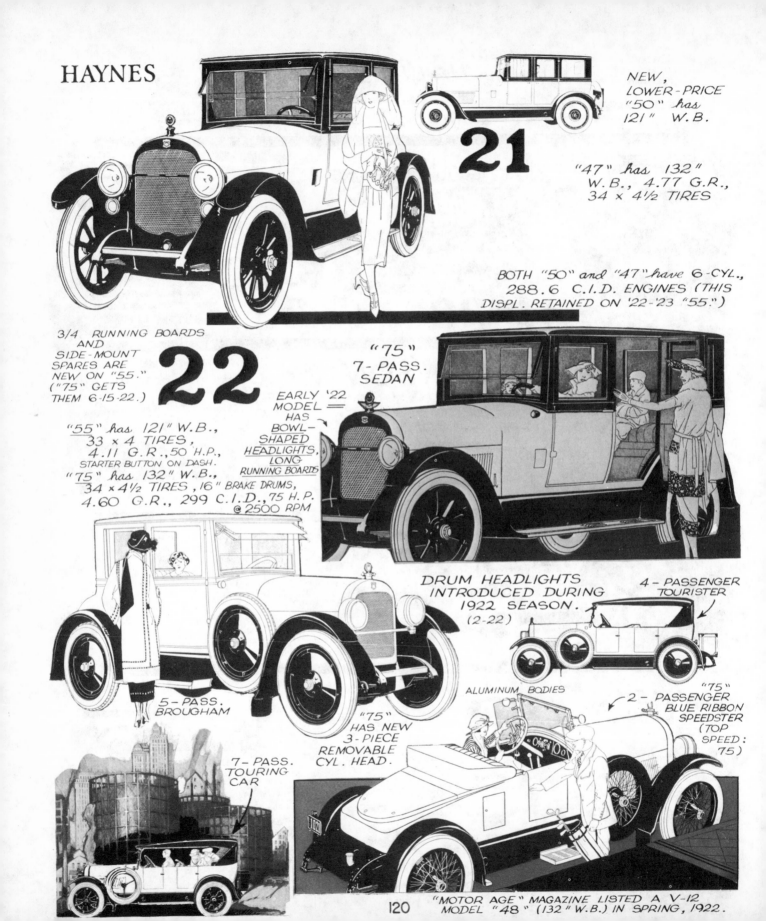

HAYNES

21

NEW, LOWER-PRICE "50" has 121" W.B.

"47" has 132" W.B., 4.77 G.R., 34 x 4½ TIRES

BOTH "50" and "47" have 6-CYL., 288.6 C.I.D. ENGINES (THIS DISPL. RETAINED ON '22-23 "55.")

22

3/4 RUNNING BOARDS AND SIDE-MOUNT SPARES ARE NEW ON "55." ("75" GETS THEM 6-15-22.)

"55" has 121" W.B., 33 x 4 TIRES, 4.11 G.R., 50 H.P., STARTER BUTTON ON DASH. "75" has 132" W.B., 34 x 4½ TIRES, 16" BRAKE DRUMS, 4.60 G.R., 299 C.I.D., 75 H.P. @ 2500 RPM

"75" 7-PASS. SEDAN

EARLY '22 MODEL HAS BOWL-SHAPED HEADLIGHTS, LONG RUNNING BOARDS

DRUM HEADLIGHTS INTRODUCED DURING 1922 SEASON. (2-22)

4-PASSENGER TOURISTER

ALUMINUM BODIES

"75" HAS NEW 3-PIECE REMOVABLE CYL. HEAD.

5-PASS. BROUGHAM

7-PASS. TOURING CAR

"75" 2-PASSENGER BLUE RIBBON SPEEDSTER (TOP SPEED: 75)

"MOTOR AGE" MAGAZINE LISTED A V-12 MODEL "48" (132" W.B.) IN SPRING, 1922.

23

HAYNES

("55" and "75" REPLACED BY "57" and "77" DURING 1923.)

The New, 1923 Haynes 55 Sport Coupelet, 3 Pass.

The New, 1923 Haynes 55 Sport Roadster, 2 Passengers

32 × 4½ TIRES CHANGED TO 33 × 5.77 DURING 1924.

("60" IS ONLY SER. FOR 1924-1925.)

"60" TOURING (STARTS 8-23)

24

121" W.B., 274.2 C.I.D. 6 CYLS.

"60" METROPOLITAN SEDAN

4.41 G.R.

50 H.P. @ 2400 RPM (MOST SPECS. AS IN '24)

25

120" W.B. ON 4-CYL. CARS

277.1 C.I.D., 4-CYL., O.H.V. WEIDELY ENGINE WITH LANCHESTER VIBRATION DAMPENER

SERIES 3 (1920-1922)

H.C.S. MOTOR CO., INDIANAPOLIS

H.C.S.

(1920-1925)

SERIES 6

126" W.B. 288.6 C.I.D. 6-CYL. ALSO AVAIL., 1923-25 (MIDWEST ENG. IN EARLY MODELS.)

SERIES 4 (1922-1925)

5-PASS. TOURING

HEINE-VELOX V-12 *(SAN FRANCISCO, 1921)*

148" W.B.

LIVERY AND FEED

Hertz Drive-it, successor to the old time livery stable.

('25)

(REPLACES 1924 AMBASSADOR "D-1")

HERTZ

YELLOW CAB MFG. CO., CHICAGO *(1925-1928)*

BUILT FOR RENTAL USE

MODEL "D-1" has 114" W.B., 31 × 4 TIRES ('25) 30 × 5.77 ('26 ON) 4.72 GEAR RATIO 195.6 C.I.D. (230.1 C.I.D., '27) 6-CYLINDER CONTINENTAL ENGINE 49 H.P. @2500 (61 H.P. @2600 RPM, '27) DELCO IGNITION

HOLMES

CANTON, OHIO *(1918-1923)*

126" W.B. 4.9 G.R.

OWN AIR-COOLED ENGINE 6 CYLINDERS, O.H.V. (259.8 C.I.D.)

34 × 4½ TIRES

EISEMANN IGN. (THROUGH '23)

21-23

20

SERIES 4 (RESTYLED FOR 1921)

121

(1909 – 1957)

HUDSON

HUDSON MOTOR CAR COMPANY
DETROIT, MICHIGAN

Look for the White Triangle

HUDSON
SUPER
SIX

(6 CYL., 288.6 C.I.D.
ENGINE, 1914 - 1929)

76 H.P.
(SINCE '16)

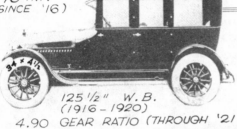

20-21

125 1/2" W.B.
(1916 - 1920)

4.90 GEAR RATIO (THROUGH '21

126 " W.B. (1921
THROUGH 1924)

76 H.P.
@ 2450 RPM

---

76 H.P. @ 2400 RPM

new
4.81 GEAR RATIO
FRONT APRONS EXTEND TO
FRONT END OF SPRING HANGERS;
SPLASH APRON *BETWEEN*
SPRING HORNS.

(PRESSED STEEL DOOR
JAMBS REPLACE WOOD.)

22

The Coach
(NEW)
←

BLUE UPHOLSTERY
IN COACH UNTIL SEPT.,
1922; THEN CHANGE TO GRAY UPH.

(9-22:
7-PASS.
SEDAN
has SLANTED
WINDSHIELD)

MAY 1, 1922 = <u>DRUM HEADLIGHTS</u>, FLAT EDGE ON
BODY, BOSCH DISTRIBUTOR, CURTAINS IN DOORS.

4.45 GEAR RATIO (THROUGH '28)
75 H.P. @ 2450 RPM (THROUGH '24)

LATE '23 COACHES UPHOLSTERED IN
BROWN.

SPECIAL
SPEEDSTER

(4- PASS. SPEEDSTER
IS SPORT TOURING)

HUDSON'S
WHITE
TRIANGLE
INSIGNIA IS
EASY TO
IDENTIFY.
→

23

4-PASS. and 7-PASS. TOURING CARS

7- PASS. SEDAN BLT. FIRST HALF OF '23
5- PASS. SEDAN " LAST " " "

ALUMINUM
BODY BY
BIDDLE and
SMART

122

THE FINEST HUDSON EVER BUILT

15½ " BRAKE DRUMS

34 × 4½ TIRES

INTERIOR
("CABRIOLET"
COUPE)

24

117-815

NEW RIDGED
FENDERS

LIMOUSINE

7- PASS.

25

33 × 6.20
(BALLOON
TIRES)

76 H.P. @ 2800 RPM
(THROUGH '26)

25½-26

(NEW WINDSHIELD)

The Brougham

(A NEW HUDSON MODEL)

HAS
ALUMINUM
BODY
PANELS,
LEATHER-
COVERED
REAR
QUARTER
SECTIONS.

33 × 6

26½ BROUGHAM
HAS ROOF-VISOR

123

HUDSON

COACH

27

F-HEAD ENGINE; 4-WHEEL BRAKES

95 H.P. @ 3100 RPM

WHEELBASES 118" = STANDARD; 127½" = CUSTOM

BROUGHAM

33 x 6 TIRES

JULY 1, 1927 = '27½ MODELS. REDESIGNED CYL. HEAD, ETC.

31 x 6.00 TIRES

RADIATOR SHUTTERS NOW VERTICAL.

CONVERTIBLE LANDAU SEDAN

ALL GAUGES UNDER ONE LONG PANEL, INDIRECTLY LIGHTED.

GEAR RATIOS
4.08 (S)
4.45 (O)

80-90 H.P.

28

MODELS "S" and "O"

31 x 6.00 TIRES

(MURPHY BODY)

(BRIGGS BODY)

WIRE WHEELS STANDARD ON LONG-WHEELBASE MODELS.

122½" OR 139" WHEELBASE
92 H.P. @ 3200 RPM

DASH

7-PASS. SEDAN

29

"THE GREATER HUDSON 6"

(BODY BY HUDSON)

4.08 GEAR RATIO
TOP SPEED = OVER 80

5-PASS. CLUB SEDAN
(BODY BY BIDDLE and SMART)

01-881

124

30 HUDSON

8 CYLS., 213.8 C.I.D.
84 H.P. @ 3400 RPM

(ALL MODELS HAD NEW STRAIGHT-8 ENGINE.)

RADIATOR FILLER UNDER HOOD

MODERNISTIC DASH

119" WHEELBASE

4.63 GEAR RATIO (THROUGH '32)
5.50 × 18 TIRES (THROUGH '31)

119" OR 126" W.B. (THROUGH '32)
233.7 C.I.D.

87 H.P. @ 3600 RPM

31

SOME 1931s HAVE 1930-STYLE HEADLIGHTS, COWL LIGHTS and WHEELS.

1931 7-PASS. PHAETON HAS 1930-STYLE DASH.

DASH

CLUB SEDAN

31½

HUDSON

HUDSON EIGHT COACH
Five Passengers . . . . 119" Wheelbase
$1025 F. O. B. DETROIT

HUDSON EIGHT BUSINESS COUPE
Two Passengers . . . . 119" Wheelbase
$995 F. O. B. DETROIT

HUDSON EIGHT TOWN SEDAN
Five Passengers . . . . 119" Wheelbase
$1050 F. O. B. DETROIT

32

HUDSON EIGHT STANDARD SEDAN
Five Passengers . . . . 119" Wheelbase
$1095 F. O. B. DETROIT

HUDSON EIGHT SUBURBAN
Five Passengers . . . . 126" Wheelbase
$1275 F. O. B. DETROIT

HUDSON EIGHT SEDAN
Seven Passengers . . . . 132" Wheelbase
$1595 F. O. B. DETROIT

"STANDARD," "STERLING," and
"MAJOR" SERIES (119, 126, 132" W.B.)

'32 INTERIOR

NEW GRILLE

PACEMAKER—Hudson Eight Standard Sedan for five passengers $1095 F. O. B. Detroit

254.4 C.I.D.   101 H.P. @ 3600 RPM   (THROUGH '33)

Hudson bodies, strong, smart and luxuriously finished, are built in Hudson's own $15,000,000 body plant. They realize in full those qualities which make steel the modern material for all structural duty in this day of high-power engine capacities and improved highways inviting to speed and demanding safety. The entire front and framework of the Hudson-built body shown here is welded into a single rattle-proof unit of unusual strength.

17 x 6.00 TIRES (17 x 6.50 ON "MAJOR")

HUDSON

VACUUM CLUTCH
FREE WHEELING

SUPER 6 = ('33 ONLY) 193.1 C.I.D. 4.64 G.R.
73 H.P. @ 3200 RPM   (6 OR 8)
5.25 × 18 TIRES   113" W.B.

PACEMAKER
EIGHT = 119" OR 132" W.B.
6.00 × 17 TIRES
"MAJOR" HAS 6.50 × 17 TIRES

33 →

'34 DASH SIMILAR TO '35, BUT ASH TRAY IS ON GLOVE-
BOX DOOR (PLUS OTHER MINOR DIFFERENCES)

"LTS" CHALLENGER ECONOMY MODEL
STARTS JUNE, 1934, WITHOUT "AXLEFLEX" SPRINGING,
DRAFTLESS VENTILATION; OR
INSIDE SUN VISORS.

34

(8-CYL. ONLY;
NO HUDSON 6
IN 1934.)
108 H.P. @ 3800 RPM

6.25 OR 6.50 × 16
TIRES

116" OR 123" WHEELBASE
"LT" = STD.   "LL" = STD.
"LU" = DLX.   "LLU" = DLX.

DELUXE MODELS HAVE RADIO

"GH" BIG 6 HAS 212 C.I.D., 93 H.P. @
3800 RPM (THROUGH '36)

BIG 6 HAS
116" W.B.

4.11 GEAR
RATIO (THROUGH '38)

35

8 = 113 H.P. @ 3800
(THROUGH '36)   8

NEW, OPTIONAL
"ELECTRIC HAND" GEARSHIFT ON STEERING COLUMN

"HT" SPECIAL 8
and
"HU" DELUXE 8
have 117" W.B.

"HHU"
CUSTOM 8
has 124" W.B.,
AS DO "HTL"
and "HUL"

DASH

IGNITION LOCK   WINDSHIELD REGULATOR   RADIO   STARTER BUTTON
                                                     GLOVE BOX

GENERATOR SIGNAL
LIGHTING SWITCH   OIL SIGNAL   FLOOD LAMP SWITCH
AUTOMATIC CLUTCH CONTROL   ASH TRAY   COWL VENTILATOR CONTROL
                    INSTRUMENT LAMP CONTROL AND SWITCH

NEW BODY

HUDSON
36

6 HAS 120" W.B.

" W.B.

HYDRAULIC BRAKES

8 HAS 120" OR 127" W.B.

"CUSTOM" STEERING
WHEEL HAS 3 SETS OF
4 CHROME-PLATED SPOKES.

OVAL SPEEDOMETER
IN CENTER OF DASH

6 HAS 101 H.P.
@ 4000 RPM
(THROUGH '39)
122" W.B.
(THROUGH '39)

8 HAS 122 H.P.
@ 4200 RPM
(THROUGH '39)
122" OR 129"
← 8 W.B.
(THROUGH
'39)

COUNTRY CLUB
8

37

New **HUDSON** Eight
122 AND 129-INCH WHEELBASE...122 HORSEPOWER

HUDSON
TERRAPLANE

HUDSON
SIX

'38
"112"
HAS
83 H.P.

"112" HAS FRONT-HINGED
HOOD. →

38

OFFICIAL AAA CAR
HUDSON 112

128

HUDSON

LOWER-PRICED "112" MODELS HAVE SEPERATE HEADLIGHTS AND DIFFERENT GRILLE. →

"PACEMAKER 91" and "92"

6 = 118" W.B.
96 H.P. @ 3900 RPM

COUNTRY CLUB 6 = ("93")
122" W.B.,
101 H.P. @ 4000 RPM

"112" (112" W.B.) ("90" SERIES)

6 CYLS., 175 C.I.D.
86 H.P. @ 4000 RPM

39

NEW DASH AND STEERING COLUMN GEARSHIFT ←

NEW DASH-LOCKING SAFETY HOOD

HOOD HINGED AT FRONT... WIND CAN'T LIFT IT...

LOCKED BY LEVER INSIDE CAR: BATTERY AND ENGINE PARTS THEFT-PROOF

NEW CARRY-ALL LUGGAGE COMPARTMENT

DASH (IN "COUNTRY CLUB" model)

6

also
8-CYLINDER
"95" COUNTRY CLUB
"97" CUSTOM
COUNTRY CLUB
122" OR 129" W.B.

4.1 GEAR RATIO

NEW AIRFOAM CUSHIONS

Airfoam is standard in new Hudson Country Club and Convertible models, optional at small cost in all other 1939 Hudsons.

Huffman 6

(1920-1925)

HUFFMAN BROS. MOTOR CO., ELKHART, INDIANA

MODEL "W" ('20)

$1895
f. o. b. Elkhart

6-CYL., 224 C.I.D.
CONTINENTAL ENGINE

120" W.B.

1921 = MODEL "R"

1923 = 241.5
C.I.D., 4.5 G.R.

FINAL HUFFMANS HAVE HYDRAULIC BRAKES, DISC WHEELS.

129

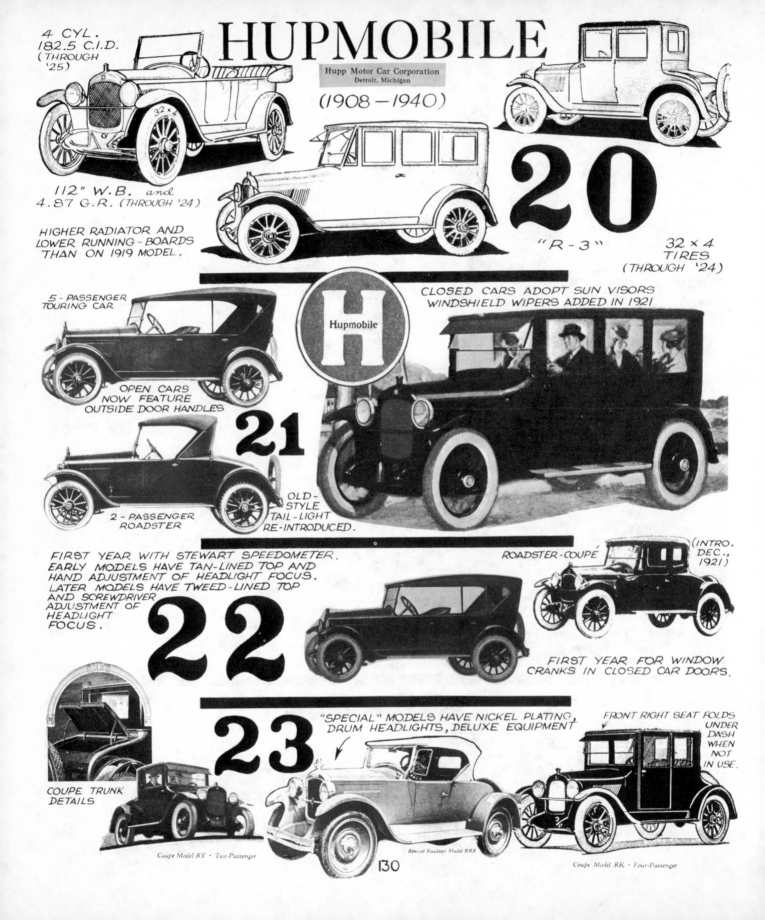

HUPMOBILE

Hupp Motor Car Corporation
Detroit, Michigan

(1908 – 1940)

4 CYL.
182.5 C.I.D.
(THROUGH '25)

112" W.B. and
4.87 G.R. (THROUGH '24)

HIGHER RADIATOR AND
LOWER RUNNING-BOARDS
THAN ON 1919 MODEL.

20

"R-3"

32 x 4
TIRES
(THROUGH '24)

Hupmobile

5-PASSENGER
TOURING CAR

OPEN CARS
NOW FEATURE
OUTSIDE DOOR HANDLES

21

2-PASSENGER
ROADSTER

OLD-
STYLE
TAIL-LIGHT
RE-INTRODUCED.

CLOSED CARS ADOPT SUN VISORS
WINDSHIELD WIPERS ADDED IN 1921

FIRST YEAR WITH STEWART SPEEDOMETER.
EARLY MODELS HAVE TAN-LINED TOP AND
HAND ADJUSTMENT OF HEADLIGHT FOCUS.
LATER MODELS HAVE TWEED-LINED TOP
AND SCREWDRIVER
ADJUSTMENT OF
HEADLIGHT
FOCUS.

22

ROADSTER-COUPÉ

(INTRO.
DEC.,
1921)

FIRST YEAR FOR WINDOW
CRANKS IN CLOSED CAR DOORS.

"SPECIAL" MODELS HAVE NICKEL PLATING,
DRUM HEADLIGHTS, DELUXE EQUIPMENT

FRONT RIGHT SEAT FOLDS
UNDER
DASH
WHEN
NOT
IN USE.

23

COUPE TRUNK
DETAILS

Coupe Model RY · Two-Passenger

Special Roadster Model RRS

Coupe Model RK · Four-Passenger

130

HUPMOBILE

24

DRUM HEADLIGHTS ON **ALL** MODELS

NEW 115" WHEELBASE

3 DOOR CLUB SEDAN ('24 and '25)

ONLY 1 DOOR ON LEFT SIDE.

(FINAL 4-CYL. MODEL (R-14) HAS 4.9 G.R.) 31 x 5.25 TIRES)

"R-14" **4**

FOURS AND EIGHTS

25

STRAIGHT-8 IS NEW FOR 1925.

"E-1" **8**

118¼" W.B. 4.63 G.R. 246.7 C.I.D.

HYDRAULIC BRAKES ON NEW 8.

"A-1" SIX

114" W.B. (THROUGH '30)

195 C.I.D. 50 H.P. @ 3000 RPM

30 x 5.25 TIRES

FRENCH-STYLE ROOF VISOR NOW AVAILABLE ON ALL CLOSED HUPMOBILES.

30 x 5.25

26

"E-2" EIGHT

"E-2" 8 BERLINE SIMILAR TO ILLUS. SEDAN, BUT HAS LIMOUSINE-TYPE CLEAR GLASS (PARTITION) BACK OF DRIVER'S SEAT.

NEW 268.7 C.I.D. 63 H.P. @ 2700 RPM NEW 125" W.B.

131

HUPMOBILE

27

"A-2" (8-26)
"A-3" (1-27, with DASH GAUGES IN ONE CENTER PANEL)

MODEL A series
6 CYLS. 195.6 C.I.D.

4.9 GEAR RATIO
114" W.B.

30 x 5.25 TIRES

BROUGHAM

7-PASS.

125" W.B.

MODEL E
8 CYLS. 268.7 C.I.D.
67 H.P. @ 2800 RPM
4.63 GEAR RATIO

(8-27 = "A-5" CONSIDERED "EARLY '28," has TRANSMISSION LOCK LIGHT.)

CUSTOM BODIES USUALLY BY DIETRICH. SPECIAL BODIES HAVE ADVANCE STYLING.

LATE MODELS HAVE IMPROVED "HYPER-EXPANSION" ENGINES.

27½

NEW 6 STARTS OCTOBER, 1927

NEW EMBLEM

ENGINE (6)

Six
(A-6)

28

NEW BODIES BY MURRAY
(COMPLETELY RESTYLED)

"CENTURY" MODELS (A, M)

("E-4" RETAINS 1927 STYLING AND ROOF-VISOR,) BUT HAS DOUBLE INTAKE MANIFOLD.)

211.6 C.I.D.
57 H.P.

4.73 GEAR RATIO

29 x 5.50

DISC WHEELS AVAILABLE, AS WELL AS WOOD OR WIRE WHEELS.

(M) **8**
268.6 C.I.D.
80 H.P.

31 x 6.00

120" W.B.

8-CYL. "M-8" INSTRUMENT PANEL

4.36 G.R.

132

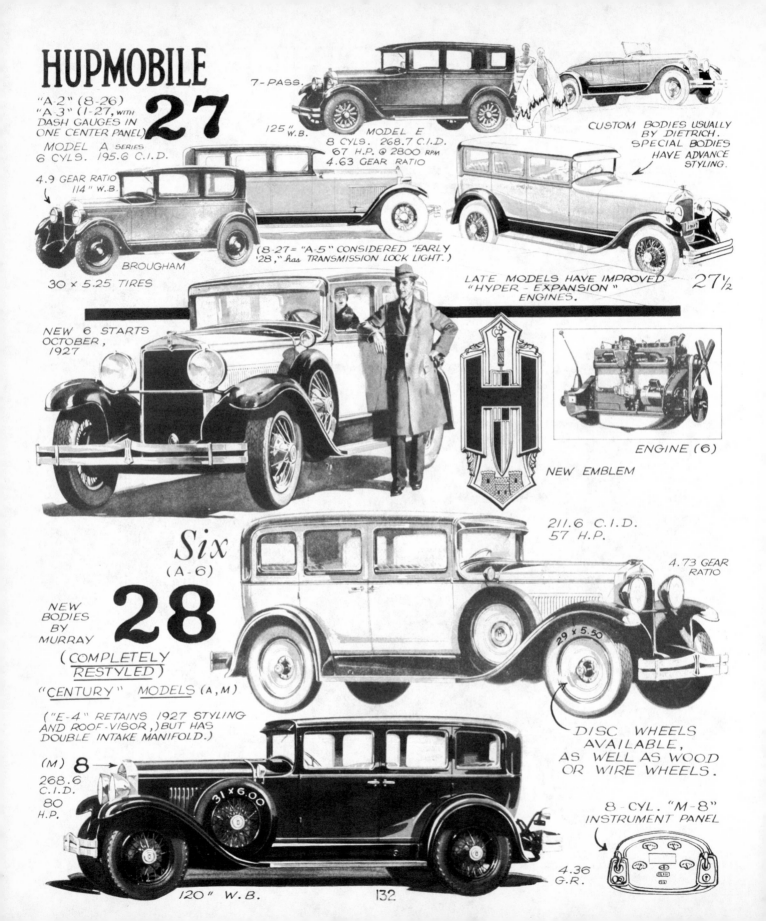

HUPMOBILE
1929 "CENTURY"
SIX & EIGHT

BODIES BY MURRAY, EXCEPT FOR BAKER-RAULANG BODIES ON "M" TOWN SEDAN, 7-PASS. SEDAN, and LIMOUSINE.

29

CURVED AND GROOVED FRONT SPLASH GUARD EXTENDS OVER SPRING HORNS.

SPECIFICATIONS SIMILAR TO 1928, BUT 1929 SIX HAS 4.7 and other GEAR RATIOS; "M" has 4.4

INSTRUMENT PANEL

BRONZE ("M")   SILVER ("A")
OXIDIZED·FINISH

HUPMOBILE

EXAGGERATED ARTIST'S RENDERING →

CENTURY · SIX

MODEL "S"
70 H.P. @ 3200
4.7 G.R.
211.6 C.I.D.
5.25 × 19 TIRES
(BEGINS 8-10-29)

6
WOOD, WIRE, OR DISC WHEELS AS BEFORE

The 1930 Hupmobile Eight Coupe showing new peaked deck and top

Instrument Panel

EARLY "S" SIX, WITH DISC WHEELS, LOW-PLACED HOOD LOUVRES

8

Inside Light

Radiator Cap   Outside Door-Handle

Fender Parking Light   Smoking Set

Inside Door Molding

30

MODEL "C"
8 CYL.
100 H.P. @
3200 RPM
268.6 C.I.D.
4.55 G.R.
6.00 × 19 TIRES
(SUPERSEDES "M," 9-18-29)

MODEL "H"
8 CYL.
133 H.P. @
3400 RPM
365.6 C.I.D.
4.07 G.R.
125" W.B.
6.50 × 19 TIRES

Inside Door-Handles

137"-W.B. MODEL "U" HAS ENGINE LIKE MODEL "H."

NO VISOR

EIGHT

CENTURY 6

'31 SPECS. SIMILAR TO '30, BUT NEW "L" has 8-CYL., 240.2 C.I.D., 90 H.P. @ 3200 RPM

31

wheelbases:
"S-2" CENT. 6   113½
"L"   "   8   118
"C"   "   121
"H"   "   125
"U"   "   137

(FREE-WHEELING AVAIL. IN ALL MODELS AS OF 1-31.)

134

HUPMOBILE

"2/6" (B)

6 CYL., 228.1 C.I.D.
75 H.P. @ 3200 RPM
4.54 G.R.

FREE-
WHEELING
AVAIL.

32

8 DIFFERENT
MODEL
SERIES!

"222" (F)
8 CYL., 250.7 C.I.D.
93 H.P. @ 3200 RPM

OTHER 1932 MODELS :

"214" (S) 6
(211.5 C.I.D.,
70 H.P.)
"218" (L) 6
(240.2 C.I.D.,
90 H.P.)
"221" (C) 8
(268.6 C.I.D.,
100 H.P.)
"225" (H) 8
(365.6 C.I.D.,
133 H.P.)
"226" (I) 8
(279.9 C.I.D., 103 H.P. — — — — and "237" (U) 8 (SAME BIG ENGINE AS "225")

GEAR RATIOS
VARY FROM
3.92 TO 4.7

SHORT FRONT FENDERS, NEW STYLING

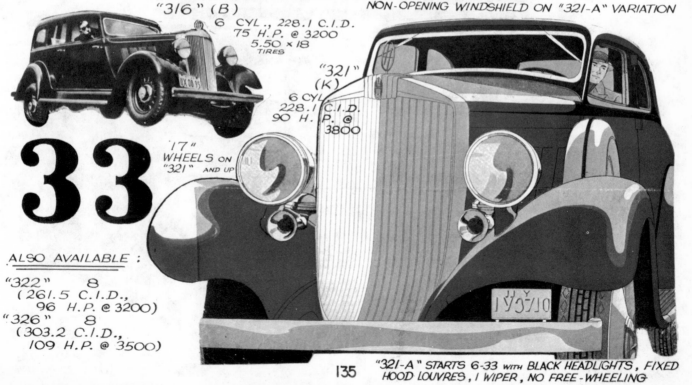

"316" (B)
6 CYL., 228.1 C.I.D.
75 H.P. @ 3200
5.50 × 18
TIRES

NON-OPENING WINDSHIELD ON "321-A" VARIATION

"321"
(K)
6 CYL.
228.1 C.I.D.
90 H.P. @
3800

33

17"
WHEELS ON
"321" AND UP

ALSO AVAILABLE :

"322" 8
(261.5 C.I.D.,
96 H.P. @ 3200)
"326" 8
(303.2 C.I.D.,
109 H.P. @ 3500)

"321-A" STARTS 6-33 with BLACK HEADLIGHTS, FIXED HOOD LOUVRES, 1 WIPER, NO FREE-WHEELING

HUPMOBILE

34

ACTUAL PHOTO →

STANDARD 6

GLAMORIZED ADVERTISING ILLUSTRATION ←

ENGINES RANGE FROM 224 C.I.D. 6 (80 H.P.) TO 303.2 C.I.D. 8 (115 H.P.)

"421-J" →

MODELS "417-W," "KK-421-A," "K-421," "421-J," (SIXES) "422," "426," "427-T" (EIGHTS)

(1ST and 2ND SERIES)

NEW "AERODYNAMIC" MODELS ARE STREAMLINED.

35

"518-D" 6 CYLS.

118" W.B.

INTRO. FEB., 1935

REAR VIEW OF "518-D" (WITH HYDRAULIC BRAKES)

91 TO 120 H.P. 4.5 G.R. ON MOST

(MECHANICAL BRAKES ON (MODELS INTRO. OCT., 1934: "517-W" (6) "521-J" (6) "527-T" (8)

8-CYL. "521-O" INTRO. MAY, 1935 (HYDR. BRAKES)

136

HUPMOBILE

35 (CONT'D.)

"527-T" COUPE
127½" W.B.

8 CYLS.
303.2 C.I.D.
120 H.P. @
3500 RPM

VACUUM MECH. BRAKES ON 527-T

36-37

6 - CYL.
SERIES
"618-G"
245.3
C.I.D.,
101 H.P. @
3600 RPM

4.27
G.R.

3 - PC. WINDSHIELD
RETAINED ON THIS
MODEL

8 - CYL. SERIES
"621-N" 303.2 C.I.D., 120 H.P. @ 3500 RPM
4.09 OR 4.27 G.R.

121 " W.B.

BECAUSE OF FINANCIAL PROBLEMS,
HUPMOBILE PRODUCTION
TEMPORARILY SUSPENDED 1936-1937
AND NO NEW "700" MODELS
ANNOUNCED FOR 1937.

38

SIX = "822-E"
245.3 C.I.D.
101 H.P. @ 3600 RPM
6.25 x 16
TIRES

4.54 G.R. (BOTH MODELS)

EIGHT =
"825-H"
303.2 C.I.D.
120 H.P. @
3500 RPM
6.50 x 16 TIRES

THIS "SENIOR" MODEL
CONTINUED INTO 1939,
WITHOUT CRANK HOLE
IN GRILLE.

OVERDRIVE
OPTIONAL

NEW
"R-915"
("SKYLARK")

CORD BODY DIES USED ON
"R-915", WITH NEW 115"
W.B. and
4.27 G.R.
6.00 x
16
TIRES

"R-915"
JUNIOR 6
(INTRO. OCT., 1938.
REPLACED BY "SKYLARK")

39

("SENIOR" MODELS
"922-E" and "925-H" ARE CONTINUATIONS of '38.)

(FINAL HUPMOBILE,
DISCONTINUED DURING 1940.)

137

"SKYLARK" 6 ONLY, IN 1940

INNES
(1921)

HENRY L. INNES,
JACKSONVILLE, FLORIDA
(COMPANY FORMED IN 1920, BUT
NO CARS ACTUALLY BUILT UNTIL
1921.)

with 4-CYLINDER
178.9 C.I.D.
SUPREME ENGINE
(3 3/8" × 5")

← ROADSTERS or 5-PASS.
TOURING CARS, *each with*
RIGID "PERMANENT TOP."

CHOICE OF
BATTERY OR MAGNETO
IGNITION.

SMALL TRUCK ALSO
(PLANNED)

JACKSON

JACKSON AUTOMOBILE CO.,
JACKSON, MICH. (1903-1923)

'20 "SPORT CAR" ("6-38")
HAS UNUSUAL TOP STYLE.

6-CYL., 3 1/4" × 5" (248.9 C.I.D.)
HERSCHELL-SPILLMAN
ENGINE ALSO LISTED,
DURING SPRING, 1922.
("6-38" SERIES
CONTINUES)

20 "6-38"
6-CYLINDER,
224 C.I.D.
CONTINENTAL
ENGINE (TO '23)

121" W.B. (TO '23)
32 × 4 TIRES
REMY IGNITION
(AUTO-LITE LOCK)

'21 "6-38"
SEMI-SPORT →

21

32 × 4 1/2 TIRES, 4.75 GEAR RATIO (TO '23)

JAEGER
(1931 — 1933)

('32)

JAEGER MOTOR CAR CO.,
BELLEVILLE and CASS CITY,
MICHIGAN

(6-CYL. CONTINENTAL
ENGINE)

JEWETT

A Thrifty Six **JEWETT** *Built by Paige*

JEWETT'S 6-CYL. ENGINE IS A DEVELOPMENT FROM THE 1921 PAIGE "6-44" ENGINE, AND HAS THE ADDITION OF FORCE-FEED OILING.

22
"6-50"

12" BRAKE DRUMS

ATWATER KENT IGNITION

112" WHEELBASE (THROUGH '24)

248.9 C.I.D. (THROUGH '25)

50 HORSEPOWER (THROUGH '24)

FIRST YEAR WITH NO SECTOR ON SPARK OR THROTTLE HAND CONTROL.

23
"6-50"

14" BRAKE DRUMS

50 HORSEPOWER

24
"6-50"

De Luxe Sedan BODY COLOR = "LOTUS BLUE"

NICKEL TRIM ON DELUXE MODELS

CARB. ON LEFT SIDE OF ENGINE. DISTRIBUTOR PUMP and GENERATOR ON RIGHT SIDE.

3-PASS. BUSINESS MAN'S CPE. INTRO. ABOUT 2-24. DURING 1924, AND 4-PASS. CPE. DROPPED. NEW 2-DR. BROUGHAM SEATS CONVERT TO A BED.

139 AUTUMN, 1924 = 32 x 4.95 BALLOON TIRES, AND "AUTUMN GREEN" SATIN BODY COLOR (MOST MODELS)

JEWETT SIX
PAIGE BUILT

DE LUXE
BROUGHAM

(STD. BROUGHAM
has PAINTED RADIATOR,
NO LANDAU IRONS.)

25

"6-50"
112" W.B.

STROMBERG CARB.
ATW. KENT IGNITION
LIGHT SWITCH
ON DASH

LOCKHEED
HYDRAULIC
4 WHEEL
BRAKES
AVAILABLE
(SINCE
1924)
($40
EXTRA)

HIGHER
HOOD
AND
LOWER
RUNNING-
BOARDS

new
"SATIN
LACQUER"
FINISH

LATER IN YEAR, EARLY
1926 "6-55" MODEL
HAS LOCKING STEERING
WHEEL. WHEELBASE
CHANGED FROM
112" TO
115", with LIGHT
SWITCH ON STEER. WH.

63 H.P.
@
2800 RPM
(ONLY 55 H.P.
CLAIMED EARLY
IN SEASON.)

CARB. MOVED
TO RIGHT SIDE
OF ENGINE,
FOR '25.

31 × 5.25

31 × 5.25

COACH ($1260.)
(LOW-PRICED MODEL of CLOSED CAR. STARTS 4-25. HAS
DOORS 3' WIDE.)

TOP SPEED = 65 MILES PER HOUR

INTERIOR

The New-Day
JEWETT SIX

SERIES "6-40"

(STARTS DEC., 1925)
THE
ONLY JEWETT WITH
NEW, NARROW
CORNER POSTS

NICKELED RADIATOR SHELL
ON DE LUXE MODELS

NEW CONTINENTAL
ENGINE HAS 169.2 C.I.D.
and 40 H.P. @ 2400 RPM
JOHNSON CARB., REMY IGN.

29 × 4.75

29 × 4.75

26

"NEW-DAY"
MODEL HAS
SHORTENED
109"
W.B.

(A VERY SCARCE MODEL)

FINAL JEWETT (1927 MODEL)
WAS INTRODUCED SEPTEMBER, 1926.
ON JANUARY 3, 1927, ITS NAME WAS CHANGED TO
THE PAIGE "6-45," APPEARANCE WAS SAME.
(SEE PAIGE, 1927 FOR PICTURE.)

JONES 6

('20-21 MODEL)

1920 MODEL 28 HAS IMPROVED RADIATOR, HIGH SHIFTING LEVER.
CONTINENTAL ENGINE (303.1 C.I.D.)

(1915 - 1920)
JONES MOTOR CAR CO., WICHITA, KANSAS
"SPEEDSTER" TOURING

126" W.B.
4.5 G.R.
AUTO-LITE IGNITION

JORDAN MOTOR CAR COMPANY, Inc., *Cleveland, Ohio*

JORDAN

('21)

224 C.I.D., 120" W.B. (1916 - 1931)
1920 "M" FEATURES ONLY MINOR IMPROVEMENTS. NEW 4-DOOR SEDAN. LIGHTWEIGHT ALUMINUM BODIES.

"F" SERIES HAS 303.1 C.I.D. ENGINE AND 127" W.B. (THROUGH '22)   Delco IGNITION (THROUGH '24 and on 6-CYL. '25)

"Silhouette" TOURING

6-CYL. CONTINENTAL ENGINES
32 × 4 TIRES (M)
32 × 4½ " (F)

PRE-1922 JORDANS have SCREW-ON (THREADED) GAS TANK CAP, AND STARTER SWITCH ON FLOOR NEAR FRONT SEAT.

NEW INSTRUMENT BOARD IN 1922, with ALL GAUGES UNDER ONE GLASS.

4.66 GEAR RATIO (M)
4.08 " " (F)

2-DOOR BROUGHAM

(1920-1923 STYLE; '16-19 MODELS HAD REAR "TURTLEBACK" DECK LIKE VICTORIA COUPE.)

"F" REPLACED BY "H" SERIES IN 1923, WITH 124½" W.B. BOTH 1923 MODELS HAVE 245.6 C.I.D. (AS "MK" CHANGED TO, IN '22.)

20-23

"M" and "F" SERIES ("M" BECOMES "MK" IN 1922)

4-DOOR BROUGHAM (INTRODUCED 1923)

EARLY TYPE HAS DASH GAUGES AT RIGHT SIDE

DISC WHEELS AVAILABLE ON 1923 "PLAYBOY"

JORDAN

"*Playboy*" SPT. ROADSTER

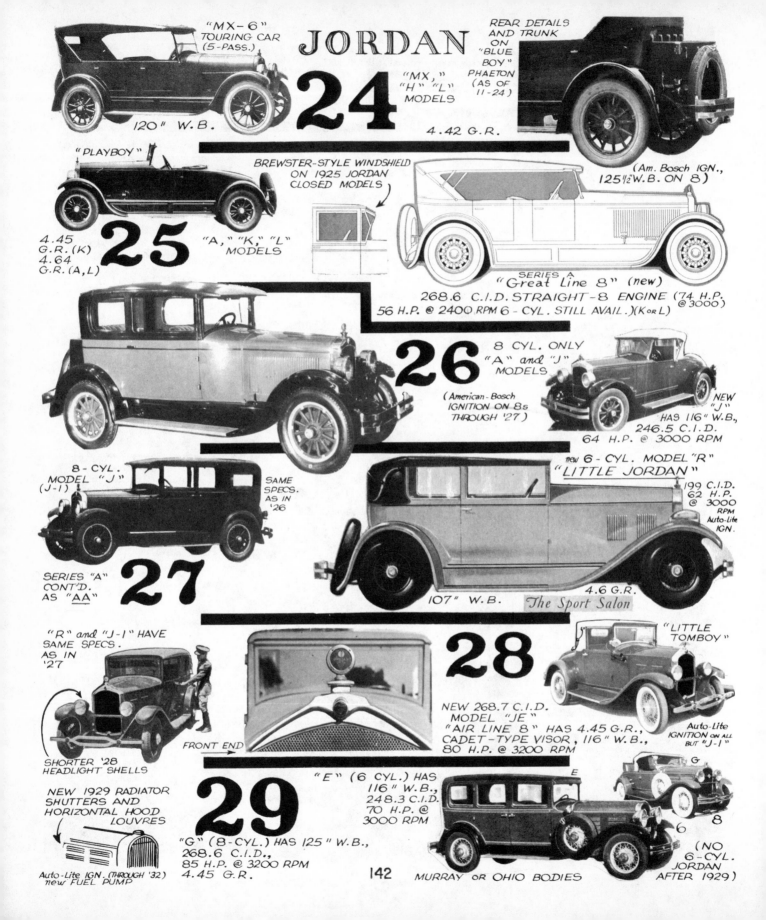

JORDAN

24

"MX-6" TOURING CAR (5-PASS.)

"MX," "H" "L" MODELS

120" W.B.

4.42 G.R.

REAR DETAILS AND TRUNK ON "BLUE BOY" PHAETON (AS OF 11-24)

(Am. Bosch IGN., 125½" W.B. ON 8)

25

"PLAYBOY"

4.45 G.R. (K)
4.64 G.R. (A,L)

"A," "K," "L" MODELS

BREWSTER-STYLE WINDSHIELD ON 1925 JORDAN CLOSED MODELS

SERIES A "Great Line 8" (new)
268.6 C.I.D. STRAIGHT-8 ENGINE (74 H.P. @ 3000)
56 H.P. @ 2400 RPM 6-CYL. STILL AVAIL.) (K or L)

26

8 CYL. ONLY "A" and "J" MODELS

(American-Bosch IGNITION ON 8s THROUGH '27)

NEW "J" HAS 116" W.B., 246.5 C.I.D. 64 H.P. @ 3000 RPM

27

8-CYL. MODEL "J" (J-1)

SAME SPECS. AS IN '26

SERIES "A" CONT'D. AS "AA"

new 6-CYL. MODEL "R" "LITTLE JORDAN"

199 C.I.D. 62 H.P. @ 3000 RPM Auto-Lite IGN.

107" W.B. *The Sport Salon*

4.6 G.R.

28

"R" and "J-1" HAVE SAME SPECS. AS IN '27

SHORTER '28 HEADLIGHT SHELLS

FRONT END

NEW 268.7 C.I.D. MODEL "JE" "AIR LINE 8" HAS 4.45 G.R., CADET-TYPE VISOR, 116" W.B., 80 H.P. @ 3200 RPM

"LITTLE TOMBOY"

Auto-Lite IGNITION on ALL BUT "J-1"

29

NEW 1929 RADIATOR SHUTTERS AND HORIZONTAL HOOD LOUVRES

Auto-Lite IGN. (THROUGH '32) new FUEL PUMP

"G" (8-CYL.) HAS 125" W.B., 268.6 C.I.D., 85 H.P. @ 3200 RPM 4.45 G.R.

"E" (6 CYL.) HAS 116" W.B., 248.3 C.I.D. 70 H.P. @ 3000 RPM

E

G

6

8

(NO 6-CYL. JORDAN AFTER 1929)

MURRAY or OHIO BODIES

142

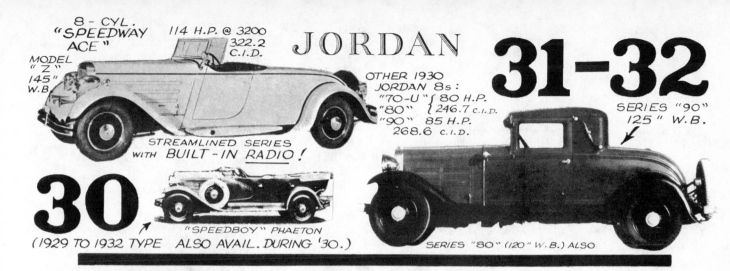

8 - CYL. "SPEEDWAY ACE"   114 H.P. @ 3200
322.2 C.I.D.

JORDAN

31-32

MODEL "Z" 145" W.B.

OTHER 1930 JORDAN 8s:
"70-U" { 80 H.P.
"80" { 246.7 C.I.D.
"90" 85 H.P.
268.6 C.I.D.

SERIES "90" 125" W.B.

STREAMLINED SERIES WITH BUILT-IN RADIO!

30

"SPEEDBOY" PHAETON

(1929 TO 1932 TYPE ALSO AVAIL. DURING '30.)

SERIES "80" (120" W.B.) ALSO

JULIAN (1922)

JULIAN BROWN, SYRACUSE, N.Y.

RADIAL ENGINE AT REAR

6 CYLS. (1921)
4 " (1922 ON)

KELSEY

FRICTION DRIVE

32 × 4 TIRES FOR '24, 206.4 CID LYCOMING REPLACES 192.4 CID G-B ENGINE.

KELSEY MOTOR CO., NEWARK and BELLEVILLE, N.J.

(1921-1924)

EARLIEST KELSEYS HAVE "OWN ENGINE" (FALLS 195.6 CID)

116" W.B.

(FACTORY IN MISHAWAKA, IND.)

KENWORTHY

KENWORTHY MOTORS OF NEW ENGLAND; BOSTON, MASS.

(1920-1922)

NOTE PEAKED RADIATOR

"8-90"
OWN STRAIGHT-8 296.9 C.I.D. (3" × 5¼")
"LINE-O-EIGHT" ENGINE
130" W.B. 4.08 G.R.
32 × 4½ TIRES

21

('22 SIMILAR)

(4-WHEEL BRAKES AVAILABLE.)

V-8 ENGINE (INTRO. 2-15)

KING

KING MOTOR CAR CO., DETROIT
(1910-1923)

(PRODUCED IN BUFFALO, N.Y., 1923-1924)

('22)

20

21-23 →

SEDANETTE (4-PASS.)

143

KISSEL

KISSEL MOTOR CAR CO.
HARTFORD, WISCONSIN

The Custom **Built Car**

(1906-1931)

SPEEDSTER

4-DR. COACH-SEDAN
(INTRO. 1-8-21)

3.62 G.R. REPLACED
BY 4.25 G.R. IN '21.

BOSCH IGNITION ('20)
REMY IGNITION
('21 ON)

4-PASS. COUPE

4-PASS. TOURSTER

124" W.B.
(THROUGH '23)
OWN 6-CYL.,
284.4 C.I.D. ENGINE
(THROUGH '23)
32 × 4 TIRES
(THROUGH '23)

19-22

'22 IS FIRST YEAR WITH SELF-LUBRICATING BRONZE BUSHINGS
ON BRAKE MECHANISM.

POPULARLY KNOWN
AS "GOLD BUG"

DRUM HEADLIGHTS, 1-PC.
WINDSHIELDS

23-24

'24 = OIL TEST
GAUGE
ROD ON
LEFT
SIDE
OF
ENG.

4.4 G.R.
IN '23

1923 "45" SERIES IS
JOINED BY
NEW "55" SERIES
NEW 121" W.B.,
SMALLER 6-CYL.
265 (264.8) C.I.D.
ENGINE (USED ON
6-CYL. CHASSIS
THROUGH '27)

BROUGHAM

6-CYL. 1925 "55" IS
FINAL KISSEL TO OFFER
2-WHEEL MECHANICAL
BRAKES.

70 M.P.H.
"6-55"

25-26

OIL TEST GAUGE ROD
IS ELIMINATED (1925)

"8-75"
STRAIGHT-8
MODEL INTRODUCED
JANUARY, 1925.
(HAS HYDR. BRAKES)
287.3 CID, 63 H.P. @ 2400 ('25)
310 CID, 71 H.P. @ 3100 ('26)
75 M.P.H. TOP SPEED

50
H.P.
@
2800 RPM
(53 @ 2300 IN '26)

Body by Kissel

2ND KICK PAD ON
8-CYL. BROUGHAM

144

KISSEL

27

HYDRAULIC BRAKES ON ALL '26-'27 KISSELS.

"6-55" 124-131" W.B. 264.8 C.I.D. 61 H.P. @2300

4.6 G.R. ("8-65") HEAVIER WHEEL SPOKES '27 ENGINES CUSHIONED IN RUBBER

"8-65" 125-132" W.B., NEW SMALL 8 (246.5 C.I.D.)(THROUGH '31) 65 H.P. @ 2000 RPM

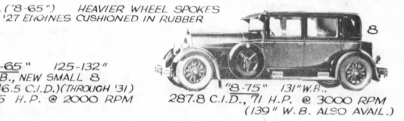

8

"8-75" 131"W.B., 287.8 C.I.D., 71 H.P. @ 3000 RPM (139" W.B. ALSO AVAIL.)

28

new, SMALL 185 C.I.D. 6 IN 117"-W.B. "6-70" 52 H.P. @ 2900 RPM (THROUGH '29) 4.63 G.R. 30 × 6.00 TIRES

(8-80) "SMALL 8" 4-DOOR BROUGHAM (REPLACES 8-65, BUT HAS 70 H.P. @2900, 4.6 G.R., 31 × 6.20 TIRES)

HYDRAULIC BRAKES CONTINUED (THROUGH '31)

"8-80-S" has 125" W.B., 30 × 6.00 TIRES, 4.8 G.R.

1928 = NEW BODIES AND ILCO-RYAN HEADLIGHTS; WATER TEMP. GAUGE ON DASH.

"8-90" →

"8-75" BECOMES "8-90" FOR '28, with 85 H.P. @ 3100 RPM, 4.89 G.R., 30 × 6.75 TIRES 131" OR 139" W.B.

SPEEDSTER

VACUUM-TANK FUEL FEED CONTINUED ON ALL MODELS (TO '31)

125-132" W.B.

"95" COUPE-ROADSTER (8 CYL.) 246.5 C.I.D. 95 H.P. @ 3200 RPM 4.8 G.R. (5.1 IN '30) 6.00 × 18 TIRES (ALSO ON "6-73")

132-139" W. B. 30 × 6.75 TIRES ('29)

"126" BROUGHAM (8 CYL.)

298.6 C.I.D. 126 H.P. 4.89 G.R. (4.8 IN '30) 7.00 × 16 TIRES IN '30)

29-31

"WHITE EAGLE" MODELS (BEGIN AUG. 15, 1928)

MODEL "73" = 6 CYL. (185 C.I.D.) 52 H.P. @ 2900 ('29) 117" W.B. 75 H.P. @ 3500 ('30-31) 4.6 G.R. (5.3 IN '30)

1931 MODEL IS FINAL KISSEL.

STARTS 7-1-30

KLEIBER MOTOR CO. (CARS = 1924–1929) ALSO BUILT TRUCKS

11th and Folsom Sts.
SAN FRANCISCO

1800 E. 12th St.
OAKLAND

11th and San Pedro Sts.
LOS ANGELES

'27
(6)

'29
(8)

CONTINENTAL "8-R" 6-CYL. 241.6 C.I.D. ENGINE
55 H.P. @ 2300 RPM
122" W.B., 32 × 6.20 TIRES

'29 DASH →
(INSTRUMENTS SET IN BLACK WOOD
PANEL; OUTDATED STYLE FOR 1929!)

KLINE KAR
(1910 – 1923)

SINCE 1912, BLT. BY KLINE MOTOR CAR CORP., RICHMOND, VA.

20-22

"6-55"   121" W.B.   224 C.I.D.
6-CYL. CONTINENTAL ENGINE

"6-60" (1923) HAS 241.5 C.I.D.

LaFAYETTE
(1919 to 1924)

LaFAYETTE MOTORS CORPORATION
Milwaukee, Wisconsin

20

V-8   100
ENGINE   H.P.
132"   348.4 C.I.D.
W.B.
(THROUGH
'24)

The Four-Door Coupe (new)

21
4.5 G.R.

(COMPANY ORIGINATED AT
INDIANAPOLIS, INDIANA)

22-23

THOUGH NEW
BODY TYPES
APPEARED,
THE
MODEL "134" DIDN'T
FEATURE
NOTEWORTHY
CHANGES
BETWEEN
1920
and 1924.

33 × 5
TIRES
ON ALL

CO. ABSORBED
BY NASH.
LA FAYETTE NAME
APPEARS
AGAIN IN
1934, ON
LOW-PRICED
CAR.

NEW
4.58 G.R.
PULL-TYPE HOOD FASTENERS and COWL BELT,
LATE 1923

FRONT
END,
SHOWING
RADIATOR
SHUTTERS

24

146

LaFAYETTE

NASH BUILT

COUPE (ACTUAL PHOTO)

34

113" W.B. (THROUGH '36)

217.8 C.I.D. (THROUGH '36)
75 H.P. @ 3200 RPM
(THROUGH '35)
4.7 GEAR RATIO (THROUGH '35)

NEW 6.00 x 16 TIRES
AUTOMATIC STARTER WITH
CLUTCH PEDAL CONTROL.
3 HORIZONTAL LOUVRES
(INSTEAD of VENT DOORS
ON HOOD)

CHASSIS

35

→

COUPE
(GROSSLY
EXAGGERATED
ARTIST'S
CONCEPTION
OF 1935.)

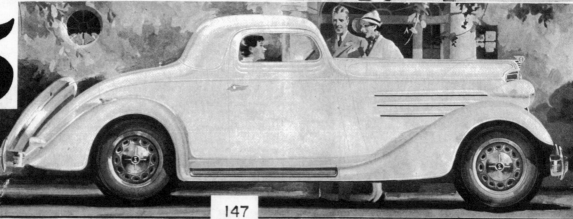

LaFAYETTE

ENGINE (7-BEARING)

NOTE HOW
ENTIRE
TRUNK BULGE
OPENS, on SEDAN

REAR SEAT,
SHOWING
UPHOLSTERY
PATTERN

36

SEAMLESS ALL-STEEL
TOP (ON LAFAYETTE
OR NASH "400")

NEW = HYDRAULIC BRAKES
4.4 GEAR RATIO

REAR
SEAT
AND
TRUNK AREA
CONVERTS TO A
6' DOUBLE BED (IN
LAFAYETTE OR NASH "400"
SEDANS)

LATE MODELS
HAVE
DIE-CAST
GRILLE.

FENDER
SKIRTS
AVAIL.

37

117" WHEELBASE AND SPECIFICATIONS
SIMILAR TO '36 NASH "400"

4.11 GEAR
RATIO

BECAME
THE
NASH-LAFAYETTE
"400"

CADILLAC MOTOR CAR COMPANY
Detroit, Michigan   Oshawa, Canada
Division of General Motors Corporation

LaSalle

INTRO.
MARCH
1927

V-8
L-HEAD
ENGINE
(all years
except
'34 THROUGH
'36)

27

303 C.I.D.
(THROUGH '28)

MODEL
"303"

SEPT., 1927 = ELECTRO
LOCK ON DASHBOARD
REPLACES
TRANSMISSION
LOCK.

OPAQUED
GLASS VISOR

28

"303"
NEW,
NARROWER
HOOD LOUVRES

"HEAT ON AND OFF" CONTROL LEVER
ADDED ON LEFT SIDE OF DASH.

80 H.P. @ 3000 RPM
4.8 COMPRESSION

4.54 OR 4.91 GEAR RATIO
(THROUGH '29)

125" OR 134" WHEELBASE (THROUGH '29)

CHROME-PLATING ON ALL BRIGHTWORK
PARKING LAMPS MOVED TO
FRONT FENDERS

FISHER OR
FLEETWOOD
BODIES

327.7 C.I.D.
86 H.P. @ 3000 RPM
5.3 and other COMPRESSION RATIOS

INSTRUMENT PANEL DESIGN
SIMILAR TO CADILLAC'S.

SYNCHRO-MESH TRANSMISSION
(ALSO ON CADILLAC)

29

"328"

REAR SECTION OF
TOP FOLDS DOWN

(FUEL PUMP USED DURING '29)

149

LaSalle

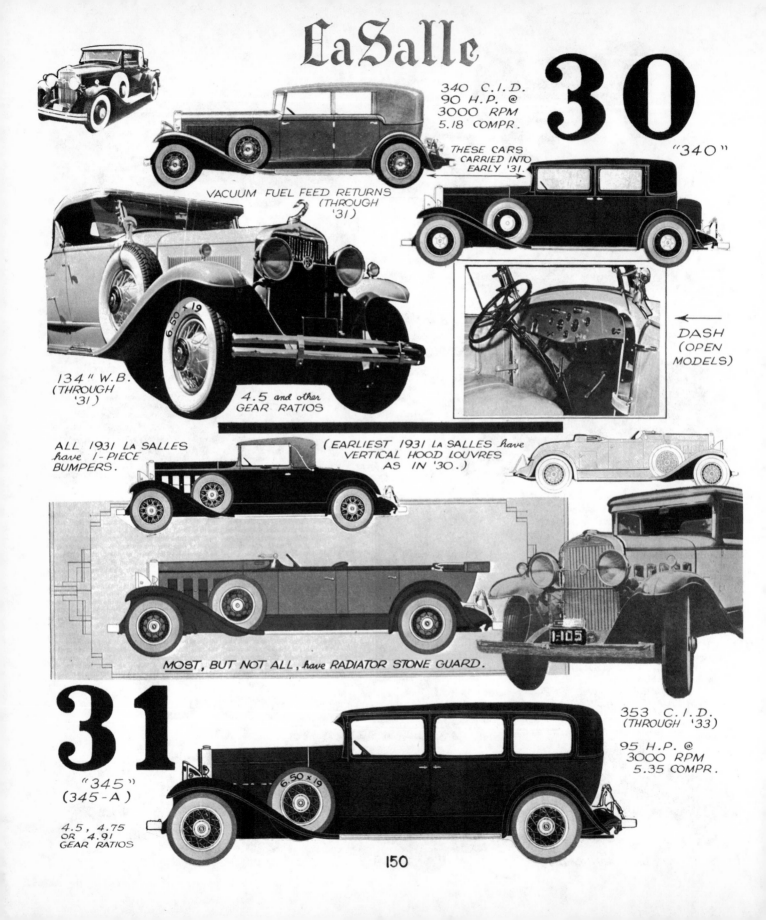

30
"340"

340 C.I.D.
90 H.P. @
3000 RPM
5.18 COMPR.

THESE CARS
CARRIED INTO
EARLY '31.

VACUUM FUEL FEED RETURNS
(THROUGH '31)

134" W.B.
(THROUGH '31)

6.50 x 19

4.5 and other
GEAR RATIOS

DASH
(OPEN
MODELS)

ALL 1931 LA SALLES
have 1-PIECE
BUMPERS.

(EARLIEST 1931 LA SALLES have
VERTICAL HOOD LOUVRES
AS IN '30.)

MOST, BUT NOT ALL, have RADIATOR STONE GUARD.

1:105

31
"345"
(345-A)

4.5, 4.75
OR 4.91
GEAR RATIOS

6.50 x 19

353 C.I.D.
(THROUGH '33)

95 H.P. @
3000 RPM
5.35 COMPR.

150

LaSalle

FUEL PUMP RETURNS

4.6 GEAR RATIO (THROUGH '33)

32 ← 115 H.P. @ 3000 RPM (THROUGH '33)

"345-B" 5.38 COMPR.

130" and 136" W.B. (THROUGH '33)

'33 DASH

"HERON" RADIATOR MASCOT with FILLER UNDER HOOD

33 → "345-C"

BENDIX POWER BRAKES

5.40 COMPR.

GRACEFUL NEW STREAMLINING
HYDRAULIC BRAKES
119" W.B.

34

MODEL "350"

7.00 x 16 TIRES (THROUGH '40)

STRAIGHT-8 ENGINE REPLACES V-8 (THROUGH '36)

240.3 C.I.D. 90 H.P. @ 3700 RPM

COUPE WITH BOTH RUMBLE-SEAT AND TRUNK ↗

6.50 or 5.75 COMPR.

4.78 GEAR RATIO ('34 and '35)

35

"50" SERIES (CONT'D. TO '40)

(PUSH-BUTTON STARTER)

120" W.B. ('35 and '36)
105 H.P. @ 3600 RPM ('35 and '36)
6.50 or 5.75 COMPR.

V-WINDSHIELD, STEEL TOP

4.55 GEAR RATIO

36

HAND-BRAKE LEVER AT LEFT SIDE OF COWL.
6.25 or 5.75 COMPR. (THROUGH '40)

LASALLE V-8 PERFORMANCE COULD ONLY
COME FROM CADILLAC—PIONEER AND
LEADER IN FINE V-8 DESIGN SINCE 1914

V·8 LaSalle

CADILLAC MOTOR

NEW ENGINE
has 322 C.I.D.
(THROUGH '40)
125 H.P.
@ 3400
RPM
(THROUGH
'39)

37

3.92 GEAR RATIO
(THROUGH '40)

'38 INTERIOR

38

HOOD HINGED AT REAR, EXTENDS TO
GRILLE WHICH IS 2" WIDER FOR 1938.

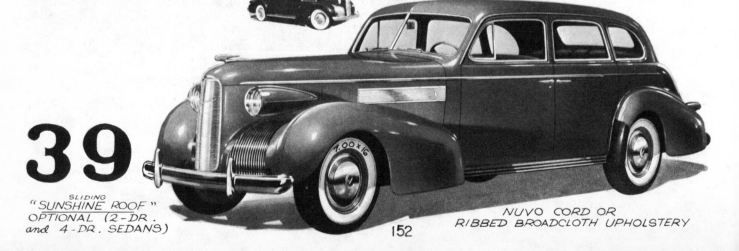

39

SLIDING
"SUNSHINE ROOF"
OPTIONAL (2-DR.
and 4-DR. SEDANS)

NUVO CORD OR
RIBBED BROADCLOTH UPHOLSTERY

152

LEACH
(1920-1923)
LEACH MOTOR CAR CO., LOS ANGELES, CALIF.

CONTINENTAL 6-CYL. 303.1 C.I.D. ENGINE IN '20 and '21

126½" W.B. ('20)
128" W.B. ('21)

BEAR RADIATOR EMBLEM (LEACH-BILTWELL)

('22) 134" W.B.

OWN "POWER PLUS 6" O.H.C. engine (347.9 CID) DELCO IGN. IN '22-'23 MODEL "999"

32 × 4½ TIRES

(FEATURED NEW "CALIFORNIA TOP" WITH SLIDING WINDOWS.)

LEON RUBAY

(1922-1924)
RUBAY CO., CLEVELAND, OHIO

118" W.B.

5.10 G.R.

32 × 4

OWN 122 C.I.D. 4-CYL. O.H.C. engine

(4-WHEEL BRAKES)

BOSCH IGNITION

20

6 CYL. L-HEAD 224 C.I.D. CONTINENTAL ENGINE

LEXINGTON
(1909-1928) = NO NEW MODEL LISTED AFTER 1926.

LEXINGTON MOTOR CO., CONNERSVILLE, INDIANA (ORIGINATED IN LEXINGTON, KY.)

"Minute Man Six" ("S")

120" W.B.

123" W.B. "U" SERIES STARTS 1-22

"MINUTE MAN" JOINED BY NEW "CONCORD" SERIES IN 1924, WITH 232.7 C.I.D. ANSTED O.H.V. 6-CYL. ENGINE

new '21 SERIES "T" (NEW ANSTED 6 CYL. O.H.V. ENGINES) (MODEL "S" CONTINUED)

128" W.B.

"Lark" MODEL 1921½-1922

119" W.B., 32 × 4 TIRES

FOLDED IN MID-20s, TAKEN OVER BY AUBURN

('23 = ABSORBED BY COLUMBIA)

"10-C" OWN 6-CYL., 230.1 CID L-HEAD ENG. (Wagner IGN.)

117" W.B.

('21)

('20)

LIBERTY SIX
Liberty Motor Car Company, Detroit (1916-1924)

DRUM HEADLIGHTS IN 1922

'22 SERIES "10-D"
4.66 G.R.

LIBERTY

4.8 G.R. IN '23-'24

32 × 4 TIRES

153

Henry M. Leland
President
and
FOUNDER

LINCOLN
MOTOR CARS
LELAND–BUILT

LINCOLN MOTOR COMPANY
DETROIT, MICH.

Wilfred C. Leland
Vice-Pres. and Gen. Mgr.

V-8
(357.8 C.I.D.)
(THROUGH 1927)

OWN
CARBURETOR
FOR 1921

7- PASS.
TOURING CAR

33 × 5

Lincoln Intake Manifold with Carburetor and Electro-Fog Producer

*In the illustration, the intake manifold is
shown in section. The upper passage (A) is
for hot water; the lower passage (C) for hot
exhaust gases, and the passage between (B)
for intake gas mixture. The retort where
fuel is converted into fog is shown at "D"*

5- PASS.
TOURING
CAR

21
(STARTS AUTUMN,
1920)

130 " WHEELBASE

(136" W. B. ON LIMOUSINE
AND TOWN CAR)
4.45 GEAR RATIO

DELCO IGNITION
(THROUGH '27)

33 × 5

154

70 MILES PER HOUR

LELAND-BUILT
LINCOLN

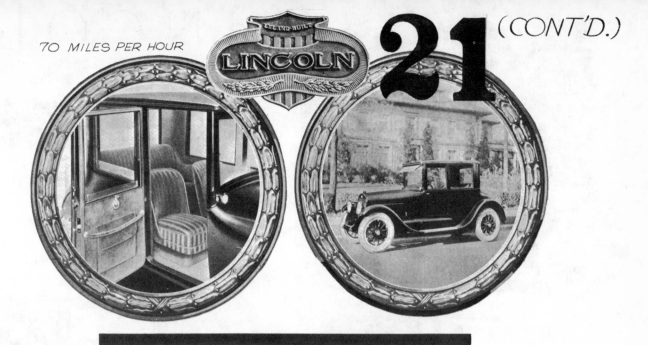

STANDARD WHEELBASE 136"
(THROUGH '30)

new STROMBERG
CARBURETOR
90 H.P.

SEVEN-PASSENGER SEDAN

22

1-22 = FORD
MOTOR CO.
PURCHASES
LINCOLN MOTOR CO.

4-PASS.
SEDAN

DRUM HEADLIGHTS
ON MOST 1923
LINCOLNS.

7-PASS. TOURING CAR

33 × 5 TIRES CONT'D. (THROUGH '27)

23

JUDKINS COUPE

(A SIMILAR COUPE WITH 1921-STYLE
"REVERSED" REAR FENDERS ALSO AVAIL.)

95 H.P. @ 2800 RPM
(THROUGH '24)

7-PASS. SEDAN

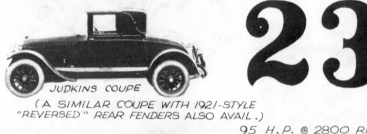

LINCOLN

MODEL "124"

24

VERTICAL
RADIATOR SHUTTERS

25

LINCOLN

MODEL "124"

JUDKINS THREE-WINDOW BERLINE

90 H.P.
@ 2800 RPM
(THROUGH '27)

156

LINCOLN

SPORT PHAETON
(LOCKE BODY)

7-PASS.
LIMOUSINE

JUDKINS 2-PASS.
COUPE

LE BARON
4-PASS. SEDAN

26

"124 - A"

"CABRIOLET" (LANDAULET) WITH
COLLAPSIBLE
REAR QUARTER

TOWN CAR

('26½)

4-WHEEL
BRAKES
NOW
ON ALL
MODELS.

GEAR RATIO 4.58 (THROUGH
1940)

27

"124-B"

90-
100
H.P.

33 × 5
TIRES

Four Passenger Two Window Sedan

157

LINCOLN

27½

The Lincoln Four-Passenger Coupe

MODEL "152"

28

33 × 5.50
TIRES
DELCO - REMY
IGNITION
(TO '31)

JUDKINS TWO-WINDOW BERLINE

Club Roadster

29

BODIES BY
JUDKINS
DIETRICH
WILLOUGHBY
BRUNN
HOLBROOK
CENTRAL
LE BARON
ETC.

1929 — LE BARON AERO-PHAETON

90 H.P. @ 2800 RPM
(THROUGH '30)

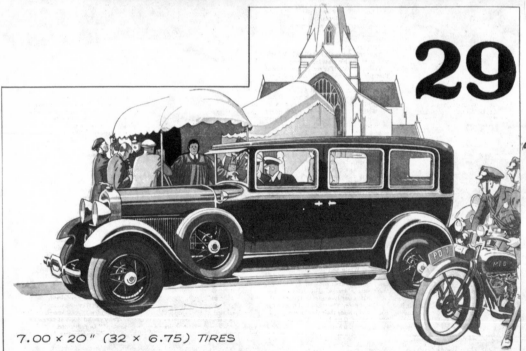

7.00 × 20" (32 × 6.75) TIRES

TOWN BROUGHAM

TOWN SEDAN

158

LINCOLN

1930 — BRUNN CABRIOLET

30

MODEL "169-B"

7.00 x 20
TIRES

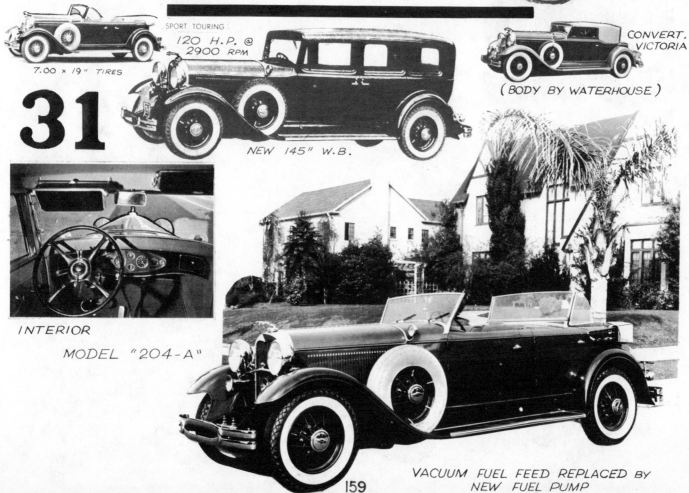

SPORT TOURING

120 H.P. @
2900 RPM

7.00 x 19" TIRES

31

NEW 145" W.B.

CONVERT.
VICTORIA

(BODY BY WATERHOUSE)

INTERIOR

MODEL "204-A"

VACUUM FUEL FEED REPLACED BY
NEW FUEL PUMP

LINCOLN

4-PASSENGER PHAETON

V-8

120-125 H.P. @ 2900 RPM

7.00 x 18" TIRES ON V-8

"2-WINDOW TOWN SEDAN"

V-12 (NEW)

136" W.B. ON V-8 "234-B"

32

V-12

WILLOUGHBY LIMOUSINE

145" W.B. ON V-12 "235" V-12 HAS 447.9 C.I.D. ENGINE, WITH 150 H.P. @ 3400 RPM

7.50 x 18

TOWN CAR

(V-12) K-B

INT.

AUTO-LITE IGN.

160

DUAL-COWL PHAETON

LINCOLN

136" and 145" WHEELBASES

33

2-TONE
HORNS
BEHIND GRILLE

381.7-C.I.D. and 447-C.I.D. V-12 ENGINES (125 and 150 H.P. @ 3400 RPM)

HOOD VENT DOORS
THERMOSTATICALLY
CONTROLLED

ALL MODELS ADOPT SAME
TYPE OF 150-H.P. (@ 3400)
V-12 ENGINE.
(414 C.I.D.)
THIS ENGINE USED WITH
SAME SPECS. IN ALL LARGE ("K")
LINCOLNS FROM 1934 THROUGH
1940.)

LeBARON CONVERTIBLE ROADSTER

custom-built types by Judkins,
Brunn, Willoughby, Dietrich and Le Baron.

7.50×18 TIRES ON
145"-W.B. CUSTOM
200 SERIES

THE TWO-WINDOW TOWN SEDAN

34

136" and 145" W.B.
(THROUGH '40)
7.00/7.50×18 TIRES
(AS IN '33) (500 SER.)
4.58 GEAR RATIO
(THROUGH '40 "K")

MECHANICAL
VACUUM BOOSTER
BRAKES

THE FIVE-PASSENGER CONVERTIBLE SEDAN-PHAETON

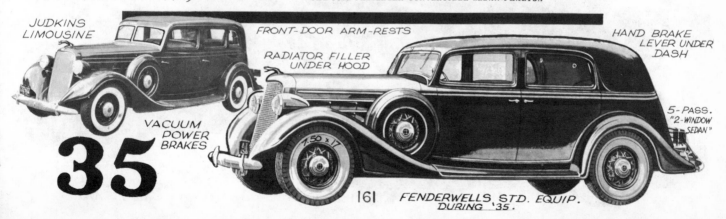

JUDKINS
LIMOUSINE

FRONT-DOOR ARM-RESTS

RADIATOR FILLER
UNDER HOOD

HAND BRAKE
LEVER UNDER
DASH

VACUUM
POWER
BRAKES

35

7.50 × 17

5-PASS.
"2-WINDOW
SEDAN"

161   FENDERWELLS STD. EQUIP.
DURING '35.

LINCOLN

Lincoln Zephyr V-12 (NEW)

BLUE EMBLEM ON GRILLE

ZEPHYR OF 1936 THROUGH 1936 HAS 267.3 C.I.D. V-12 ENGINE (110 H.P. @ 3800 - 3900 RPM)

4.33 GEAR RATIO, 122" W.B. (THROUGH '37)
7.00 x 16" TIRES (THROUGH '41)

BRUNN "CABRIOLET"

7.50 x 17

23 511

36

BRUNN CVT. VICTORIA

MECHANICAL BRAKES (all)

BRIGHT METAL SPOKES ON STEERING WHEEL

37

ENTIRE LUGGAGE / TIRE COMPART. NOW ACCESSIBLE THROUGH THE TRUNK DOOR.

RED EMBLEM ON GRILLE

7124

ZEPHYR

new QUIETER FAN has ALTERNATE LONG and SHORT BLADES.
MECHANICAL BRAKES

162

new V-SHAPED WINDSHIELD (K)

LINCOLN

37

(CONT'D.)

2-WINDOW BERLINE

BRUNN TOURING CABRIOLET

LIMOUSINE (WILLOUGHBY BODY)

HEADLIGHTS SUNKEN IN FENDERS →

VACUUM BOOSTER ON MODEL "K" BRAKES

ZEPHYR HAS NEW 125" W.B. AND 4.44 GEAR RATIO

38

LE BARON CONVERTIBLE SEDAN

The LINCOLN

ZEPHYR (RESTYLED)

STROMBERG CARB. (SINCE '22)

ZEPHYR HAS OWN IGNITION SYSTEM (SINCE '36)

CONTINUED USE OF AUTO-LITE IGNITION and 7.50 x 17" TIRES ON LARGE LINCOLNS

ZEPHYR

LARGE "K" TYPE DISCONTINUED AFTER '40

ZEPHYR GETS HYDRAULIC BRAKES

39

163

LOCOMOBILE

LOCOMOBILE CO.
OF AMERICA, INC.
BRIDGEPORT, CONN.
(1899 – 1929)

SPECIAL LOCOMOBILE SEDAN

"GUNBOAT" ROADSTER

17-29

(6 CYL.) MODEL "48"
OWN T-HEAD ENG.

TYPICAL
HEADLIGHTS →

524.8 C.I.D.
(THROUGH '29)
103 H.P. @ 2100 RPM ('25-'26)
105 " ('27 ON)

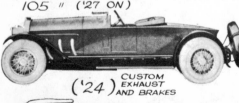

('24) CUSTOM
EXHAUST
AND BRAKES

('25)

SPECIAL GROWLER COUPE
A type adapted from the old London Four Wheeler

NO DRASTIC MODEL CHANGES IN MODEL "48"
DURING MOST YEARS IT WAS AVAILABLE, BUT
GRADUAL REFINEMENTS WERE INCORPORATED.
THE "48" WAS LOCOMOBILE'S LARGEST CAR.
142" W.B.

AFTER EARLY 1920s, ('22)
DRUM HEADLIGHTS
USED FREQUENTLY →

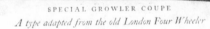

('23)

4-WHEEL
MECHANICAL BRAKES
ON ALL MODELS,
STARTING 1925.

LATE "48s", LOWER-PRICED
MODELS ON
FOLLOWING PAGE.

3.5 GEAR RATIO ('24 ON)
BERLING IGN. REPLACED BY DELCO ('23 ON)
("48")

164

Locomobile Junior Eight

OWN STRAIGHT-8, L-HEAD
181.5 C.I.D. ENGINE   5.12 G.R.
63 H.P. @ 2800 RPM   124" W.B.

25

"J-6" ALSO AVAIL.   6 CYL. OWN ENG.,
195.6 C.I.D.   4.77 G.R.
115" W.B.   30 × 5.77 TIRES

DE JON IGNITION USED ON
MOST '25-29 LOCOMOBILES (EXCEPT "48")

26-27

JUNIOR 8 KNOWN
AS
"LOCOMOBILE
STRAIGHT 8"
IN 1927. →

"90" has OWN
L-HEAD, 371.5 C.I.D.
ENGINE
86 to 90 H.P.
138" W.B.
4.5 and other G.R.s
(THROUGH '29)

33 × 6.75 TIRES
ON "90"

MODEL "90"
(INTRO. LATE 1925)
NOTE UNUSUAL STYLING
OF FRONT
PILLARS.

"48"
SPORTIF
(1927) →

LYCOMING
STRAIGHT-8
ENGINES ON
'27-'29 "8-80"
AND '29 "8-88"

124" W.B.
"8-66 IS
AVAIL.'27 (63 HP)
OWN O.H.V. ENG.

246.7 C.I.D., 4.77 G.R.
70 H.P. @ 3000

1928 "8-80" HAS WINDSHIELD
PILLARS AKIN TO MODEL 90.

28

130" W.B.
298.5 CID
90 H.P.
@ 3200
4.81 G.R.
32 × 6.00 TIRES
(THROUGH '29)

"8-80"

CONTINENTAL-ENGINED
1928 "8-70" HAS ROOF-VISOR, 122" W.B.
DRUM HEADLIGHTS, HOOD LOUVRES
LIKE 1927 "8," BUT RADIATOR SHAPED LIKE '29 (BUT WITH RADIMETER.)

LOCOMOBILE OR
CENTRAL
BODIES
"8-88"

130"
W.B.

"6-90"

SHOWN WITH OWNER:
GEO. BANCROFT (FILM STAR)

115 H.P.
@ 3300 RPM

29   (FINAL YEAR)

7-PASSENGER
SUBURBAN

SERIES 8
"48"

165

LORRAINE
(1920-1922)

LORRAINE MOTORS CORP.,
GRAND RAPIDS, MICH.; DETROIT

4-CYL., 192.4 C.I.D. HERSCHELL-SPILLMAN ENGINE

114" W.B.

"21-R" ('21)

Maibohm

BUILT BY MAIBOHM, SANDUSKY, OHIO
(1916 TO 1922)

6-CYL.
195.6 C.I.D.
FALLS ENGINE

20-22

MODEL "B"
116" W.B.

(REPLACED
BY
COURIER)

16-21

MARMON
(1902-1933)

NORDYKE and MARMON, INDIANAPOLIS

136" W.B. (THROUGH '28)

MODEL "34"
(THROUGH '24)

('20)

6-CYL., O.H.V., 339.7 C.I.D.
(THROUGH '28)

DELCO IGNITION on ALL

3.75 G.R. and 32 x 4½ TIRES (THROUGH '23)

MODEL "34"
CONTINUES
FROM 1916.

EARLY '22 = DOES NOT
HAVE DRUM
HEADLIGHTS

22-23

HOOD LOUVRES
(INTRODUCED
DURING 1921.)

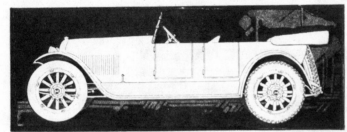

MARMON

7-PASS. PHAETON

4-WHEEL BRAKES
OPTIONAL, IF DESIRED

NEW 4.10 GEAR RATIO (TO '26)
32 × 4½ OR 33 × 5 TIRES
(BALLOON TIRES AVAILABLE)

24

FINAL YEAR OF "34" SERIES

DURING LATE FEBRUARY, 1926,
MANUFACTURER CHANGED NAME TO
MARMON MOTOR CAR CO.

'25 HAS 82 H.P.
@ 2650 RPM

25-26

"74" SERIES

"4 DOOR
BROUGHAM
COUPE"
('25)

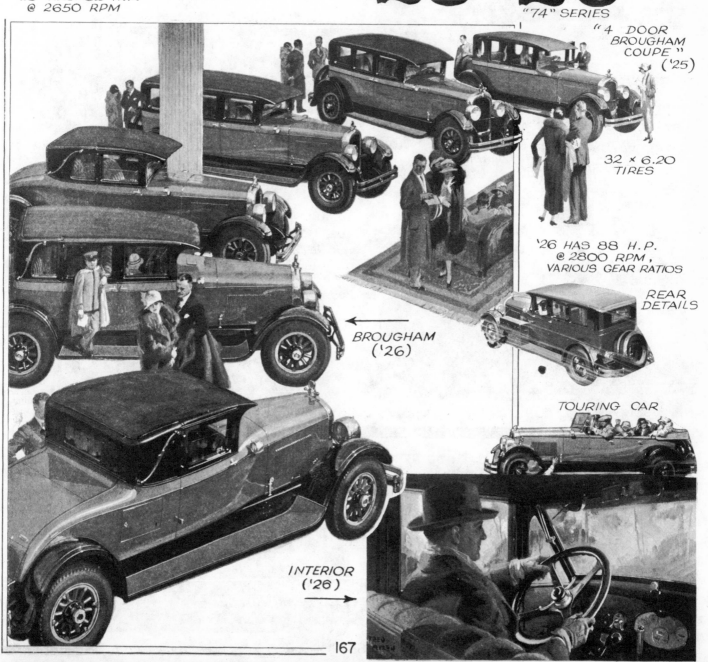

32 × 6.20
TIRES

'26 HAS 88 H.P.
@ 2800 RPM,
VARIOUS GEAR RATIOS

REAR
DETAILS

BROUGHAM
('26)

TOURING CAR

INTERIOR
('26)

the little MARMON 8
AMERICA'S FIRST TRULY FINE SMALL CAR

(INTRO. JAN., 1927)

COUPE (WITH RUMBLE SEAT)

2-DOOR SEDAN

4-DOOR SEDAN

COLLAPSIBLE COUPE-ROADSTER (WITH R.S.) →

29 x 5.25

4-PASS. SPEEDSTER (PHAETON)

new STRAIGHT-8, O.H.V.
190.1 C.I.D. ENGINE
64 H.P. @ 3200 RPM
116" W.B. 5.1 G.R.
70-75 MILES PER HOUR

2-PASS. SPEEDSTER (WITH RUMBLE SEAT) →

HYPOID GEAR DRIVE

FEDCO I.D. NUMBERS

ELECTRIC CLOCK

27

8

4-WHEEL BRAKES ON BOTH SERIES —

LATE '27s FEATURED UNUSUAL MARMON-VALENTINE "JEWEL COLORS."

6

84 H.P. @ 2700 RPM ('27)

32 x 6.75 TIRES
4.1 G.R.

THIS 339.7 C.I.D. "E-75" 6-CYL. MODEL CONT'D. INTO 1928, BUT WITH LOWER H.P. RATING OF 75 @ 2800.

COUPE-ROADSTER (NEW)

28

"68"
L-HEAD STR.-8
201.9 C.I.D.
72 H.P. @ 3200 RPM
114" W.B.
29 x 5.25 TIRES

4.9 GEAR RATIO

"78" O.H.V. STR.-8
216.8 C.I.D.
86 H.P. @ 3400 RPM

120" W.B., 29 x 5.50 TIRES

168

MARMON

THE NEW MARMON 68
THE NEW MARMON 78

"68" DASH

"68"

29

(STRAIGHT–8
ENGINES ONLY)
MOST SPECS.
AS IN 1928
HORIZONTAL HOOD LOUVRES
HAYES BODIES

"68" DISPLACEMENT UP TO 211.2 , H.P. UP TO 76.
29 × 5.50 TIRES
(29 × 6.00 ON "78")

"78" DASH has CLOCK AT LEFT CENTER (BY SPEED-OMETER)

"8-69" = 118" W.B.
211.2 C.I.D.
84 H.P. @ 3400 RPM
4.9 G.R.   5.50 × 19 TIRES

"8-79" = 125" W.B.
303.2 C.I.D.
110 H.P. @ 3400 RPM
4.45 G.R.
6.00 × 19 TIRES

NEW HOOD VENT DOORS

30

ALL 1930 MARMONS HAVE
STRAIGHT-8 , L-HEAD ENGINES.

"BIG 8" =
136" W.B.
315.2 C.I.D., 125 H.P.
@ 3400 RPM, 4.45 G.R.
6.50 × 19 TIRES

8
('31)

"8-69" BECOMES "70"
"8-79"
"BIG 8" BECOMES
"88" DURING 1931.

(8 - CYL. SERIES DROPPED DURING 1932.)
'32 "8-125" has 130-136" W.B., 315.2 C.I.D., L-HEAD ENG. 125 H.P. @ 3400 RPM

NOTE V-GRILLE
ON '32 "8-125"

31-33

7.00 × 18 TIRES

200 - H.P.
V-16
490.8 C.I.D., OHV, 145" W.B.

3.69 G.R.
IN '31 ;
3.78 ('32 ON)

"1934" MODEL ALSO

169

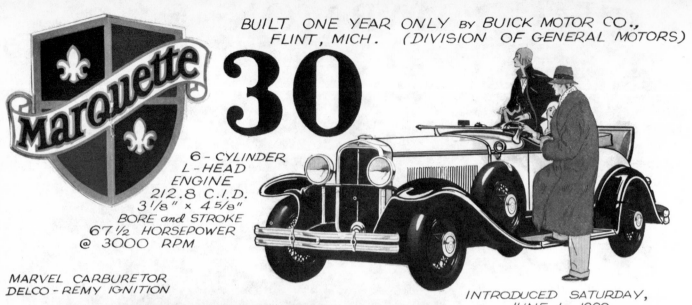

Marquette 30

BUILT ONE YEAR ONLY by BUICK MOTOR CO., FLINT, MICH. (DIVISION OF GENERAL MOTORS)

6 - CYLINDER
L - HEAD
ENGINE
212.8 C.I.D.
3 1/8" × 4 5/8"
BORE and STROKE
67 1/2 HORSEPOWER
@ 3000 RPM

MARVEL CARBURETOR
DELCO - REMY IGNITION

INTRODUCED SATURDAY, JUNE 1, 1929.

114" WHEELBASE   4.54 GEAR RATIO
5.25 × 18 TIRES

BODY BY FISHER

MASTERBILT 6 (1926)
(AIR COOLED)

GOVRO - NELSON CO., DETROIT

ENGINEERED BY VICTOR GAVREAU, FORMERLY CHIEF ENGINEER OF THE PAN CAR.

MAINLY AN EXPERIMENT. NO DEALERSHIPS KNOWN TO HAVE EXISTED.

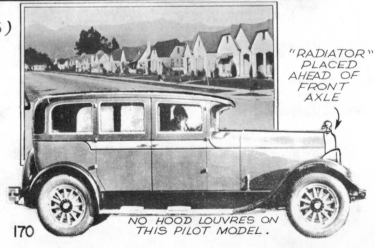

"RADIATOR" PLACED AHEAD OF FRONT AXLE

NO HOOD LOUVRES ON THIS PILOT MODEL.

170

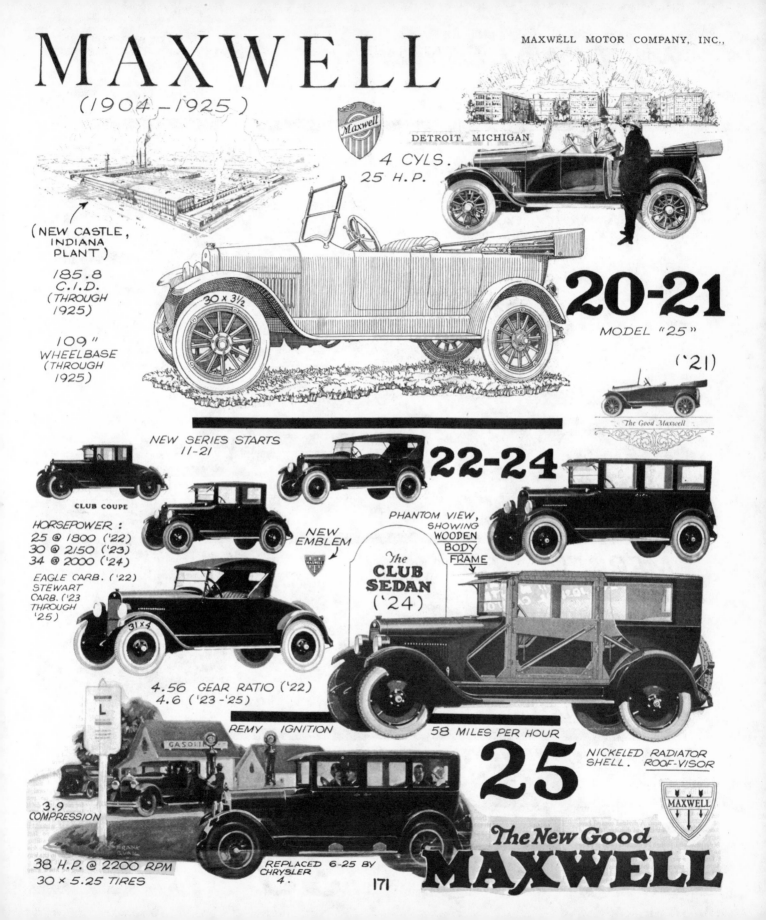

MAXWELL

(1904 – 1925)

MAXWELL MOTOR COMPANY, INC.,

DETROIT, MICHIGAN

4 CYLS.
25 H.P.

(NEW CASTLE, INDIANA PLANT)

185.8 C.I.D. (THROUGH 1925)

109" WHEELBASE (THROUGH 1925)

30 x 3½

20-21

MODEL "25"

('21)

The Good Maxwell

NEW SERIES STARTS 11-21

CLUB COUPE

22-24

HORSEPOWER:
25 @ 1800 ('22)
30 @ 2150 ('23)
34 @ 2000 ('24)

EAGLE CARB. ('22)
STEWART CARB. ('23 THROUGH '25)

NEW EMBLEM

PHANTOM VIEW, SHOWING WOODEN BODY FRAME

The CLUB SEDAN ('24)

31 x 4

4.56 GEAR RATIO ('22)
4.6 ('23 -'25)

REMY IGNITION

58 MILES PER HOUR

25

NICKELED RADIATOR SHELL. ROOF-VISOR

3.9 COMPRESSION

GASOLINE

38 H.P. @ 2200 RPM
30 x 5.25 TIRES

REPLACED 6-25 BY CHRYSLER 4.

The New Good
MAXWELL

MAXWELL

171

MacDONALD (1923-1924)

MacDONALD STEAM AUTOMOTIVE CORP.,
GARFIELD, OHIO

(STEAMER) "BOBCAT" ROADSTER

McFARLAN
(1910-1928)

McFARLAN MOTOR CAR CO.,
CONNERSVILLE, IND.

TYPE "157"
"T.V." 6
('22)

7-PASS.
SUBURBAN SEDAN

6-CYL. T-HEAD
572.5 C.I.D.
ENGINE
140" W.B.
3.5 G.R.

(SV)"LIGHT 6" ALSO AVAIL.
IN 1924, WITH 127" W.B.
268.4 C.I.D. WISCONSIN ENG.
5.10 G.R.

'25 TOWN CAR

STRAIGHT-8
LYCOMING
ENGINE
70 H.P. ('26)
79 H.P. ('27)

'26-7
8-IN-LINE "872"
TOWN COUPE
131" W.B.

4-PASS.
SPORTING

132" W.B.   ('23)

MERCER
(1910-1925)

MERCER AUTOMOBILE CO.,
TRENTON, N.J.

SERIES 5=4 CYLS.(298.2 C.I.D.)
LARGER SERIES 6 (331.3 C.I.D.,
6 CYL.) JOINS SERIES 5 IN '23

(2 1931 MERCER 8s
BUILT BY ELCAR.)

RACEABOUT
('21)

SPORTS
ROADSTER
('22)

MERCURY 8

(BEGINS WITH 1939 MODEL)

A PRODUCT OF THE ~~~~~~~ COMPANY
FORD MOTOR CO

239 C.I.D. V-8

39

95 H.P.
@ 3600
RPM

116"
W.B.

→ REAR
DETAILS
(TRUNK
OPEN)

MERCURY

MERCURY CARS, INC.
HOLLIS, N.Y.
(1918-1920) (4 CYL.)

METEOR

(1914-1930)
SHELBYVILLE, IND. and PIQUA, O.

('21)

MILBURN
ELECTRIC

('21)

(1914-1922) MILBURN WAGON CO.,
TOLEDO, OHIO

MODEL
"27-L"

MILLER

(CUSTOM-BUILT)
V-8 OR
V-16

HARRY A. MILLER
(RELLIMAH, INC.)
LOS ANGELES,
CALIF.

FRONT-WHEEL
DRIVE
SPEEDSTER

31

"SPECIAL"

NEW, SLANTED
STYLING

MITCHELL
20-21

(1903-1923)

MITCHELL MOTORS CO.,
RACINE, WIS.
(MFR. NAME AS OF 1916-1923)

120" W.B.

"F-40" 6-CYL., 248.9 CID
L-HEAD ENGINE   4.41 G.R.

FINAL "50" MODELS HAVE
CONVENTIONAL STYLING.

MONITOR

(1915-1922)

MONITOR MOTOR CAR CO.,
COLUMBUS, OHIO

20

6-CYL. CONTINENTAL
"7-R" ENGINE
121" W.B.   DISC WHEELS   MODEL "M"

"B-50" and
"B-52" MODELS
IN 1921 (SAME
121" W.B.,
CONTINENTAL ENG.)

20

MONROE

FLINT, MICH.
(1914-1924)
(4 CYL.)

(CONTROLLED BY
PREMIER,
1923-24)

24

111" W.B.   ('24)

('20)

173

MOON (1905-1929)

Built by
Moon Motor Car Company, St. Louis, U. S. A.

MOON HOOD LOUVRES ARE PUNCHED INWARD. CHARACTERISTIC PEAKED RADIATOR, 1919 THROUGH 1926

Moon's Ten Proven Units

1. Continental Red Seal Motor.
2. Delco Starter and Ignition.
3. Timken Axles.
4. Spicer Universal Joints.
5. Brown-Lipe Transmission.
6. Borg & Beck Clutch.
7. Rayfield Carburetor.
8. Exide Battery.
9. Fedders Radiator — Nickel-Silver.
10. Gemmer Steering Gear.

20

"6-48" VICTORY 122" W.B. 224 C.I.D. (THROUGH '22) 4.75 G.R.

32 × 4 TIRES   4.75 G.R.

"6-68" 125" W.B. 303.1 C.I.D. 33 × 5 TIRES 4.45 G.R.

(6-CYL. ONLY, UNTIL 1928)

21-22

('21 = DRUM HEADLIGHTS)

"6-75" ('22 ONLY) HAS 135" W.B., 325.1 C.I.D., 32 × 4½ TIRES 4.45 G.R.

"6-48" →

Actual Photograph of the Six-48 Touring

(115" W.B.) "6-40"

(46 - H.P.) "6-40" STARTS 2-22

('24)

NEW "A" SERIES INTRODUCED 1924 113" W.B. LOCKHEED HYDRAULIC 4-WHEEL BRAKES ALSO AVAILABLE (OPTIONAL).

("A" CONT'D. INTO '28)

("6-58" STARTS AUG., 1922 HAS 128" W.B. 241.6 C.I.D. "8-R" ENGINE (TO '26)

D-27

115" W.B. "6-40" (U) STARTING 8-23, REPLACES 195.6 C.I.D. "6-Y" ENG. WITH 195.6 "7-U" ENG. 5.10 G.R.

23-24

("6-50" INTRO. DURING '24)

60 M.P.H.

25-26

('26 HAS HIGHER, NARROWER RADIATOR, CROWN FENDERS.)

6-40 "NEWPORT" ('25) 50 H.P. @ 2600 RPM
6-50 "METROPOLITAN" ('25) 52 H.P. @ 2600 RPM
6-58 "LONDON" 56 H.P. @ 2300 RPM

(HYDRAULIC BRAKES, NEW ROOF-VISOR)

One of the Moon innovations of the year is this new Cabriolet roadster. The deck lid opens up a fully upholstered rear seat "a deux." With the lid down the car is a closed roadster. Concealed compartment for golf bag and other luggage. Rear window may be lowered for communication between passengers.   (Patents applied for)

"A" HAS 113" W.B., CONTINENTAL "7-Z" ENG. 50 H.P. @ 2600 RPM 30 × 5.25 TIRES

27

RADIATOR DESIGN IS NEW. USED 1 YEAR ONLY.

NEW "BULLET" HEADLAMPS

"6-60" (new)

HAS 110" W.B. 185 C.I.D. CONTINENTAL "26-L" ENG. 47 H.P. @ 2600 RPM 29 × 4.75 TIRES (CONT'D. INTO 1928)

FINAL "A" ('28) SOMETIMES KNOWN AS 6-A.

new "6-72" (ROYAL) HAS OLD-STYLE BODY AND ROOF-VISOR BUT NEW RADIATOR DESIGN.

28

6 OR 8 CYL.

NEW STRAIGHT-8 "8-80" HAS 125" W.B., 268.6 C.I.D. CONTINENTAL ENG., 86 H.P. @ 3200 RPM, 31 × 6.20 TIRES, 4.63 G.R.

STARTING AUGUST, 1928, A RE-STYLED "6-72" CONT'D. INTO '29 WITH SAME 120" W.B., 214.7 C.I.D. "11-E" CONTINENTAL ENG., 66 H.P. @ 3150 RPM, 29 × 5.50 TIRES, 4.9 G.R.

('29-'30 WINDSOR CARS ALSO)

"6-72"

29

"AEROTYPE" 8-80 (DISC. LATE '28)

PETITE SEDAN

BODY BY UNION CITY

174

20 FOR 1920, 8 HOOD LOUVRES ON EACH SIDE, LARGER RADIATOR

MODEL "F-30"

106" W.B.

30 x 3½

MOORE (1916-1921)
MOORE MOTOR VEH. CO., DANVILLE, ILLINOIS

4- CYL. GOLDEN, BELKNAP and SCHWARTZ ENGINE *
3¾" x 4¼" B.+s. 22 H.P.
4.25 G.R.
*-NEW TURNER and MOORE ENGINE ALSO.

FOR EXPORT TO ENGLAND   BRITISH BODIES INSTALLED ON MOST.

114" W.B.
4 CYL.

MORRISS - LONDON (1919-1925)
CROW-ELKHART MOTOR CAR CO.; CENTURY MOTOR CO., ELKHART, IND.

NASH (1917-1957)

THE NASH MOTORS COMPANY, KENOSHA, WISCONSIN

THE NASH SIX

"SPORT"

('20)

"681" SERIES = 261.3 C.I.D.
(MODELS 681-687)

19-20

("685" COUPE)
('20)

(6 CYL.)

"681" 6 CYL. O.H.V.
248.9 C.I.D.
55 H.P. @ 2400 RPM
121" WHEELBASE
4.50 GEAR RATIO

33 x 4

7 - PASS. SEDAN

"41"   (NOTE THINNER HOOD LOUVRES)

112" WHEELBASE

4 - CYL. SERIES
(INTRODUCED LATE IN 1920, CONTINUED INTO 1924.)
'21 = 165.9 C.I.D., 35 H.P. @ 2200 RPM
LATER = 178.9 C.I.D., 37 H.P. @ 2800 RPM

22½ ('23)

21-22

(1922 6- CYL. SERIES BEGINS OCT., 1921, WITH MODELS "691" THROUGH "698;" GAS GAUGE ON DASH; NEW, MORE POWERFUL EMERGENCY BRAKE ON TRANSMISSION.)

(NOTE NEW DRUM HEADLIGHTS)

The New Five Passenger Six Cylinder Sedan

NASH

Nash Leads the World in Motor Car Value

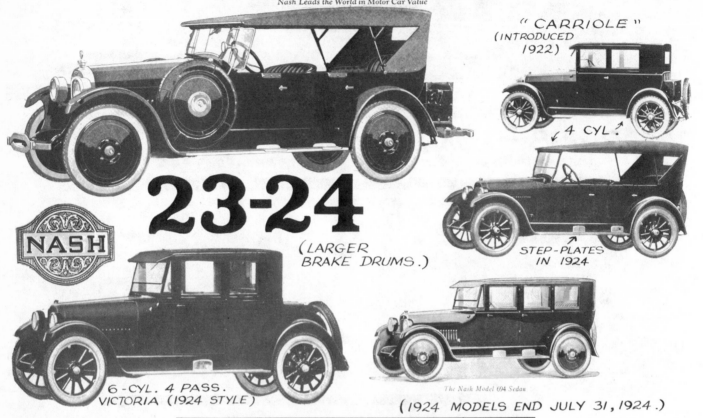

"CARRIOLE"
(INTRODUCED
1922)

4 CYL.

STEP-PLATES
IN 1924

23-24

(LARGER
BRAKE DRUMS.)

NASH

6-CYL. 4 PASS.
VICTORIA (1924 STYLE)

The Nash Model 694 Sedan

(1924 MODELS END JULY 31, 1924.)

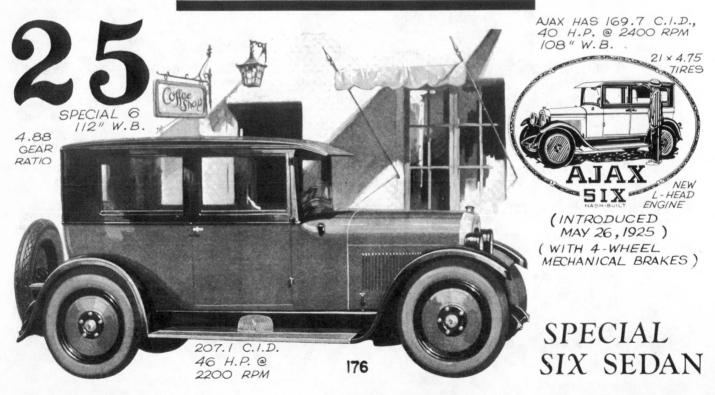

25

SPECIAL 6
112" W.B.

4.88
GEAR
RATIO

AJAX HAS 169.7 C.I.D.,
40 H.P. @ 2400 RPM
108" W.B.

21 x 4.75
TIRES

AJAX
SIX
NASH-BUILT

NEW
L-HEAD
ENGINE

(INTRODUCED
MAY 26, 1925)
(WITH 4-WHEEL
MECHANICAL BRAKES)

207.1 C.I.D.
46 H.P. @
2200 RPM

176

SPECIAL
SIX SEDAN

NASH

Leads the World in Motor Car Value

25 (CONT'D.)

ADVANCED SIX

OVERHEAD-VALVE, 6 CYLS.
248.9 C.I.D.
60 H.P. @ 2400 RPM

"4-DOOR COUPE"

4-Wheel Brakes

127-inch Wheelbase
Five Passengers

121" W.B. ON SOME BODY TYPES

4.50 GEAR RATIO

26

Light Six
4-Door Sedan

LIGHT 6 (REPLACES AJAX)

The New
Special Six Series

112½" W.B.

31 × 5.25

New Special Six Sedan
(JULY, 1925)

The New
Advanced Six Series

"4-DOOR COUPÉ"

177

NASH

Leads the World in Motor Car Value

27

108" W.B.
170 C.I.D.
40 H.P. @ 2400

LIGHT 6

4.77 GEAR RATIO

DELUXE LIGHT 6

(WITH BUMPERS)

30 x 4.75

SPEC. 6 WITH CONVENTIONAL ROOFLINE →

31 x 5.25

4.67 GEAR RATIO

112½" W.B.

SPECIAL 6

224 C.I.D. (THROUGH '29)
52 H.P. @ 2600

CAVALIER SEDAN (WIRE WH. AVAIL.)

"241"

New Nash Attractions

7-bearing crankshaft motor —world's smoothest type— powers all new Nash models.

New-type crankcase "breather" which prevents crankcase dilution.

Rubber insulated motor supports—(standard Nash practice for some time).

New-design motor muffler deepening operative quietness.

Motor heat control by new thermostatic water regulator.

Oil screen "agitator" preventing oil coagulation in coldest weather.

And many other new improvements.

A NEW Instrument Board

and Greater
Front Compartment Convenience

178

27 (CONT'D.)

69 H.P. @ 2500 RPM

AMBASSADOR

AMBASSADOR

ADVANCED 6

VICTORIA
127" W.B.

AMBASSADOR
(ADVANCED 6)
and
CAVALIER
(SPECIAL 6)
SEDANS INTRODUCED
AT CHICAGO AUTOMOBILE
SHOW, JANUARY 29, 1927.

EMBLEM AND MASCOT (ABOVE)

LIGHT 6 REPLACED BY
STANDARD 6 ("321")

108 1/4" W.B. 4.77 GEAR RATIO
184.1 C.I.D. 30 × 5.00
45 H.P. @ 2600 TIRES (THROUGH
'29)

"325" COUPE

SPECIAL 6 ("331")
HAS 224 C.I.D.
52 H.P. @ 2600 RPM
4.88 GEAR RATIO (THROUGH '29)
112 3/4" (TIRES = 30 × 5.25)
W.B.

28

ADVANCED 6 "SEDAN FOR 5"
(COACH) RESEMBLES ABOVE CAR (AND
ALSO HAS SAME FRENCH ROOF-LINE.)

32 × 6.00 TIRES' (THROUGH '29)
("361" SERIES)
ADVANCED 6 HAS 70 H.P.
@ 2400 RPM

"AMBASSADOR" →
("367")

THE NEW NASH "400" SERIES

184.1 C.I.D.
50 H.P. @
2800 RPM
112 1/4" W.B.
4.77 G.R.

STANDARD 6
(30 × 5.00 TIRES)

THE WORLD

HAS A NEW AND FINER

MOTOR CAR

Advanced Six Coupe

SPECIAL 6
(DUAL ROWS OF
HOOD LOUVRES)
65 H.P. @ 2900 RPM
116" W.B.   29 × 5.50 TIRES

ADVANCED 6
78 H.P. @ 2900 RPM

29

ADVANCED 6   AMBASSADOR

NASH RADIATOR,
FITTED WITH USEFUL
ACCESSORY "ALLEN
VERTICAL SHUTTERS"
(SOLD SEPERATELY.)

BODIES BY NASH
OR SEAMAN

new = 2 SPARK PLUGS PER CYLINDER

Advanced Six Sedan

**TWIN IGNITION
MOTOR**

29½ NASH

FINAL YEAR FOR VACUUM FUEL FEED.

FINAL YEAR OF 6-CYL. NASH CHOICES ONLY.

NEW "400" ROADSTER

1930

STARTER CONTROL ON DASH

114" W.B. SINGLE 6 (201.3 C.I.D., 60 H.P. @ 2800 RPM ("450" SERIES)
118" W.B. TWIN IGNITION 6 (241.6 C.I.D., 74½ H.P. @ 2800 ("480" ")
124" W.B. TWIN IGNITION 8
(298.6 C.I.D., 100 H.P. @ 3200
("490" SERIES)

4.5 GEAR RATIO
(4.7 ON STD. 6)

new FUEL PUMP

Illustrating the Nash New 400 equipped with Pines Automatic Winterfront. Fulton Sylphon Thermostat is used in this Winterfront

5.1, 5.1, 4.45, 4.5 RESPECTIVE GEAR RATIOS ON "6-60," "8-70," "8-80" and "8-90" SERIES

(INTRO. 10-30)

31

JAN., '31 = NEW "CONVERTIBLE SEDAN" (871 or 881)

"8-70"

8 TWIN IGN.
8-80 = STRAIGHT-8, O.H.V.
240.3 CID   87 H.P. @ 3400
121" WB, 5.50 × 18 TIRES
(94 H.P., 6.00 × 18 TIRES ON '32 "980")

6-60 = 6 CYL., L-HEAD
201.3 CID   65 H.P.
114¼" WB, 5.00 × 19
TIRES (SPECS. THROUGH EARLY '32 "960")

new
L-HEAD
STRAIGHT-8 "8-70"
227.2 CID   78 H.P.
(SPECS. THR. '32 "970")

116¼" WB
5.25 × 19 TIRES

TWIN IGN.
8-90 = STRAIGHT-8, O.H.V.
298.6 CID, 115 H.P. @ 3600 RPM
124-133" WB, 6.50 × 19 TIRES
(SPECS. THROUGH EARLY '32 "990")

NASH

(INTRODUCED JUNE 28, 1931)

NEW "V" GRILLE →

31½-32

EARLY '32s IN "900" MODEL SERIES

new SILENT-2ND SYNCHRO-SHIFT TRAN. and FREE-WHEELING

AMBASSADOR 8

32½

NEW BODY DESIGNS

STANDARD 8

INTRODUCED SATURDAY, FEB. 27, 1932

Beavertail Back of the new Nash Slip-Stream Body

RIDE CONTROL AVAIL.

5 NEW SERIES NAMES (AS IN '33)

EARLY '33 LOW-PRICED MODELS HAVE VERTICAL HOOD LOUVRES.

IN 5 SERIES :

BIG 6 = 116" WB, 75 H.P. @ 3200 RPM (217.8 CID)
STANDARD 8 = 116" WB, 80 H.P. @ 3200 RPM (247.4 CID)
SPECIAL 8 = 121" WB, 85 H.P. @ 3200 RPM   "   "
ADVANCED 8 = 128" WB, 100 H.P. @ 3400 RPM (260.8 CID)
AMBASSADOR 8 = 142" WB, 125 H.P. @ 3600 RPM (322 CID)
(OR 133")

33

MODEL "1194" AMB. 8 7-PASS.

142" W.B.

NASH

88-H.P.
BIG 6
(234.8 C/D)

34

IN ABOVE INTERIOR VIEW NOTE THE GROSS EXAGGERATION OF HOOD LENGTH (FROM AN ORIGINAL ADVERTISEMENT.)

AMBASSADOR

new HYDRAULIC BRAKES

35

BIG 6 BECOMES ADVANCED 6 :

6.25 x 16 TIRES 120" W.B. (EARLY MODELS = 88 H.P. @ 3200 RPM) 4.4 G.R. (AS IN '34)

Super-Hydraulic Brakes
Automatic Cruising Gear
All-Steel, One-Piece Bodies
Synchronized Springing
Ball-Bearing Steering
Mid-Section Seating
Balanced Ride

Aeroform Design
Flying Power (Developed from Twin Ignition)

ADVANCED SIX VICTORIA $895	ADVANCED EIGHT VICTORIA $1115	AMBASSADOR EIGHT VICTORIA $1240
120" Wheelbase — 90 Horsepower	125" Wheelbase — 102 Horsepower	125" Wheelbase — 102 Horsepower

(EARLY MODELS OF ADV. 8, AMB. 8 100 H.P. @ 3400 RPM)

STARTING 1935, 1ST TWO DIGITS OF MODEL NO. INDICATES YEAR, BEGINNING WITH 3500 SERIES FOR 1935. SYSTEM USED ON NASH AND SUBSEQUENT AMERICAN MOTORS CARS.

183

NASH 36

ENGINE

NEW! NASH "400" MONITOR-SEALED MOTOR $675

EARLIEST "400" MODELS (STARTING AT # C-1001) ARE SOMETIMES LISTED AS LATE 1935 MODELS.

("400" (STARTS MAY, 1935)

"400" HAS 117" W.B., 6 CYL. 234.8 C.I.D., 90 H.P. @ 3400 RPM

4.1 GEAR RATIO

'400' has 6.00 x 16 TIRES

L-HEAD ENGINE ON "400"

"400" DELUXE

60½ IN

SAME C.I.D. ON "400" and AMB. 6

6.25 x 16 TIRES ON AMBASSADOR 6;

6.50 x 16 ON 8

ADVANCED 6 BECOMES AMBASSADOR 6

NASH AUTOMATIC CRUISING GEAR! Available at slight extra cost. Reduces engine revolutions about ⅓ at high speeds. Gives you an entirely new ride sensation. Saves 15% to 25% in gasoline; as much as 50% in oil!

AMBASSADOR 6 : 93 H.P. @ 3400 RPM

260.8 C.I.D. AMBASSADOR 8 : 102 H.P. @ 3400 RPM

125" W.B. ON AMBASSADOR 6 OR 8

184

NASH 37

"LAFAYETTE" GRILLE MEMBERS ARE HORIZONTAL.

"37/3" 2-DOOR

"3788"

"3782"

AMBASSADOR

CHAS. W. NASH (FOUNDER)

"LAFAYETTE" BECOMES A 117"-W.B. SERIES OF NASH, (1937 THROUGH '40) (L-HEAD)

BABE RUTH

7.00 x 16 TIRES ON AMBASSADOR 8 (THROUGH '39)

"3781" CONVERTIBLE

"3815"

95 H.P. @ 3400 RPM (AS ON '37 AMB. 6)

AMBASSADOR 6

105 H.P. @ 3400 RPM (AS ON '37 AMB. 8) 4.11 G.R. (SINCE '37)

117" W.B.

"LAFAYETTE"

NASH Worlds FIRST CAR With CONDITIONED AIR For Winter Driving

38

JAN. 4, 1938 : 1ST ANNIVERSARY OF 1937 NASH-KELVINATOR MERGER

OPTIONAL VACUUM SHIFT HAS CONTROL LEVER PROTRUDING FROM CENTER OF DASH.

← AMBASSADOR 8

115 H.P. @ 3400 RPM (4.1 G.R. (THROUGH FINAL STRAIGHT-8 SINCE '35) NASH OF 1942)

LAFAYETTE has 99 H.P. @ 3400 RPM (THROUGH '40)

39

LAST STOP GAS

AMBASSADOR = 121" W.B. ON 6 ; 125" ON 8 (SINCE '37)

new 4.1 G.R. ON 6s, 4.4 ON AMBASSADOR 8.

The NATIONAL SEXTET

NATIONAL MOTOR CAR
and VEHICLE CORP.,
INDIANAPOLIS

(1900-1924)

OVERHEAD-VALVE
6-CYLINDER 301.3 C.I.D.
ENGINE NEW
FOR 1920;
REPLACES THE
former L-HEAD
6-CYL. and V-12 TYPES.

130" W.B.,
32 × 4½ TIRES,
4.08 GEAR RATIO
ON "SEXTET" (BB)
(THROUGH '24)

National

FIVE CUSTOM BUILT BODY STYLES

DASH

FRONT END ('23)

20-24

WITH
TOP DOWN

7-PASSENGER
TOURING CAR

NOTE THE
UNUSUALLY
LONG
REAR
QUARTER
WINDOWS →

7-PASSENGER
SEDAN

IN '23, 112"-W.B. "6-31" and 121"-W.B. "6-51" MODELS ALSO,
WITH 155 CID (OWN) and 241.6 CID (CONT.) ENG. "6-71" IS BB SERIES.

MODEL "D" UNCHANGED
FROM 1919
            104" W.B.
OWN 4-CYL., O.H.V.
145.7 C.I.D. ENGINE
4.25 G.R.
12-VOLT BOSCH IGNITION

32 × 4 TIRES

NELSON

(1917—1921)

E.A. NELSON
MOTOR CAR CO.,
DETROIT

(WITH DOUBLE-DROP
FRAME!)

('22)

32 × 4½ TIRES, 128" W.B.

NOMA 6   (1919-1923)

NOMA MOTORS CORP., N.Y.C.
224 CID CONTINENTAL OR BEAVER ENGINES
("3-C")   (364.5 CID, "I-D")

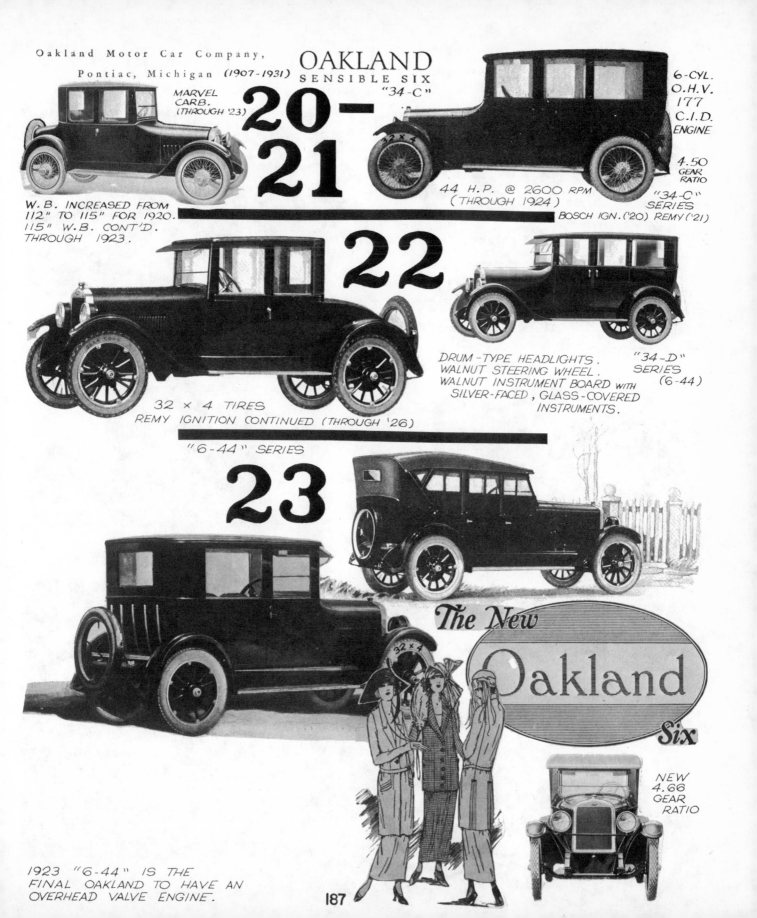

Oakland Motor Car Company,
Pontiac, Michigan (1907-1931)

OAKLAND
SENSIBLE SIX
"34-C"

MARVEL CARB. (THROUGH '23)

20-21

6-CYL.
O.H.V.
177
C.I.D.
ENGINE

4.50 GEAR RATIO

44 H.P. @ 2600 RPM (THROUGH 1924)

"34-C" SERIES
BOSCH IGN.('20) REMY('21)

W.B. INCREASED FROM 112" TO 115" FOR 1920. 115" W.B. CONT'D. THROUGH 1923.

22

DRUM-TYPE HEADLIGHTS. WALNUT STEERING WHEEL. WALNUT INSTRUMENT BOARD WITH SILVER-FACED, GLASS-COVERED INSTRUMENTS.

"34-D" SERIES (6-44)

32 × 4 TIRES
REMY IGNITION CONTINUED (THROUGH '26)

"6-44" SERIES

23

The New

Oakland Six

NEW 4.66 GEAR RATIO

1923 "6-44" IS THE FINAL OAKLAND TO HAVE AN OVERHEAD VALVE ENGINE.

187

OAKLAND

PRODUCT OF GENERAL MOTORS

(STARTS 9-8-23)

113" W.B. (THROUGH 1927)

BLUE DUCO ON BODIES

The True Blue Six

24

"6-54" SERIES
(ADOPTS L-HEAD
VALVE ARRANGEMENT)

4-WHEEL BRAKES

STROMBERG CARB. (THROUGH '26)

'24 DASH GAUGES ON DARK RECTANGULAR PANEL, BEHIND GLASS PANE.

Oakland

PRODUCT OF GENERAL MOTORS

COUPE WITH LANDAU IRONS AND OVAL QUARTER WINDOWS

HEADLIGHT TIE-BAR ELIMINATED

25

"6-54"

185 CU. IN. DISPL.
5 TO 1 COMPRESSION

4.7 GEAR RATIO

44 H.P. @ 2600 RPM
5 TO 1 COMPRESSION   60 M.P.H.

OAKLAND

EARLIEST LANDAU SEDANS
HAVE OVAL REAR QUARTER
WINDOWS. IN AUTUMN,
1925, WINDOW STYLE IS
LIKE '27.

DASH
(RADIO,
WATER
TEMP.
GAUGE
NOT
ORIG.)

26 "OS"

(INTRO. 7-25)

45 H.P. @ 2600 RPM
(THROUGH '27)
new HARMONIC BALANCER
AIR CLEANER
5.0 COMPR.

4.8 COMPR.
MARVEL CARB.
(THROUGH '31)

27 "OS"

(INTRO. 7-26)

DELCO-
REMY
IGNITION
(THROUGH
'31)

FROM JULY 29, 1926 TO JAN. 9, 1927, THIS
'27 "GREATER OAKLAND 6" WAS RUN (IN DETROIT)
CONTINUOUSLY ON A TREADMILL, ON PUBLIC
DISPLAY, FOR A 100,000-MILE ENDURANCE
TEST. AVG. SPEED 25.49 M.P.H.,
AVG. 34.09 MILES PER GALLON.

COMPARE THE ACTUAL PHOTO ABOVE
WITH THE GLAMOURIZED ADVERTISING
ILLUSTRATION AT LEFT!

4.7 G.R.   FOOT-DIMMER FOR HEADLIGHTS
"RUBBER-SILENCED" CHASSIS   189   NATURAL-FINISH WOOD WHEELS

OAKLAND MOTOR CAR COMPANY, PONTIAC, MICHIGAN

OAKLAND
ALL-AMERICAN SIX
PRODUCT OF GENERAL MOTORS

NEW 117" WHEELBASE
211.5 C.I.D.
60 H.P. @ 2800 RPM
4.8 COMPRESSION
4.41 GEAR RATIO

The Cabriolet
Body by Fisher

28

"212" SERIES

FUEL PUMP REPLACES VACUUM TANK

Body by Fisher

Body by Fisher

2-DOOR SEDAN

190

OAKLAND

SMOOTH GLOSS-BLACK
INSTRUMENT PANEL WITH
SMALL, INDIVIDUAL CIRCULAR
BLACK-FACED GAUGES.

DASH/MAP
LIGHTS

INDIRECT LIGHTING ALSO

ROADSTER and PHAETON
have BODY BY OAKLAND.
FISHER BODY ON
OTHERS.

117" W.B.

4.72 GEAR RATIO
228.1 C.I.D.   68 H.P. @ 3000 RPM

OAKLAND'S FINAL "ALL-AMERICAN SIX"

29

THE MOST RELIABLE AND
DURABLE OF OAKLANDS.
MORE 1929s HAVE SURVIVED
THAN ANY OTHER YEAR MODEL
OF THIS MAKE.

CONVERTIBLE
LANDAU SECTION

29 × 5.50 TIRES

EIGHT
(V-8)

117" WHEELBASE,
251 C.I.D.   (THROUGH
1931)

30

NEW
MOLDINGS
ON
INSTRUMENT
PANEL

82 H.P. @ 3000 RPM
4.42 GEAR RATIO

5.50 × 18 TIRES
(1930 and 1931)

85 H.P. @ 3400 RPM
4.55 GEAR RATIO

31
(THE FINAL
OAKLAND)

MAKING NEW FRIENDS AND KEEPING THE OLD

OGREN (1915-1923)

OGREN MOTOR CAR CO., MILWAUKEE, WIS.

(NICKELED RADIATOR SHELL ON '22 MODEL.)

BOSCH IGNITION

6-CYL. CONTINENTAL ENGINE
(325.1 C.I.D.)
('22-'23)
80-90 H.P.
TOP SPEED = 68 M.P.H. (ROADSTER, 90 MPH)

134" W.B.
33 × 5 TIRES

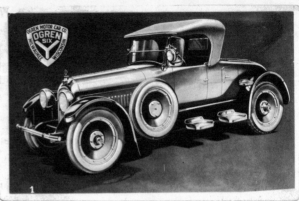

RAYFIELD CARB.

20 TO 23

OLDS MOTOR WORKS, LANSING, MICH. (EST. 1897)

Product of GENERAL MOTORS SINCE '09

Oldsmobile

6

→ MODEL "37-A"
112" W.B.
6 CYLS. (O.H.V.)
177 C.I.D.
4.58 GEAR RATIO
32 × 4" TIRES
44 H.P. @ 2600 RPM

JOHNSON CARB.

6-CYL.
OR
V-8
(SINCE '17) 8

20

MODEL "45-B"
122" W.B.
V-8 (T-HEAD)
246.7 C.I.D.
4.91 GEAR RATIO
33 × 4½" TIRES
58 H.P. @ 2600 RPM
BALL CARB.

4 (NEW)

"43-A"
224.3 C.I.D., 43 H.P., 115" W.B.
REMY IGN.
4.66 GEAR RATIO
ZENITH CARB.

21

"46"
V-8
SIMILAR SPECS. AS '20 "45-B" BUT HAS 58 H.P. @ 2510 RPM

8

"47"
STARTS March, 1921

OLDSMOBILE

22

REMY IGN. ON "43-A"
DELCO IGN. (OTHERS)

4-CYL.
Semi-Sport
44 H.P. @ 2000 RPM

CARBURETORS:
"43-A" ZENITH
"47" JOHNSON
"46" BALL + BALL
(SAME IN '23)

(FINAL YEAR
FOR 4 and
V-8)

"46" V-8,
122" w.b., 4.93 GEAR RATIO
"43-A" = 4-CYL.,
115" w.b., 4.66 G.R.
"47" = V-8,
115" w.b., 5.10 G.R.
(THROUGH 1923)

"47" HAS 233.7 C.I.D.
V-8 ENGINE WITH
60 H.P. @ 2710 RPM

The Four Cab—2 passengers—

The Four Sedan—5 passengers—

The Four Coupe—4 passengers—

4-CYL. "43-A" HAS 4.70 GEAR RATIO, 40 H.P.
@ 1800 RPM

"47"
(V-8) 63 H.P. @
2710 RPM

23

PHANTOM VIEW
OF
"4" Brougham (AVAIL. 9-22)

4.92 G.R. ON
V-8 "46"

ALL MODELS have
DELCO IGN. (THROUGH '26)

PRODUCT OF GENERAL MOTORS

(FROM '24 THROUGH '31,
6 CYL. ONLY)
(3-WINDOW BUSINESS COUPE
KNOWN AS "CAB.")
110" W.B. (1924
and 1925)
ZENITH CARB. (THROUGH '25)

42 H.P. @
2600 RPM

169.3 C.I.D. (THROUGH
'26)

SPORT
TOURING

STD. TOURING

SIX 24 MODEL "30"

31 x 4 TIRES IN
1924 and 1925, AS
WELL AS 5.10 GEAR RATIO

New Beauty outside — but same good chassis 40,000 owners know!

25

MODEL "30"

41 H.P. @ 2600 RPM (THROUGH '26)

DISC WHEELS AVAIL.

new RADIATOR DESIGN (THROUGH '27)

WALNUT-FINISH INSTRUMENT PANEL ('27)

DELCO-REMY IGN. ('27 ON)

26-27

30-D   30-E

Chromium Plating (1927)

1927½ VISOR

110½" W.B.

30 x 4.95

'27 HAS 185 C.I.D., 40 H.P. @ 2600 RPM
30 x 5.25 TIRES,
4-WHEEL BRAKES (STARTING 1-27)
CARTER CARB. ('26) JOHNSON CARB. ('27)

4.73 GEAR RATIO

194

OLDSMOBILE

28

55 H.P. @ 2700 RPM
(THROUGH '29)

MODEL "F-28"
113½" WHEELBASE and
197.5 C.I.D.
(THROUGH 1931)

28 x 5.25 TIRES IN 1928 and 1929
4.41 GEAR RATIO IN 1928 and 1929
SCHEBLER CARB. (THROUGH '29)

LATE MODEL =
NOTE LONGER ROW
OF HOOD LOUVRES

ON '28 OLDSMOBILES,
FUEL PUMP REPLACES VACUUM TANK

This emblem identifies
the new 1929 Oldsmobile

(ON RADIATOR)

29

MODEL "F-29"

OLDSMOBILE
PRODUCT OF GENERAL MOTORS

30
"F-30"

62 H.P. @ 3000 RPM
JOHNSON CARB.

DASH
GAUGES, LEFT TO RT.:
AMMETER, WATER TEMP.,
SPEEDOMETER-ODOMETER,
OIL PRESSURE, GASOLINE

5.25 × 18 TIRES IN
1930 and 1931

4.54 GEAR RATIO

65 H.P. @ 3350 RPM

31
"F-31"

STROMB.
CARB.
(THROUGH
'35)

'31 DASH

4.56
GEAR RATIO
(THROUGH '33)

6.00 × 17 TIRES, 116½" W.B.

6 "F-32"

32

6 HAS 213.3 C.I.D.
and 71 H.P.
@ 3200 RPM

8
(NEW)
"L-32"

STRAIGHT-
8 HAS
240.3 C.I.D.
and 82
H.P. @
3200 RPM

DASH

196

OLDSMOBILE

4.56 GEAR RATIO

240.3 C.I.D. CONTINUED ON 8 (THROUGH '36)

8 HAS 90 H.P. @ 3350 RPM (THROUGH '34)

119" W.B. (THROUGH '34)

33

6 INCREASED TO 221.4 C.I.D. FOR '33 ONLY. 80 H.P. @ 3200 115" WHEELBASE

5.50 × 17 TIRES ON 6, 6.00 × 17 ON 8

THE NEW EIGHT . . . THE NEW SIX . . . TWO GENERAL MOTORS VALUES

6 HAS 5.50 × 17 TIRES, 8 HAS 7.00 × 16 TIRES, 4.56 GEAR RATIO 4.78 GEAR RATIO 213.3 C.I.D., 84 H.P. @ 3250

HYDRAULIC BRAKES

34

"L-34" 8

"F-34" (114" W.B.) 6

WOOD-GRAINED dash

'34 DASH

'35 DASH

8 HAS 100 H.P. @ 3400 RPM (THROUGH '36)

"L-35" 8

"F-35" 6

6 HAS 213.3 C.I.D. and 90 H.P. @ 3400 RPM (THROUGH '36)

7.00 × 16 TIRES (8) 121" W.B. (THROUGH '36)

35

6.25 × 16 TIRES ON 6

115" W.B. (THROUGH '36)

197

OLDSMOBILE

TOURING SEDAN (W. TRUNK)

INTERIOR

6 "F-36"

GAS FILLER LOCATED HIGHER ON RT. REAR FENDER.

3-WINDOW SPORT COUPE

FRONT DOORS NOW HINGED AT FRONT.

8 "L-36"

36

7.00 x 16 TIRES ON OLDSMOBILE 8 FOR 1936 and 1937

8 has FENDER PARKING LIGHTS, and 5 HORIZONTAL CROSS-MEMBERS VISIBLE IN GRILLE.

CARTER CARB. (BOTH MODELS, STARTING '36)

6 HAS 229.7 C.I.D. (THROUGH '40) and 95 H.P. @ 3400 (THROUGH '38)

TAIL-LIGHTS MOVED UP TO SIDES OF BODY

6   117" W.B. (THROUGH '38)

8 NOW USES 257.1 C.I.D.

110 H.P. @ 3600 RPM

8

37

124" W.B. (THROUGH '38)

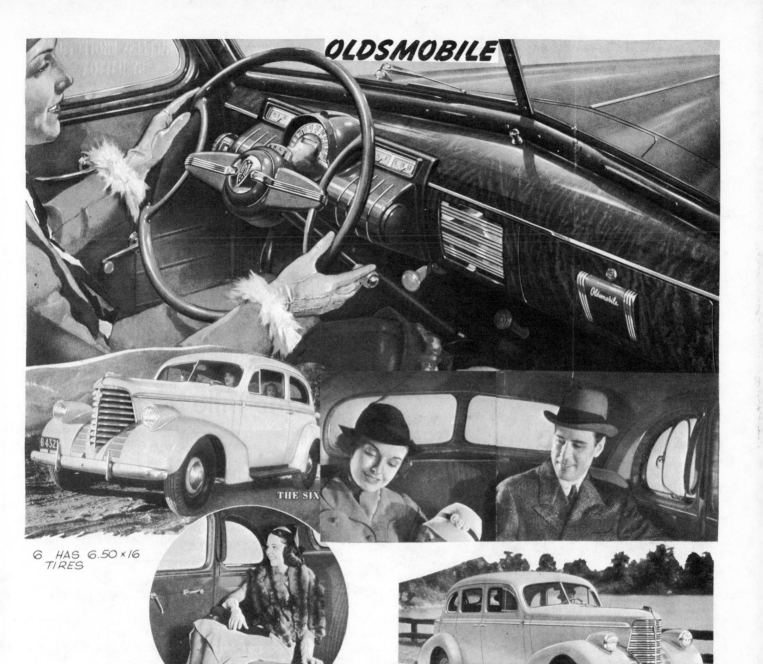

OLDSMOBILE

THE SIX

6 HAS 6.50 × 16
TIRES

THE EIGHT

OPTIONAL === AUTOMATIC TRANSMISSION!

38

OLDSMOBILE

6-CYL. "60" HAS 215.8 C.I.D. and 90 H.P. @ 3200 RPM

NEW "60" 4-DOOR SEDAN

39

"F-39" and "G-39" (6)
"L-39" (8)

1-PIECE REAR → WINDOW

6-CYL. "60" and "70" SERIES 115" and 120" W.B.

6

6-CYL. "70" HAS 229.7 C.I.D. and 95 H.P. @ 3300 RPM

8

8-CYL. "80" HAS 257.1 C.I.D. and 110 H.P. @ 3500 RPM

200

Series 80

120" W.B.

Overland

(1903-1926) (1939 ALSO*)

* - SEE WILLYS

WILLYS-OVERLAND, INC., TOLEDO, OHIO
Sedans, Coupes, Touring Cars and Roadsters
Willys-Overland, Limited, Toronto, Canada
The John N. Willys Export Corporation, New York

20-21

(4 CYLS.,
143.1 C.I.D.)
27 H.P.
4.5 GEAR
RATIO

100" W.B. CONT'D.
THROUGH '26 (ON 4-CYL.)

with NEW, DIAGONALLY-MOUNTED
"TRIPLEX" SPRINGS

REAR
DETAILS

HOOD LOUVRES
NEW FOR
1920

Rides as if Every Bump Had Springs

22 27 H.P. @ 2400 RPM

OVERLAND TRADE MARK REG.

22½

23

27 H.P. @ 2200 RPM

30 × 3½ TIRES AND TRIPLEX SPRINGS UNTIL 1926 (ON 4-CYL. SERIES)

24 NEW 153.9 C.I.D. and 30 H.P. (THROUGH '26) @ 2400 RPM

SPECIAL MODEL "92" "RED BIRD" TOURING HAS OWN 106" W.B. INTRO. MAY, 1923 (NICKEL RADIATOR ON EARLY MODELS.)

SPRING-SUMMER, 1924 = "BLUE BIRD" SPECIAL TOURING HAS NICKEL TRIM; DISC WHEELS OPTIONAL.

"CHAMPION" 3-DOOR SEDAN INTRODUCED OCT. 6, 1923.

COUPE

THE **Overland**

CHAMPION

"91"

OVERLAND

BUDD
(LIGHTWEIGHT, ALL-STEEL
BODIES ON 4-CYL.
MODELS, STARTING
AUGUST,
1924)

MODEL "91"

25

4

4 "91"

BUDD-BODIED 1925
"91s" ARE EASILY IDENTI-
FIED BY NARROW
WINDSHIELD CORNER-POSTS.
(ON COUPES and SEDANS.)

MODEL
"93"

new
OVERLAND SIX

NEW
'25 and '26 MODEL "93" 6-CYLINDER
OVERLANDS HAVE 169.6 C.I.D. ENGINE
WITH 38 H.P. @ 2800 RPM (30 × 5.25 TIRES)
and 112 3/4" W.B.

1926 4-CYL.
"91"
HAS BODY
SIMILAR TO 6.

26

The seats are wider, the windows larger, the doors much broader than other cars of this size and price

REPLACED BY
WHIPPET

203

OWEN MAGNETIC-
(1914 – 1922)

THE CAR OF A
THOUSAND SPEEDS

OWEN MAGNETIC MOTOR CAR CORPORATION, BROADWAY AT 57TH STREET, NEW YORK

(AND WILKES-BARRE, PA.)

19 – 21

142" WHEELBASE
6 - CYL. WEIDELY ENGINE
(4" × 5½" BORE and STROKE)

CLOSE - COUPLED ('20)
(NOT LISTED EARLY IN SEASON.)

HAD A UNIQUE ELECTRO -
MAGNETIC GEAR-SHIFT,
CONTROLLED FROM QUADRANT
ON STEERING WHEEL.

(KNOWN AS THE
"CROWN MAGNETIC"
FOR 1922 SEASON)

PACKARD

V-12
75 H.P. @ 2000 RPM
424.1 C.I.D.
136" W.B.
4.36 GEAR RATIO
35 x 5" TIRES

PACKARD MOTOR CAR COMPANY, Detroit

"Ask the Man   *Who Owns One"*

DELCO IGN.
(THROUGH '27)
OWN CARB.
(THROUGH '29,
31-32)
(1899-1958)
("3-25" MODELS HAVE
128" W.B.)

SOME MODELS WITH 136" W.B.

18
TO
20
TWIN
6
(V-12)

21

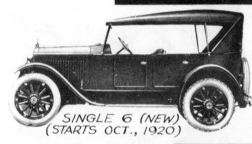

SINGLE 6 (NEW)
(STARTS OCT., 1920)

NEW SINGLE SIX has
6-CYL., L-HEAD
241.6 C.I.D. ENGINE with
52 H.P. @ 2600 RPM (THROUGH '22)

TWIN 6
(85 H.P.)

SINGLE
6

116" W.B. ON 6,
AS IN 1921

22

TWIN 6
(DISCONTINUED
DURING
1923)
85 H.P.
@ 2600
RPM

THE
TWIN-SIX
SPECIAL

205

PACKARD

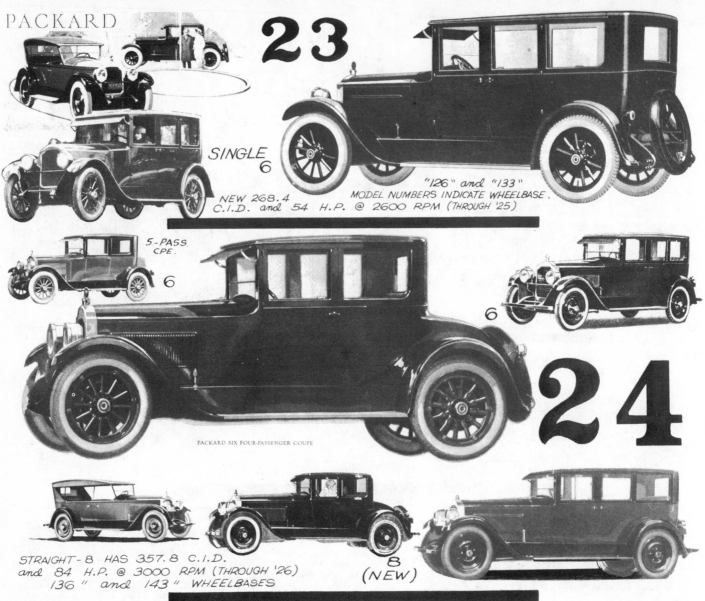

23

SINGLE 6

NEW 268.4 C.I.D. and 54 H.P. @ 2600 RPM (THROUGH '25)

"126" and "133" MODEL NUMBERS INDICATE WHEELBASE.

5-PASS. CPE.

6

6

24

PACKARD SIX FOUR-PASSENGER COUPE

STRAIGHT-8 HAS 357.8 C.I.D. and 84 H.P. @ 3000 RPM (THROUGH '26) 136" and 143" WHEELBASES

8 (NEW)

70 M.P.H. TOP SPEED OF 1925 "8" (4.7 GEAR RATIO)

ONLY PACKARD CAN BUILD A PACKARD

8

25

6

8 7-PASS.

206

75 M.P.H. 4.66 GEAR RATIO

PACKARD SIX and EIGHT

PACKARD

6

8

26

"426" and "433" are 6-CYL. MODELS WITH 288.6 C.I.D., 82 H.P. @ 3200

27

"336" and "343" STRAIGHT-8 INCREASED TO 384.8 C.I.D. and 106 H.P. @ 3200 RPM

(27½)

P A C K A R D

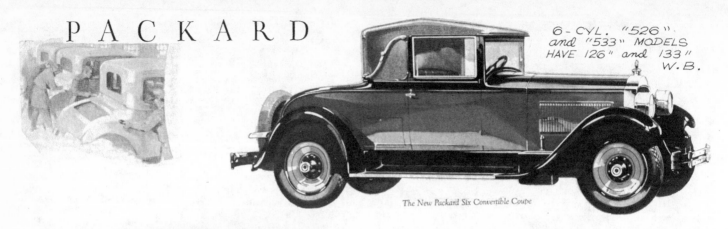

6-CYL. "526" and "533" MODELS HAVE 126" and 133" W.B.

The New Packard Six Convertible Coupe

UNTIL 1937, THE "526" and "533" OF 1928 WERE PACKARD'S FINAL 6-CYL. MODELS. 288.6 C.I.D., 82 H.P. @ 3200 RPM

28

(FINAL YEAR FOR DRUM HEADLIGHTS.) DELCO-REMY IGN.

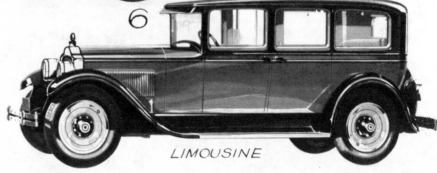

6

LIMOUSINE

1928 8-CYL. "443" HAS 143" WHEELBASE, VENT DOORS ON HOOD.

384.8 C.I.D. STRAIGHT-8 106 H.P. @ 3200 (THROUGH '30)

8

208

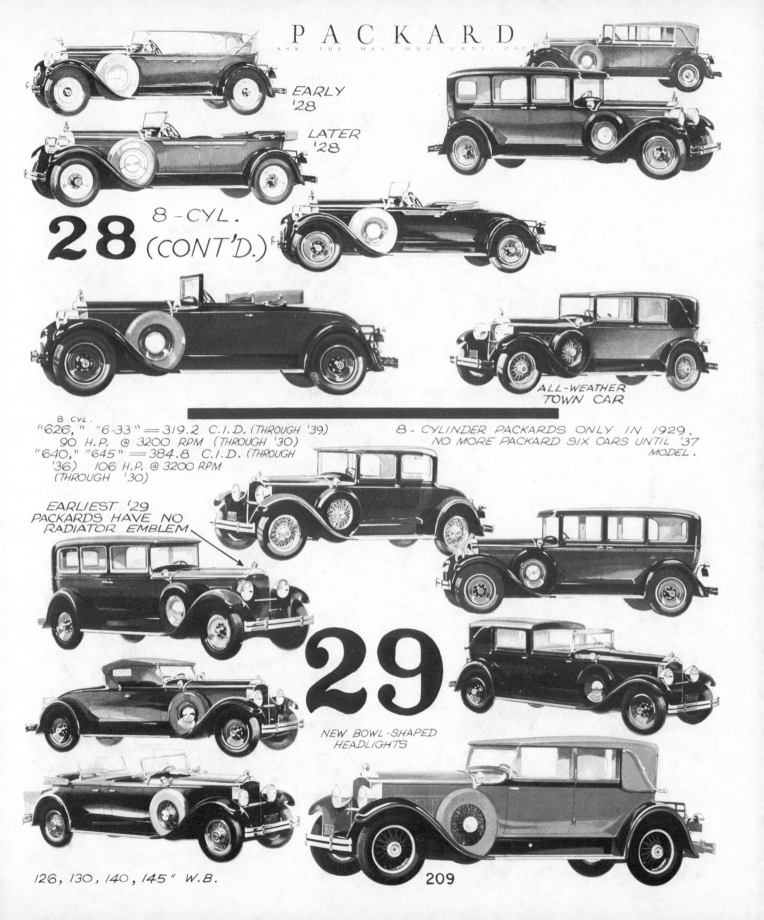

EARLY '28

LATER '28

28 8-CYL. (CONT'D.)

ALL-WEATHER TOWN CAR

8 CYL.
"626," "6-33" = 319.2 C.I.D. (THROUGH '39)
90 H.P. @ 3200 RPM (THROUGH '30)
"640," "645" = 384.8 C.I.D. (THROUGH '36) 106 H.P. @ 3200 RPM (THROUGH '30)

8-CYLINDER PACKARDS ONLY IN 1929. NO MORE PACKARD SIX CARS UNTIL '37 MODEL.

EARLIEST '29 PACKARDS HAVE NO RADIATOR EMBLEM

29

NEW BOWL-SHAPED HEADLIGHTS

126, 130, 140, 145" W.B.

209

PACKARD

STD. 8

STEWART CARB. LISTED FOR '30 (ALL SERIES)

DELUXE 8

(ENGINE SPECS. AS IN '29)

127½, 134½, 140½, 145½" WHEELBASES (THROUGH '31)

30

"726," "733," "740," "745" MODELS

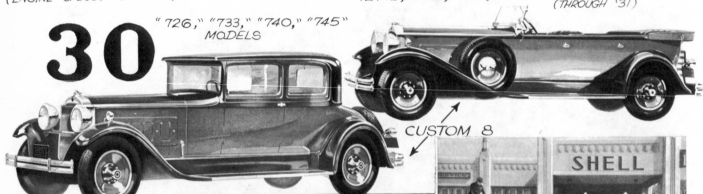

CUSTOM 8

OWN CARB. (THROUGH '32)

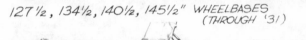

NEW MECHANICAL FUEL PUMP REPLACES VACUUM TANK.

31

"826," "833," "840," "845" MODELS

100 or 120 H.P. @ 3200 RPM

31½ NEW SERIES (CONTINUES INTO 1932)

210

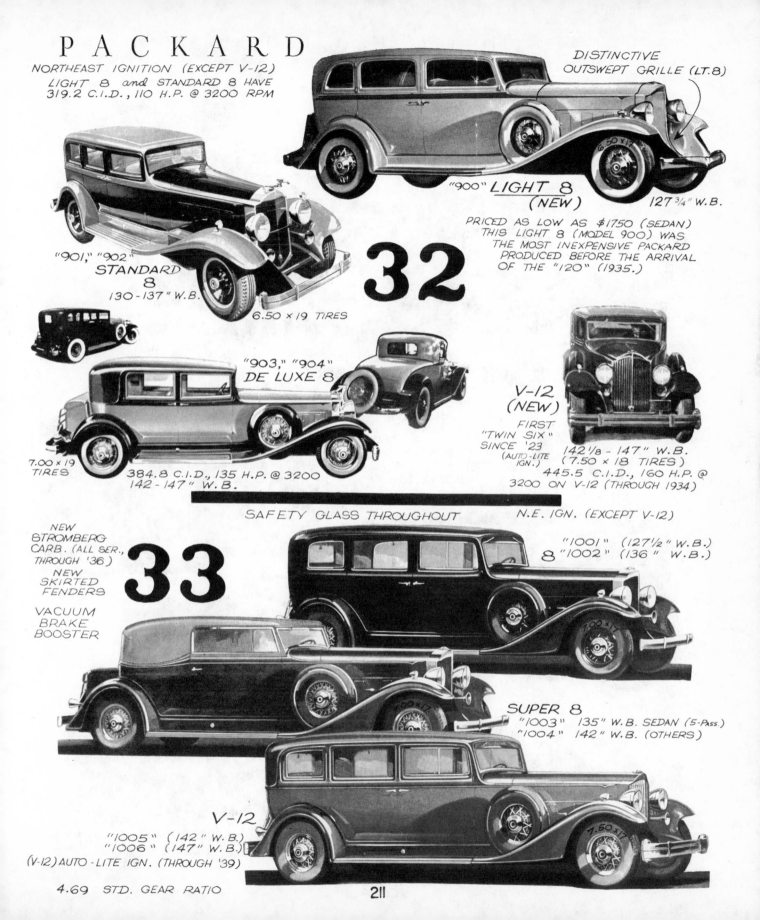

PACKARD

NORTHEAST IGNITION (EXCEPT V-12)
LIGHT 8 and STANDARD 8 HAVE
319.2 C.I.D., 110 H.P. @ 3200 RPM

DISTINCTIVE
OUTSWEPT GRILLE (LT.8)

"900" LIGHT 8
(NEW)

127 3/4" W.B.

PRICED AS LOW AS $1750 (SEDAN)
THIS LIGHT 8 (MODEL 900) WAS
THE MOST INEXPENSIVE PACKARD
PRODUCED BEFORE THE ARRIVAL
OF THE "120" (1935.)

"901," "902"
STANDARD
8
130-137" W.B.

32

6.50 x 19 TIRES

"903," "904"
DE LUXE 8

7.00 x 19
TIRES

384.8 C.I.D., 135 H.P. @ 3200
142-147" W.B.

V-12
(NEW)

FIRST
"TWIN SIX"
SINCE '23
(AUTO-LITE
IGN.)

142 1/8 - 147" W.B.
(7.50 x 18 TIRES)
445.5 C.I.D., 160 H.P. @
3200 ON V-12 (THROUGH 1934)

SAFETY GLASS THROUGHOUT

N.E. IGN. (EXCEPT V-12)

NEW
STROMBERG
CARB. (ALL SER.,
THROUGH '36)
NEW
SKIRTED
FENDERS

VACUUM
BRAKE
BOOSTER

33

"1001" (127 1/2" W.B.)
8 "1002" (136" W.B.)

SUPER 8
"1003" 135" W.B. SEDAN (5-Pass.)
"1004" 142" W.B. (OTHERS)

V-12
"1005" (142" W.B.)
"1006" (147" W.B.)
(V-12) AUTO-LITE IGN. (THROUGH '39)

4.69 STD. GEAR RATIO

PACKARD

THE YARDSTICK WITH WHICH TO MEASURE ALL FINE CAR VALUES

4.69 STANDARD GEAR RATIO ON 8s

8 HAS CHROME-PLATING ON RADIATOR SHELL. →

SUPER 8 "1103" and "1104" have 384.8 C.I.D. and 145 H.P. @ 3200 RPM

135," 142," 147" WHEELBASES ON SUPER 8s. 147"– W.B. "1105" SUPER 8 AVAILABLE with DIETRICH or LE BARON BODIES.

NORTHEAST IGN. (EXCEPT V-12)

34

DASH

V-12

4.41 OR 4.69 GEAR RATIOS ON V-12

142 OR 147" W.B. ON V-12

PACKARD

HYDRAULIC BRAKES ON "120" ONLY.

NEW LOW-COST 120

"120" HAS 8-CYL. 257.1 C.I.D. ENGINE,

110 H.P. @ 3850 RPM

120" W.B.

4.36 GEAR RATIO

6.50 x 16

"120" IS LOWEST-PRICED PACKARD EVER, AT ONLY

$980 to $1095

"120" SEDAN

"1203," "1204," "1205" HAVE 132, 139, 144" W.B.

35

SUPER 8

SUPER 8 HAS 384.8 C.I.D., 150 H.P. @ 3200 RPM 4.41 G.R.

EIGHT ("1200","1201","1202") HAS 127,134, 139" W.B., 319.2 C.I.D., 130 H.P. @ 3200 RPM 4.69 GEAR RATIO

"1207" 139" W.B.
"1208" 144" W.B.
4.41 GEAR RATIO

V-12

V-12 has NEW 473.3 C.I.D. WITH 175 H.P. @ 3200 RPM

new AUTO-LITE IGN. ON "120" and "V-12" (THROUGH '39) OTHERS have NORTHEAST IGN. (FINAL YEAR)

PACKARD SKIPPED 1300 SERIES AND MOVED ON TO 1400 MODEL NUMBERS IN '36.

30-569

213

PACKARD

"120" B

NEW 282 C.I.D. 120 H.P. @ 3800 RPM (THROUGH '38 "1601")

SUPER 8

SU. 8 has DELCO-REMY IGN. (THROUGH '37)

36

V-12

MECHANICAL "POWER" BRAKES ON LARGE 8s AND V-12.

HYDRAULIC BRAKES ON ALL MODELS.

37

DE LUXE "120-CD" and "138-CD" (138" W.B.) HAVE AUTOMATIC RADIATOR SHUTTERS, OTHER SPECIAL FEATURES.

NEW 6 HAS 236.7 C.I.D. 100 H.P. @ 3600 RPM

SIX (NEW) MODEL 115-C

115" W.B. 4.36 GEAR RATIO

6 has DELCO-REMY IGN. (THROUGH '38)

120 C

120" W.B. (CARTER CARB. ON '37 "120")

"1500" (127"W.B.,) "1501" (134" W.B.,) and "1502" (139" W.B.) ARE SUPER 8 MODELS, WITH 319.2 C.I.D. and 130 H.P. @ 3200 RPM 4.69 G.R., 7.50 x 16 TIRES STROMBERG CARB.

6.50 x 16

V-12 STROMBERG CARB.

214

PACKARD
38

NEW 245.3 C.I.D.,
STILL RATED AT 100 H.P.
@ 3600 RPM

6

122" W.B.

MODEL
"1600"

8
"120" REPLACED
BY THIS "1601"
(127" W.B.) MODEL.

"1602" HAS 148"
W.B.

STROMBERG CARB. (ALL SERIES
EXCEPT 6)

SUPER 8

12

BODIES BY BRUNN

1938
MODEL NUMBERS
IN 1600 SERIES.

215

P A C K A R D

38

12 (CONT'D.)

AUTO-LITE IGN. ON ALL '38 MODELS EXCEPT 6.

SIX

6 has CHANDLER-GROVES CARB. (SINCE '37)

39

"CONTROLLED OVERDRIVE" OPTIONAL ON ALL MODELS.

1939 MODEL NUMBERS IN 1700 SERIES

120

EIGHT "1701" and "1702" (127" and 148" W.B.)

319.2 C.I.D. ENGINE (SINCE '29) 130 H.P. @ 3200 RPM (SINCE 1935 "EIGHT")

SUPER-8

AUTO-LITE IGN. ON ALL 1939 PACKARDS.

12

(FINAL V-12)

216

The Most Beautiful Car in America

PAIGE (1909 – 1930)

PAIGE-DETROIT MOTOR CAR COMPANY, DETROIT, Michigan

Manufacturers of Paige Motor Cars and Motor Trucks

19-20

PAIGE TRUCK →

"LARCHMONT" 4-PASS.

"GLENBROOK" 5-PASS.

"6-42" = 119" W.B. = OWN 6-CYL.; 230.1 C.I.D. ENG.
"6-55" = 127" W.B. = 303.1 C.I.D. 6-CYL. CONTINENTAL ENG.

"6-66" 7-PASS. SEDAN

On January 21st, the Paige, Daytona Model, 6-66 broke every stock car record for speed when it covered a measured mile in 35.01 seconds—a speed of 102.8 miles an hour.

119"-W.B. "6-42" CONTINUED IN 1921; IS "6-44" IN 1922.

21-22

"6-66"
131" W.B.
70 H.P.

1922-STYLE TOP BOWS
331.4 C.I.D. CONT. ENG. (THROUGH '25)

JULY, 1922 =
new series "6-66"
has NEW CLUTCH AND TRANSMISSION THAT PERMITS DOWN-SHIFTING FROM HIGH TO 2ND GEAR AT 35 M.P.H.

PAIGE

23 "6-66" BECOMES "6-70" IN 1923.

"6-70" DASH

131" WHEELBASE

"6-70"

24

NIGHT VIEW OF PAIGE FACTORY ←

4.6 GEAR RATIO

331.4 C.I.D. 6-CYLINDER CONTINENTAL "10-A" ENGINE 73 H.P. @ 2400 RPM 131" W.B.

TOP SPEED = 75 M.P.H.

NOTE DIFFERENT QUARTER-WINDOW STYLE

MODEL "21-24" 4.9 G.R.

25

The New Paige Standard Brougham ('25½)

218

PAIGE

26

MODEL "24-26"
6 CYL.
248.8 C.I.D.
63 H.P. @
2800 RPM
HYDRAULIC BRAKES

125" W.B.

32 × 6.00 TIRES

The Most Beautiful Car in America

4.9 GEAR RATIO
109" W.B.

4.45 GEAR RATIO
115" W.B

HYDRAULIC BRAKES

MODEL "6-45"
(FORMERLY "JEWETT")

185 C.I.D.
CONTINENTAL
SPECIAL ENGINE
43 H.P. @
2600 RPM
"6-45" COUPE

27

"6-65"
249 C.I.D., 63 H.P. @
2800 RPM

"6-75"
268 C.I.D., 68 H.P.
@ 3000 RPM
4.82 GEAR RATIO
125" W.B.

There are in the new Paige line 20 charming body types and color combinations on 4 chassis from $1095 to $2795—all prices f. o. b. Detroit

1927
INSTRUMENT PANEL

NEW NAME FOR
1928:
GRAHAM-PAIGE

STRAIGHT-8
"8-85"
4.82 G.R. ➤
298.6
C.I.D. LYC.
ENG.
80 H.P.
@ 3000

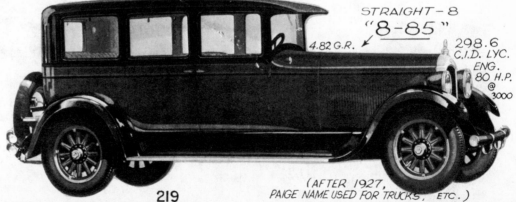

219

(AFTER 1927,
PAIGE NAME USED FOR TRUCKS, ETC.)

PAN (1918-1922)

108" W.B.
MODEL "A"

4 CYL., 165.9 C.I.D.
OWN O.H.V. ENGINE
33 x 4 TIRES
4.9 G.R.

PAN MOTOR CO.,
ST. CLOUD, MINN.

(SEATS COULD BE FOLDED, TO FORM A BED.)

PARENTI (1920-1922)

125" W.B.
32 x 4 TIRES

OWN AIR COOLED V-8

PARENTI MOTORS CORP., BUFFALO, N.Y.

2 3/4" x 4 1/4" BORE and STROKE

PATERSON 6

W. A. PATERSON CO., FLINT, MICH.
(1908 - 1923)

22 "22-6-52"

('21)

21 "6-50"

4.5 G.R.
120" W.B.
6-CYL. CONTINENTAL ENGINE
(THROUGH '23)
224 C.I.D. (ALSO ON
'20 "6-47")

DELCO IGNITION (THROUGH '23)

('23)

32 x 4 1/2 TIRES
(THROUGH '23)
298.2 C.I.D.

23 "23-6-52"
242 C.I.D.

PEERLESS

7-PASS. SEDAN
SERIES 7
(V-8) ('21)

PEERLESS MOTOR CAR COMPANY, CLEVELAND, OHIO
Peerless Eight

(1900-1932)

MODEL "56"
('20)

19-22 "56-7"
CONT'D.
INTO 1922.

125" W.B. (THROUGH '22)
AUTO-LITE IGNITION AND 4.54 G.R. (THROUGH '20)
ATWATER-KENT IGNITION ('21-'22)
4.9 G.R. (TO '26)

OWN 331.8 C.I.D., V-8 L-HEAD ENGINE
(THROUGH '28)
34 x 4 1/2 TIRES (THROUGH '22)

PEERLESS

23

(INTRODUCED
AUGUST,
1922)

NEW
128" W.B.
(THROUGH '25,
ON V-8)

TOWN COUPE
(4-PASS.)

DELCO IGN.
(ON 8s, THROUGH '29)

33 × 5 TIRES

24

6 CYL. "70"
V8 ═ "66"

PAINTED
RADIATOR SHELL

new
"70" has OWN 288.6 C.I.D.
ENGINE (USED THROUGH '29)
126, 133" W.B. (THROUGH '26)
4.63 G.R., 32 × 4½ TIRES

("EQUIPOISED 8")
V-8 "67"

BALLOON TIRES, HYDRAULIC BRAKES

(INSTRUMENTS IN 3 OVALS,
2 GLASSED-IN)

70 H.P. @ 2500
RPM
(THROUGH
'26)
NEW RADIATOR DESIGN

65 MILES PER HOUR

25

(STYLE OF 6 - CYL. "70"
SIMILAR TO 1924)
70 H.P. @ 2500 RPM
(THROUGH '29)
4.45 G.R.
33 × 6.20 TIRES

PEERLESS

6 - CYL., 230.2 C.I.D.
CONTINENTAL "8-U"
ENGINE ON NEW "6-80"
Auto-Lite IGNITION
30 × 5.77 TIRES ('26)
32 × 6.00 ('27)

The Remarkable Six ~ 80
$1395 to $1795

116" W.B.
54 H.P. ('26)
63 " ('27)

26-27

FRENCH-STYLE
ROOF VISOR
(IN VOGUE ON
MANY AMERICAN
CARS OF 1925
TO 1928.)

The Powerful Six ~ 72
$1895 to $2995

126" W.B.
70 H.P.

DELCO IGN.
ON 6-72, 8-69

288.5 C.I.D.
70 H.P. @ 2500
(120" W.B. "6-90"
7-WINDOW LANDAULET
SEDAN (WITH CONVERTIBLE
REAR QUARTERS) ALSO
AVAIL. IN 1927.

133½" W.B. 70 H.P. ('26)
80 " ('27)

The 90° V-type Eight-69
$2995 to $3795

SMALL REAR QUARTER
WINDOWS ON MOST
PEERLESS COUPES
OF LATE 1920s.

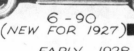

6 - 90
(NEW FOR 1927)

116"-W.B. "6-60" IS NEW FOR '27, has 199.1 C.I.D. CONTINENTAL eng.,
52 H.P. @ 3000 RPM

EARLY 1928 MODELS : "6-60"   "6-80"
          "6-90"   "8-69" (V-8)

28 (EARLY)

← MODEL "6-60"
(INTRODUCED EARLY
SUMMER, 1927, WITH
ROOF-VISOR AS ON
'27 MODELS.)

62 H.P. @ 3000 RPM
(ALSO ON '29-30 "6-61")

222

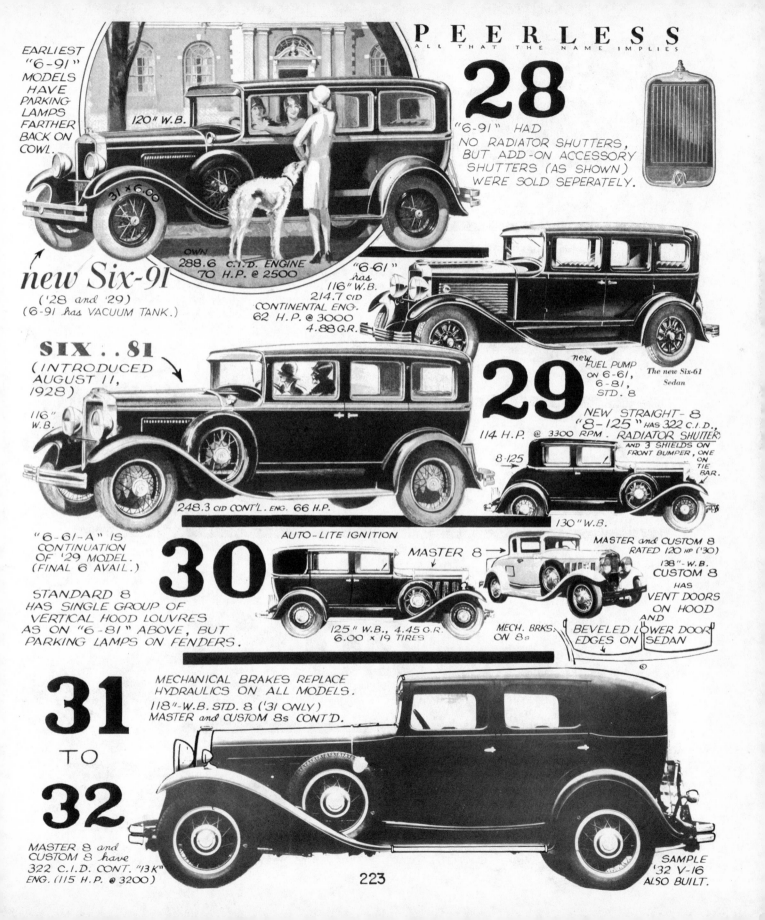

PEERLESS
ALL THAT THE NAME IMPLIES

28

EARLIEST "6-91" MODELS HAVE PARKING LAMPS FARTHER BACK ON COWL.

120" W.B.

31 × 6.00

OWN 288.6 C.I.D. ENGINE 70 H.P. @ 2500

new Six-91

('28 and '29)
(6-91 has VACUUM TANK.)

"6-91" HAD NO RADIATOR SHUTTERS, BUT ADD-ON ACCESSORY SHUTTERS (AS SHOWN) WERE SOLD SEPERATELY.

"6-61" has 116" W.B. 214.7 CID CONTINENTAL ENG. 62 H.P. @ 3000 4.88 G.R.

SIX .. 81

(INTRODUCED AUGUST 11, 1928)

116" W.B.

248.3 CID CONT'L. ENG. 66 H.P.

29

new FUEL PUMP ON 6-61, 6-81, STD. 8

The new Six-61 Sedan

NEW STRAIGHT-8 "8-125" HAS 322 C.I.D. 114 H.P. @ 3300 RPM. RADIATOR SHUTTERS AND 3 SHIELDS ON FRONT BUMPER, ONE ON TIE BAR.

8-125

130" W.B.

AUTO-LITE IGNITION

30

"6-61-A" IS CONTINUATION OF '29 MODEL. (FINAL 6 AVAIL.)

STANDARD 8 HAS SINGLE GROUP OF VERTICAL HOOD LOUVRES AS ON "6-81" ABOVE, BUT PARKING LAMPS ON FENDERS.

125" W.B., 4.45 G.R. 6.00 × 19 TIRES

MASTER 8

MASTER and CUSTOM 8 RATED 120 HP ('30)

138"- W.B. CUSTOM 8 HAS VENT DOORS ON HOOD AND BEVELED LOWER DOOR EDGES ON SEDAN

MECH. BRKS. ON 8s

31 TO 32

MECHANICAL BRAKES REPLACE HYDRAULICS ON ALL MODELS.
118"-W.B. STD. 8 ('31 ONLY)
MASTER and CUSTOM 8s CONT'D.

MASTER 8 and CUSTOM 8 have 322 C.I.D. CONT. "13K" ENG. (115 H.P. @ 3200)

SAMPLE '32 V-16 ALSO BUILT.

223

The
PETERS
AUTOMOBILE
"Everybody's Car"

Peters Motor Corporation
Trenton   New Jersey

(1921–1922)

BUDDY MODEL   90" W.B.

IN 1919, PEAKED RADIATOR AND LOUVRELESS HOOD ADOPTED, IN ROLLS-ROYCE STYLE.

PHIANNA
NEW SERIES
The Highest Type of Motor Car Construction

(1916–1922)
(PHIANNA MOTORS CO., NEWARK, N.J. === TO 1918

M. H. CARPENTER, LONG ISLAND CITY, N.Y. === 1919 ON)

('19–'21)

"1922" PHIANNAS BUILT FROM 1921 PARTS ON HAND.

(1917–1922) PIEDMONT

Piedmont
MOTOR CAR CO. INC.
LYNCHBURG VIRGINIA

PIEDMONT MOTOR CAR CO., LYNCHBURG, VA.

MODEL E

THE PIERCE-ARROW MOTOR CAR COMPANY, *Buffalo, N.Y.*

PIERCE-ARROW

(1901 TO 1938)

"38" 134" W.B.

20
(RIGHT-HAND DRIVE)

"48" 142" W.B.

1921 === NEW MODEL "33" (138" W.B.) LEFT-HAND DRIVE REPLACES 2 PREVIOUS MODELS

DUAL-VALVE ENGINE

4.28 G.R.

6 CYLS., 414.7 C.I.D.

21-23

('23)

224

PIERCE-ARROW

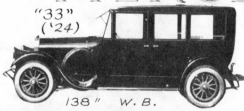

"33"
('24)

138" W. B.

"33" ('25)

100 H.P. @ 2600

24-26

LOWER-PRICED SERIES "80"
INTRODUCED
MID-1924.

Body by Pierce-Arrow   Series 80

1925-6
"80"
HAS 288.6
C.I.D., 6 CYLS.,
70 H.P. @ 2600 RPM
130" W. B.

COACH
('25½)

27

"80"
(130" W.B.)

"36"
(138" W.B.)

PIERCE-ARROW

28

"81" REPLACES "80"

"36"
7-PASSENGER TOURING CAR
4.29 G.R.

"6-81" INSTRUMENT PANEL

75 H.P. @ 3200 RPM

130" W.B.

4.45 G.R.

29

"143"
(HOOD VENT DOORS)

143" W.B.

NEW STRAIGHT-8 ENGINE
365 CU. IN. DISPL.
125 H.P. @ 3200 RPM
new FUEL PUMP

INSTRUMENT PANEL

"133"
(7 GROUPS of VERTICAL HOOD LOUVRES)

133" W.B.

4.08 and 4.42 G.R.

30

"B"

340, 366
and 385 C.I.D. STRAIGHT-8s,
DEVELOPING 115, 125, 132 H.P.
@ 3000 RPM

132³⁄₈, 134, 139, 144" W.B.

31

"43" = 125 H.P.
134-7" W.B.
"42," "41" =
132 H.P.
142-7" W.B.

PIERCE ARROW

"54" STRAIGHT-8 HAS
366 C.I.D., 125 H.P. @ 3000

"53" V-12 =140 H.P. @ 3100
"52," "51" V-12 =150 H.P. @ 3100

4.42 GEAR RATIO

32

8

V-12 (NEW) 398 and
429 C.I.D.

7.00 × 17 TIRES
7.50 × 17 ON LARGE V-12.

"SILVER ARROW" HAS SMALL REAR WINDOW

"836"
136-9" W.B.

135-H.P. 8

POWER BRAKES
"1236" = 136"
or 139" W.B.
"1247," "1242" =
137" or 142" W.B.

33

429 and 462-C.I.D. V-12s (160 and 175 H.P.)

"SILVER ARROW" AND ITS INTERIOR

34

MODIFIED "SILVER ARROW" OFFERED FOR 1934.

"836-A"
DIFFERENT GRILLE,
NO HOOD VENTS.*
(LOWER-PRICED
MODEL,
STARTS APRIL, 1934.)

8 = 385 C.I.D.,
140 H.P. @ 3400

V-12 = 462 C.I.D.,
175 H.P. @ 3400

"836-A" DASH

* = HOOD VENTS
OPTIONAL ON SOME
"836-A" MODELS.

"1240-A"

PIERCE-ARROW

35

CHOICE OF STR.8
V-12, CONT'D.
THROUGH '38.

"845," "1245," OR "1255"

17" WHEELS AS BEFORE,
CONT'D. THROUGH '38.

36

"1601" STRAIGHT-8
HAS 139" OR 144" W.B.,
150 H.P. @ 3400 RPM

"1602," "1603" V-12s HAVE
139," 144," 147" W.B.,
185 H.P. @ 3400 RPM

BACK SEAT OF
1936 MODEL

MECHANICAL BRAKES STILL RETAINED.

37-38

'37 = 1700 SER.

'38 = 1800 SER.

DISCONTINUED 1938

PILOT (1909-1924)

PILOT MOTOR CAR CO.,
RICHMOND, IND.

120" W.B.
(THROUGH '20)

"6-45" (SINCE '16)
HAS TEETOR 6-CYL.
ENG. (230.1 CID)

('19-21)

126" W.B., 6-CYL.,
248.9 C.I.D.
HERSCH.-SPLM.
ENGINE (IN '21)

('22)

('23)

126" W.B.
('21 THROUGH '24)

('24)

"6-50"
CUSTOM SEDAN
6-CYL.
HERSCH.-SPLM.
"E" ENGINE
288.6 C.I.D.

"6-56"

PLYMOUTH

A CHRYSLER
M O T O R S   P R O D U C T

EARLY
EMBLEM
(CHRYSLER
PLYMOUTH)
MODEL
"Q"

IN JAN, 1929,
MODEL "U"
BEGINS, WITH
THE ABOVE
EMBLEM

STARTS JUNE, 1928 (MODEL Q)

29

"NARROW
PROFILE"
RADIATOR
SHELL

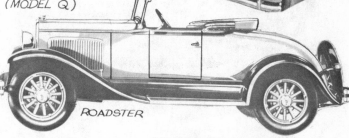

ROADSTER

REPLACES 1928
CHRYSLER "52"
(4 CYLS.)

MODEL
"Q"

(170.3
C.I.D.)

(4.6
COMPR.)

45 H.P. @ 2800 RPM

BUSINESS COUPE (METAL BACK)

GAS
GAUGE
ON
TANK

109" WHEELBASE
4.3 GEAR RATIO

FEDCO I.D.
PLATE

DASH

SOFT-TOP
COUPE IS
VERY SCARCE.

MODEL "U" STARTS 1-29,
WITH IMPROVED 175.4 C.I.D.
ENGINE (HAS NEW
SQUARED-OFF CORNERS
ON CYLINDER
HEAD.)

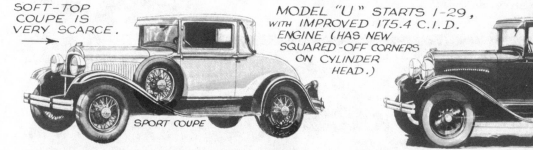

SPORT COUPE

DELCO-REMY IGNITION (THROUGH '34)

(EARLY '30 IS SIMILAR TO '29 MODEL.)

30
LATE
MODEL

STARTS APRIL, 1930 (EARLY '31 SIMILAR)

"NEW FINER" series

4.33
GEAR RATIO

EARLY TYPE WITH RECTANGULAR REAR
WINDOW

GAS
GAUGE
ON DASH

(OVAL REAR WINDOW
AFTER SUMMER, 1930)
109" W.B.

196.1 C.I.D.   48 H.P. @ 2800 RPM   4.6 COMPR.
FUEL PUMP REPLACES VACUUM TANK

229

PLYMOUTH

COWL VENTS
ARE DELUXE
EQUIPMENT

NEW
GRILLE

31½-32

MODEL "PA"

STARTS JUNE, 1931

109 ³/₈" W.B.
56 H.P. @
2800 RPM
NEW 4.9 COMPRESSION

"*NEW* Floating Power"

FLEXIBLE ENGINE
MOUNTS, "EASY-SHIFT"
CONSTANT-MESH TRANSMISSION,
AND
FREE WHEELING

SCREEN-TYPE
STONE GUARD IS
OPTIONAL

NEW
SHIELD-
SHAPED
RADIATOR EMBLEM,
NEW MASCOT,
NEW HUB CAPS

NEW
CIRCULAR
DASH GAUGES
(5 IN A
ROW)

INTERIOR
("PA")

WIRE WHEELS STANDARD EQUIPMENT

"PA" "THRIFT" SEDANS
(WITH ONLY 3 DASH GAUGES)
AVAILABLE AFTER "PB" MODELS INTRODUCED.

32½

MODEL "PB"

INTRODUCED APRIL, 1932

WALTER P.
CHRYSLER
(FOUNDER OF
CHRYSLER
CORP.)
SHOWING
1932
PLYMOUTH
MASCOT

FINAL 4-CYLINDER SERIES
NEW 112 ³/₈" WHEELBASE
65 H.P. @ 3400 RPM

INTERIOR
("PB")

COUPE
SEAT BACK
FOLDS,
FOR
EXTRA
STORAGE

(5.6-COMPRESSION "Red Head" OPTIONAL)

NEW BODY
DOORS HINGED AT REAR

230

PLYMOUTH

33
(FIRST 6-CYL. PLYMOUTH)

NEW 4.38 GEAR RATIO

"PC" MODEL (10-32 TO 3-33) CHROME ON RADIATOR SHELL 107" W.B.

189.8 C.I.D. 70 H.P. @ 3600 RPM WITH 5.5-COMPR. "SILVER DOME" HEAD, OR 76 H.P. @ 3600 RPM WITH 6.5-COMPRESSION "Red Head"

33½
"PD" (3-33 TO 12-33. PAINTED RADIATOR SHELL)

STD. 107¾" W.B. DE LUXE 113½" W.B.

34
"PF" "PG" MODELS 107¾" W.B.

"PE" DE LUXE has 113½" W.B.

4.11 GEAR RATIO

new 201.3 C.I.D. (THROUGH 1941)

NEW VENT WINDOWS ROLL DOWN INTO DOORS.

77 H.P. @ 3600 RPM WITH 5.8 COMPRESSION OR 82 H.P. @ 3600 WITH 6.5 ALUMINUM CYL. HEAD

DIP IN BUMPER

HOOD VENT DOORS NOT ON STD. MODELS.

35
"PJ"

4.13 GEAR RATIO

113" W.B. 85 H.P. @ 3600 RPM

6.7 COMPR. (THROUGH '41)

LATE '35 MODEL (EARLY '35s [SHOWN AT LEFT] HAVE CHROMED HOOD "PORT-HOLES.")

AUTO-LITE IGNITION REPLACES DELCO-REMY.

PLYMOUTH

82 H.P. @ 3600 RPM (THROUGH 1939)

P-1 = "BUSINESS"
P-2 = "DE LUXE"

36

4.125 GEAR RATIO

X 54724

37

4.1 GEAR RATIO

SAFETY INTERIOR—Nothing protrudes on instrument panel

P-3 "BUSINESS" (STD.) MODEL

P-4 DE LUXE MODELS HAVE BUTTERFLY VENT WINDOWS, GRAINED EFFECT on DASH.

X 82578

112" W.B.
(1937 and 1938)

LATE '37 DOES NOT HAVE DRAWER-TYPE SAFETY KNOBS on DASH.

1938 WINDSHIELDS DO NOT OPEN

38

(1937 to 1939 SEDANS HAVE 2-PC. REAR WINDOW; 1-PIECE ON COUPES.)

"ROADKING" (STD.)
P-5

REGISTERED REST ROOM

309,816

3.9 OR 4.1 GEAR RATIO

HAND-BRAKE UNDER DASH

"DE LUXE"
P-6

PLYMOUTH

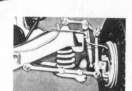

New AMOLA STEEL Coil Springs...

3.9, 4.1, OR
4.3 GEAR RATIO

PERFECTED Remote Control Shifting with new All-Silent Auto-Mesh Transmission.

NEW "SAFETY SIGNAL" SPEEDOMETER

NEW "ROADKING" (P-7)
NEW "DELUXE" (P-8)

Indicator Light shows green up to 30 miles per hour...from 30 to 50, amber ...above 50, a warning red.

NEW 114" W.B.

39

TURN A SWITCH AND THE TOP GOES UP OR DOWN—BY ITSELF!

AN "ECONOMY" ENGINE
WITH 5.2 COMPR. and
65 H.P. WAS
AVAIL. IF
DESIRED,
FROM 1935
THROUGH
1940.

PONTIAC SIX
CHIEF · OF · THE · SIXES

PONTIAC INTRODUCED 1926, BY GENERAL MOTORS, AS A LOWER-PRICED COMPANION TO OAKLAND CAR.

EARLIEST PONTIACS OF 1926 AVAILABLE ONLY WITH 2-DOOR COACH OR COUPE BODIES.

COACH

"STEP-UP" IN BELT MOULDING (CONT'D. ON EARLY '27 COUPE AND COACH)

6 CYLINDERS
186.6 C.I.D.
36 H.P. @
2400 RPM
(THROUGH '27)

26

110" WHEELBASE (THROUGH 1930)

4.18 GEAR RATIO (THROUGH 1929)

27

FINAL YEAR WITH 2-WH. BRAKES and VACUUM TANK.

H.P. INCREASED TO 37 @ 2400

28

new "TRI-CLUSTER" DASH

new = FUEL PUMP

new = 4-WHEEL BRAKES

ACTUAL '28 ROOFLINE IS NOT AS LOW AS THIS ORIGINAL ADVERTISEMENT SUGGESTS.

234

PONTIAC

EARLY SERIES 29

(HORIZONTAL → HOOD LOUVRES)

RDSTR. and PHAETON have BODY BY OAKLAND-PONTIAC. FISHER BODY ON OTHERS.

200.4 C.I.D. (THROUGH '32)
57 H.P. @ 3000 RPM
OVAL REAR WINDOW

← **29½**

(VERTICAL HOOD LOUVRES)

29 × 5.00 TIRES

60 H.P. @ 3000 RPM (THROUGH '31)

4.42 GEAR RATIO

30

"6 - B"

SLIGHTLY SLANTED WINDSHIELD

5.00 × 19

4.55 GEAR RATIO

112" W. B.
5.00 × 19 TIRES

31

"6 - 401"

PONTIAC

32

(6 HAS INDIAN HEAD MASCOT, V-8 HAS BIRD.)

CHIEF OF VALUES

"6-402" OR "8-302"

6 CYL. OR V-8

251 C.I.D. V-8 (1 YEAR ONLY)

65 H.P. @ 3200 (6)

85 H.P. @ 3400 (V-8)

5.25 × 18 TIRES (6)
6.00 × 17 TIRES (V-8)

114" W.B. (6)
117" W.B. (V-8)

4.55 (6) OR 4.22 (8) GEAR RATIOS

(NO 6-CYLINDER PONTIACS FOR 1933 OR 1934)

33

MODEL "8-601"

(STRAIGHT-8)

223.4 C.I.D. (THROUGH 1935)

75 H.P. @ 3600 RPM

115" WHEELBASE
4.44 GEAR RATIO

5.50 × 17 TIRES ('33)

6.00 × 17 TIRES ('34)

34

(STRAIGHT-8)
"8-603"

84 H.P. @ 3600 RPM

117 1/4" W.B.
4.55 GEAR RATIO

PONTIAC

Silver Streak SIXES AND EIGHTS

8 HAS LEAPING FIGURE HOOD ORNAMENT; 6 HAS INDIAN HEAD IN CIRCLE.

(INTRODUCED DEC. 29, 1934)

STARTING 1935, 6 HAS 6.00 × 16 TIRES, 8 HAS 6.50 × 16

35

6 - CYL. MODEL AVAILABLE ONCE AGAIN. STRAIGHT-8 CONTINUED.

HYDRAULIC BRAKES

TAIL / STOP LIGHT ON LEFT SIDE OF TRUNK DOOR.

Pontiac's ridged Silver Streak and "V" windshield diffuse and deflect sun-glare.

1935 MODEL WAS FIRST TO USE FAMOUS "SILVER STREAK" BANDS OF CHROME ALONG CENTER OF HOOD (A PONTIAC TRADEMARK UNTIL MID-'50s.)

"6-701" OR "6-AB" (6) 112" W.B. 208 C.I.D.* 80 H.P. @ 3600*

"8-605" OR "8-AA" (8) 116 5/8" W.B. 84 H.P. @ 3800

* - THROUGH '36

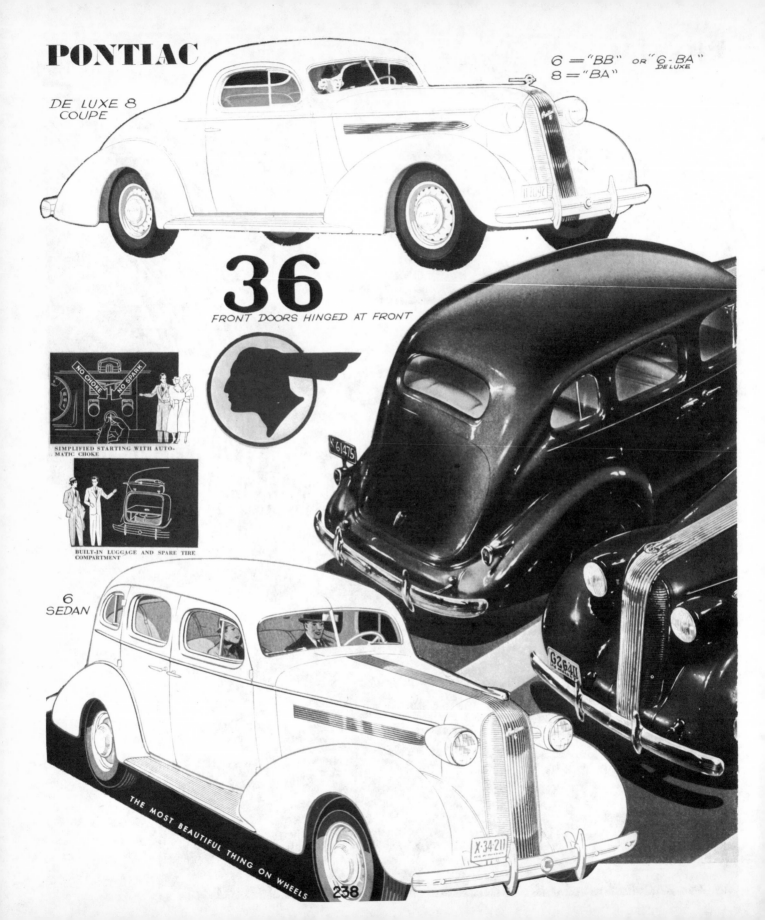

PONTIAC

DE LUXE 8
COUPE

6 = "BB" or "6-BA" DE LUXE
8 = "BA"

36
FRONT DOORS HINGED AT FRONT

SIMPLIFIED STARTING WITH AUTO-MATIC CHOKE

BUILT-IN LUGGAGE AND SPARE TIRE COMPARTMENT

6
SEDAN

THE MOST BEAUTIFUL THING ON WHEELS

238

PONTIAC

37

HIGH ORNAMENT →
8

FROM 1934 ON, "TOURING SEDANS" (2-DR. and 4-DR.) have EXTENDED TRUNK

INDIAN HEAD HOOD MASCOT IS HIGHER ON 8 THAN ON 6.

4.38 GEAR RATIO

"CA" 6 OR 8

117" (6) OR 122" (8) WHEELBASE (THROUGH '38)

FASTBACK STYLE (WITHOUT EXTENDED TRUNK)

LOW ORNAMENT ↘ 6

Front Compartment ↗

"6" OR "8" ON THIS MEDALLION.

6 and 8-CYL. PONTIAC CONVERTIBLE SEDANS AVAIL. IN 1937 and 1938.

8 HAS NEW 248.9 C.I.D. 99 H.P. @ 3800

6 HAS 222.7 C.I.D. (THROUGH 1940) and 85 H.P. @ 3520 RPM (THROUGH '39)

239

PONTIAC

38⁶

GENERAL MOTORS TERMS TO SUIT YOUR PURSE

| NEW SAFETY SHIFT GEAR CONTROL* | NEW SILVER STREAK BEAUTY | NEW ENGINE FEATURES | NEW SAFETY STYLED INTERIORS | NEW EASIER CLUTCH ACTION | NEW BATTERY LOCATION | NEW KNEE-ACTION FEATURES | IMPROVED CENTER-POINT STEERING | VENTILATED TRIPLE-SEALED HYDRAULIC BRAKES | MORE LUXURIOUS UNISTEEL BODIES | NEW INTERIOR ROOMINESS | NEW MORE POWERFUL GENERATOR |

8

8 HAS 100 H.P. @ 3700 RPM (THROUGH '40)

4.38 GEAR RATIO

* STEERING COLUMN GEARSHIFT OPTIONAL AT EXTRA COST

6 EA "QUALITY" 115" W.B.
6 EB "DE LUXE" 120" W.B.
8 EA "DE LUXE" 120" W.B.

4.1 (6) OR
4.3 (8) GEAR
RATIOS

39

RUNNING BOARDS OPTIONAL

PORTER
MODEL "45" ('20)

(1919 - 1922)
AMERICAN AND BRITISH MFG. CORP., BRIDGEPORT, CONN.

OWN 4-CYL.,
478.4 C.I.D. ENGINE
125 H.P.
12-VOLT ELECTRICAL SYS
3.0 GEAR RATIO
142"
WHEELBASE

MODEL "46"
(3.25 G.R.) ('21)

PREMIER
(1903 - 1925)
MOTOR CORP
INDIANAPOLIS···USA
THE ALUMINUM SIX WITH MAGNETIC
GEAR SHIFT

EASILY IDENTIFIED BY V-SHAPED
RADIATOR AND STREAMLINED
COWL
LAMPS.

EXHAUST (RT.) SIDE
OF PREMIER'S OWN
ALUMINUM ENGINE (295.3 C.I.D.,
THROUGH 1925)

CUTLER-HAMMER MAGNETIC GEARSHIFT
CONTROLLED FROM STEERING WHEEL

('20)
"6-D"
126 3/4"
WHEELBASE
(THROUGH
1925)

STARTING 1922, CLOCK
and SPEEDOMETER ARE
COMBINED, AND C-H
MAGNETIC GEARSHIFT
BECOMES OPTIONAL,
AT $200. EXTRA.

6 CYL.

('21)(6)

"6-D" 7-PASS.
CLOSED CAR

"NEW SERIES"
"D-24"
('24)

7-PASSENGER SED.

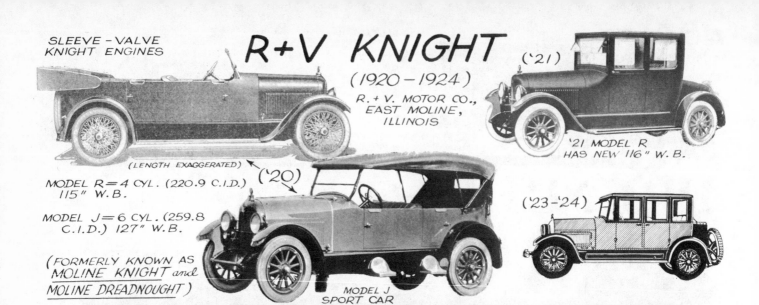

R+V KNIGHT

SLEEVE - VALVE
KNIGHT ENGINES

(1920 – 1924)

R. + V. MOTOR CO.,
EAST MOLINE,
ILLINOIS

('21)

'21 MODEL R
HAS NEW 116" W.B.

(LENGTH EXAGGERATED)

MODEL R = 4 CYL. (220.9 C.I.D.)
115" W.B.

MODEL J = 6 CYL. (259.8
C.I.D.) 127" W.B.

(FORMERLY KNOWN AS
MOLINE KNIGHT and
MOLINE DREADNOUGHT)

('20)

('23 –'24)

MODEL J
SPORT CAR

RAUCH + LANG ELECTRIC

(1905 – 1928)

BAKER, RAUCH and LANG,
CLEVELAND, OHIO (UNTIL '22)
CHICOPEE FALLS, MASS. (TO '28)

also known as
"R + L" OR
"RAULANG"

('21)
"C-55"

('20 MODEL
IS SIMILAR)

('24 –25)

6- CYLINDER
ENGINES
(THROUGH '30)

"THE GOLD STANDARD OF VALUES"

REO

2- WHEEL MECH. BRAKES (THROUGH '25)
4.66 G.R. (THROUGH '21)
33 × 4 TIRES
(THROUGH
'22)

(AUTOMOBILES = 1904 – 1936)

REO MOTOR CAR COMPANY, Lansing, Mich.

SEDAN AND
VICTORIA COUPE
HAVE SLANTING
WINDSHIELD.

20-21

"T-6" SERIES
6 CYL. F-HEAD ENGINE,
239.4 C.I.D., and
120" W. B. (THROUGH 1926)

NORTHEAST IGNITION (THROUGH '26)

REO22

"T-6" has 50 H.P. @ 2000 RPM, 33 × 4 TIRES

New 4-Passenger Coupe

"(B) T-6" and "U-6" MODELS LISTED DURING 1922.

4.7 G.R. (TO '26)

New Business Coupe

ALSO NEW: "LIGHT 7" SMALL 7-PASS. TOURING

"T-6" 23-24

33 × 4½ TIRES ALSO AVAILABLE IN 1924. (BALLOON TIRES OPTIONAL)

32 × 4

25

"T-6"

50 H.P. @ 2000 RPM (THROUGH '26)

32 × 6.20 BALLOON TIRES (THROUGH '26)

25½

Series G SEDAN

1-PC. WINDSHIELD, FULL-LENGTH BELT MOLDING

NEW ROOF-VISOR

50 H.P.

26

"T-6"

COUPE WITH WEDGE-SHAPED QUARTER WINDOWS AND DECORATIVE LANDAU IRONS

4-WHEEL MECHANICAL BRAKES

243

REO
FLYING CLOUD

SEDAN · VICTORIA
BROUGHAM
SPORT COUPE

27

SPORT COUPE

VICTORIA

NEW
"A"
SERIES

6 CYLS.   121" WHEELBASE
249 CUBIC IN. DISPLACEMENT
65 H.P. @ 2800 RPM
4.58 GEAR RATIO

HYDRAULIC BRAKES
(THROUGH '36)

30 x 6.20

27½

COACH
DASH

WOLVERINE

INTRO. MAY 5,
1927

FINAL
"1929"(Summer, '28)
MODELS HAVE MILITARY-
STYLE PILLARS,
CADET VISOR.

114" W.B.
4.45 G.R.

28

"FLYING CLOUD" has 6-CYL., 249 C.I.D.
OWN ENGINE   DELCO-REMY IGNITION
73 H.P. @ 2800 RPM   121" W.B.
4.58 and other GEAR RATIOS

FLYING CLOUD

WOLVERINE has
6-CYL.   28 x 5.25 and other TIRES
199 C.I.D.
CONTINENTAL "15-E" ENGINE
NORTHEAST IGNITION   50 H.P. @ 2400 RPM

30 x 6.20 TIRES

244

REO

MATE →

4.45 G.R., 30 × 6.00 TIRES (Mate)

"MATE" EASILY IDENTIFIED BY THIS UNIQUE CURVED MOLDING.

FLYING CLOUD "MATE"
(REPLACES "WOLVERINE" DECEMBER, 1928.)

"MATE" HAS MURRAY BODY, 115" W.B., 6-CYL., 214.7 C.I.D. CONTINENTAL "16-E" ENGINE 65 H.P. @ 2800 RPM new FUEL PUMP

29

1929 "FLYING CLOUD" RADIATOR, FITTED WITH OPTIONAL
ALLEN SHUTTERFRONT ↙

MASTER →

Delco-Remy IGNITION on both "MATE" and "MASTER" and on cars that follow.

121" W.B. OWN 6-CYL. 268.3 C.I.D. ENGINE (USED ON CERTAIN MODELS THROUGH '35) 80 H.P. @ 3200 RPM

1929 ("MASTER") REO ANNOUNCED MARCH, 1928!

"MASTER" RETAINS VACUUM TANK.

30 × 6.20 TIRES

FLYING CLOUD ("MASTER" AS OF DEC., 1928.)

MASTER "FLYING CLOUDS" have BUDD OR HAYES-IONA BODIES.

4.42 G.R.

30

"25" has 124" W.B., VACUUM TANK OWN 6-CYL., 268.3 C.I.D. ENGINE 80 H.P. @ 3200 RPM 4.42 G.R., 6.50 × 18 TIRES

"15" has 115" W.B. SAME 65-H.P. CONT. "16-E" ENG. AS '29 Mate 4.25 GEAR RATIO 6.00 × 18 TIRES (SAME TIRES ON "20") FUEL PUMP

MODEL "20" SPORT COUPE (SAME ENGINE as "25") 120" W.B., 4.07 G.R.

245

FLYING CLOUD 8

(6 ALSO) **REO**

6-CYL. "25-N" has 125" W.B., 268.3 C.I.D., 85 H.P. 4.42 G.R. 6.50 × 17 TIRES

FLYING CLOUD "8-21" CUSTOM SEDAN

(SOME FLYING CLOUDS HAVE ROYALE-STYLE AERODYNAMIC BODIES AND V-SHAPED GRILLES, BUT RETAIN EARLY '31 HOOD LOUVRES AS SHOWN ABOVE AND AT RIGHT.)

"8-21" SERIES CONT'D. INTO '32 (INSTRUMENT PANEL) (STD. MODEL HAS MESH V-GRILLE, PARK. LIGHTS ON FENDERS ONLY.)

1931½ "15" SERIES has 116" W.B., 4.27 G.R.

THE

Reo-Royale

EIGHT

1931 ROYALE 8 "N-35" (INTRODUCED OCTOBER, 1930.) has 135" W.B., STRAIGHT-8 357.8 C.I.D. ENG. 125 H.P. @ 3300 RPM (THROUGH '34) 4.07 G.R. 6.50 × 18 TIRES

31

ROYALE INTERIOR

ROYALE VICTORIA

"N-30" EIGHT has SAME ENGINE, TIRES, G.R. as "ROYALE," BUT has 130" W.B.

ROYALE CABRIOLET INTRODUCED APRIL, 1931.

STRAIGHT-8 REO ENGINES AVAILABLE 1931 THROUGH 1934.

REO

"6-21," "6-25" have
268.3 C.I.D., 85 H.P.
@ 3200 RPM, 4.07 G.R.
6.00 × 17 TIRES

"8-21," "8-25" have
268.6 C.I.D., 90 H.P.
@ 3300 RPM, 4.42 G.R.
6.00 × 17 TIRES

"8-31," "8-35" have
357.8 C.I.D., 125 H.P.
@ 3300 RPM, 4.07 G.R.
6.50 × 18 TIRES

FLYING CLOUD
MODEL "S"

32

(6 CYL "S" → HAS OUTSWEPT GRILLE)

REO FLYING CLOUD 8-25 COUPE

REO-ROYALE 8-35 SEDAN

REO-ROYALE 8-31 VICTORIA

1932 MODEL NUMBERS INDICATE NO. OF CYLINDERS, and WHEELBASE

1933 "S" has SAME ENGINE SPECS., SAME TIRE SIZE as '32 "6-21,"
but has 117½" W.B., 4.3 G.R. (STARTS 1-33, as "S-2;"
FREE-WHEELING.) ("8-131" ALSO STARTS 1-33.)

"8-131"
"ROYALE" 8 has SAME
ENGINE SPECS., SAME TIRE
SIZE as PREVIOUSLY. 131" W.B.
4.42 G.R. DELUXE MODELS
KNOWN as <u>ELITE</u> SERIES

* "<u>SELF-SHIFTER</u>"
AUTOMATIC TRANSMISSION
INTRODUCED BY
REO IN SPRING, 1933.
(AVAIL. FOR BOTH 6 and 8.)

AN AMAZING NEW INVENTION*

?

33

247

34 REO

"S-2" FOR '34 STARTS 8-33.

NO GEARSHIFT LEVER
33⅓ % easier to drive

2 LARGE, ROUND DASH INSTRUMENTS at CENTER

SIX (S-6) has 118" W.B., 268 C.I.D., 85 H.P. @ 3200 RPM, 4.3 G.R., 6.00 × 17 TIRES ("S-4" STARTS 12-33, HORIZONTAL LOUVRES.)

"ROYALE" 8 (N2-1) has SAME SPECS. as '33 MODEL; REO'S FINAL STRAIGHT-8.

131" W.B., but "CUSTOM" MODELS have 135" W.B.

MODELS ABOVE SERIAL NO. 5S-28677 START 7-34, CAN BE CONSIDERED "EARLY 1935."

35

NEW STREAMLINED MODELS START 2-35.

6 CYLINDER CARS ONLY; NO MORE CONVERTIBLES.

FLYING CLOUD "6-A" 228 C.I.D. 90 H.P. @ 3400 RPM 115" W.B.

REO SELF SHIFTER OPTIONAL IN 1935 REOS

DASH GAUGES MOVED TO LEFT.

("6-75") ROYALE "S-7" 268 C.I.D. 95 H.P. @ 3200 RPM 118" W.B. 6.50 × 16 TIRES BOTH SERIES have 4.3 G.R.

6.25 × 16 TIRES ON "FLYING CLOUD" (1935 and 1936)

COUPES AVAIL., BUT ONLY IN THE Royale '35 SERIES.

NO MORE COUPES, ONLY ONE REMAINING 1936 "FLYING CLOUD" SERIES

6 CYL. 228 C.I.D. 90 H.P. @ 3400

115" W.B. 4.27 G.R.

(STARTS 11-35)

36

248

AFTER 1936, REO TRUCKS ONLY.

4-CYL. DUESENBERG ENGINE (TO '23)

REVERE (1917-1926)

131" W.B. (THROUGH '26)

('20) MODEL "C"

32 × 4½ TIRES ON "C" and "M" SERIES

"M" SERIES ('24-'26) has 4-CYL., 360.8 C.I.D. MONSEN/REVERE O.H.V. ENG., 2-WHEEL BRAKES

"25" SERIES ('25-'26) has 6-CYL., 331.4 C.I.D. CONT'L. "6-J" 70-H.P. ENG., and 4-WHEEL BRAKES (32 × 6.20 BALLOON TIRES)   BOSCH IGNITION (ALL MODELS)

RICHELIEU (1922-1923)

(NOTE SIMILARITY TO REVERE CAR, ABOVE LEFT. RICHELIEU DESIGNED BY N. VAN ZANDT, FORMERLY WITH REVERE.)

RICHELIEU MOTOR CAR CORP., ASBURY PARK, N.J.

4-CYLINDER ROCHESTER-DUESENBERG 340.4 C.I.D. ENGINE

78 H.P. @ 2500 RPM   EISEMANN IGNITION

131" W.B. 32 × 4½ TIRES 2-WHEEL BRAKES

Rickenbacker

A · CAR · WORTHY · OF · ITS · NAME

Rickenbacker Motor Company
Detroit   Michigan

(FLYWHEEL AT EACH END OF CRANKSHAFT.)

(1922-1927)

('23) "HAT-IN RING" EMBLEM

'22 has 6-CYL., 218 C.I.D. ENGINE, 58 H.P. @ 2800 RPM, 4.63 G.R., 32 × 4 TIRES, 4-WHEEL BRAKES, 117" W.B.

IGNITION: AUTO LITE ('22) ATW. KENT ('23) BOSCH ('24-'27) DELCO ('25-27)

The only 4-door Coach-Brougham on the American Market

('23)

('25)

32 × 4

6-CYL. ONLY (THROUGH '24)

AM. BOSCH (6-70) OR DELCO-REMY ('27) IGNITION

('25) 117"-WB "E-6" OR 121½"-WB "B-8" IN '26

"D" = 6 CYL., 236.4 CID 70 HP @ 3000 "8" = STRAIGHT-8 268.6 CID BOTH HAVE 70 HP @ 3000, 117" WB

'27 SPECS.
"6-70" = 118½"WB 236.4 CID 70 HP @ 3000
"8-80" = 119½"WB 268.5 CID 80 HP @ 3000
"8-90" = 136"WB, 315.2 CID, 95 HP @ 3000

ROAMER (1916-1930)

BARLEY MOTOR CAR CO., KALAMAZOO, MICH.

4-CYL. ROCH.-DUES. ENG. ALSO

128"-WB "6-54" ('20)

6-CYLINDER, 303.1 CID CONT'L. ENGINE

('22) "6-54"

LYCOMING STRAIGHT-8 ENGINES

('27)

4-PASS. CLUB SEDAN "8-78" (120"-WB) "8-88" (136"-WB)

"65" (110" W.B.)
189.9 C.I.D., 65 H.P. @ 3200 RPM
4.27 G.R.

"75" (114" W.B.)
205.3 C.I.D., 72 H.P. @ 3200 RPM
4.73 G.R.

(AUTO-LITE IGN. ON ALL)

ROCKNE 6
(1932-1933)
BY
(STUDEBAKER)

5.25 × 18 TIRES (5.50 ON "75")

('32)

"6-10" IS 1933 MODEL.

SPECS. AS '32 "65,"
BUT H.P. UP TO
70 @ 3200

ROLLIN
(LATE '23 TO 1925)

ROLLIN MOTORS CO.,
CLEVELAND, OHIO

IGNITION = O.D. ('24) CONNECT. ('25)

31 × 5.20 TIRES   4-WHEEL BRKS.

COUPE DETAILS
('24)

W.B. = 112"   5.1 G.R.,
149.3 C.I.D., 41 H.P. @ 2750 RPM (THROUGH '25)

('25)

6 CYL. ALSO

60 M.P.H.

'25 BELT MOLDING
RUNS FULL LENGTH OF CAR.

ROLLS-ROYCE

BEST CAR IN THE WORLD

6 CYL., 453 C.I.D.,
143½" W.B. ('25)

('23)

BUILT
IN
ENGLAND
SINCE 1904.

AMERICAN
FACTORY AT
SPRINGFIELD, MASS.
(1920-1931)

144¾" W.B.

('30)

"PHANTOM"
MODEL

'25 HAS
80 H.P. @
1800 R.P.M.,
3.25 GEAR RATIO
73 M.P.H.
SPEED

"SILVER GHOST"
MODEL

("SILVER GHOST"
SUPERSEDED 1927
BY "PHANTOM")

7.00 × 20

THIS
1931 MODEL
"DERBY (BREWSTER)
SPEEDSTER" PHAETON
IS THE
FINAL AMERICAN-BUILT
ROLLS-ROYCE.

6 CYLINDERS (468 C.I.D.)
OVERHEAD VALVES (SINCE '29)
100 H.P. @ 2250 RPM

146½" WHEELBASE
3.72 GEAR RATIO
De JON IGNITION

Roosevelt

MARMON-BUILT

A CAR FOR ALL

(1929-1930*)

(INTRODUCED MARCH, 1929)

NAMED FOR THEODORE ROOSEVELT, PRESIDENT OF U.S.A. FROM 1901 TO 1909.

DELCO-REMY IGN.

STRAIGHT 8 engine.

201.9 C.I.D.
77 H.P. @ 3400
5.50 × 19 TIRES
4.9 GEAR RATIO

* = LISTED AS MARMON, '30-'31

RUGBY (1927)

BUILT BY DURANT, PRIMARILY FOR EXPORT. COMPARABLE TO STAR.

NOTE THE RIGHT-HAND DRIVE

RUXTON (1929-1931)

(NEW ERA MOTORS, N.Y.C. "IN COOPERATION WITH" MOON and KISSEL.)

PHAETON, FITTED WITH TYPICAL "WOOD-LITES"

RAINBOW-COLORED BANDS OF PAINT

FRONT-WHEEL-DRIVE STRAIGHT-8 CONTINENTAL ENGINE (268.6 C.I.D. "18-S" with 100 H.P. @ 3400 RPM)
130" or 140" W.B.   4.4 G.R.
SEDAN has BUDD BODY
RDSTR." BAKER RAULANG BODY
PHAETON" KISSEL BODY
CUSTOM MODELS ALSO

SEDAN, FITTED WITH CONVENTIONAL-STYLE HEADLIGHTS

6.00 × 19 TIRES
HYDRAULIC BRAKES
Auto-Lite IGNITION

SAXON (1913-1923)

SAXON MOTOR CAR CO., DETROIT, MICH. and YPSILANTI, MICH.

(6 CYLS. IN 1920)

FOR 1922, 178.9 C.I.D., O.H.V. 4-CYL. ROOT and VAN. ENG. REPLACED BY 192.3 C.I.D. GRAY ENGINE.
WAGNER IGNITION

SAXON-DUPLEX 4 CYL. "BLACKSTONE" (5-PASS.) →

('21-23) "125" SERIES

32 × 4 TIRES

4.75 G.R.

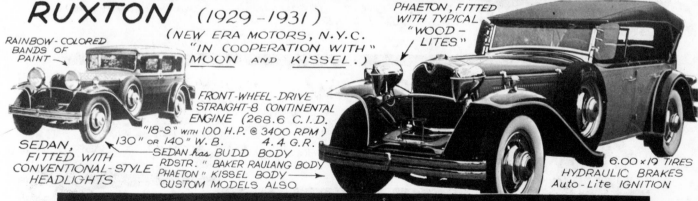

SAYERS 6 (1917-1924)

DELCO IGNITION
STROMBERG
CARB. ('21)

(SAYERS and SCOVILL CO., CINCINNATI, OHIO)

FOR 1924, NAME CHANGED TO

S. + S. (1924 - 1930)

new 136" W.B. (TO '27)
new 33 × 5 TIRES (THROUGH '25)

('24)

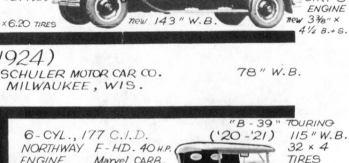

S + S "BRIGHTON" 8 PASS. (6 CYL.)
new 331.4 C.I.D. CONT'L. 6-CYL. "6-J" ENG. (TO '27)

"AVONDALE" 5-PASS.

118" W.B. (THROUGH '23)
6-CYL. 224 C.I.D. CONTINENTAL
ENGINE (THROUGH '22)
241.6 C.I.D. IN '23

'25 and '26 "ELMWOOD" SIMILAR TO '24, BUT HAS OVAL REAR QTR. WINDOWS, LANDAU IRONS (34 × 7.30 TIRES IN '26)

MILITARY CADET VISOR and BOWL HEADLIGHTS FOR 1929

('29)

"42" SUPERLINE 8-PASS. "LAKEWOOD" SEDAN

STR.-8 ENGINE
new 3⅜" × 4½ B.+S.

FOR '28, "Washington 8" S.+S. HEARSE has 141" W.B., STR.-8
ENG. (3" × 4¾" B.+S.) ROOF-VISOR, DRUM ILCO-RYAN LITES, 33 × 6.20 TIRES

new 143" W.B.

7.00 × 20

SCHULER (1924)

(2 CYL.)

SCHULER MOTOR CAR CO. MILWAUKEE, WIS.

78" W.B.

6-CYL., 177 C.I.D. NORTHWAY F-HD. 40 H.P. ENGINE   Marvel CARB.
4.5 G.R. CHANGED TO 4.87 FOR '21.
SINCE '19, CHASSIS SIMILAR TO OAKLAND.

"B-39" TOURING ('20-'21) 115" W.B. 32 × 4 TIRES

SCRIPPS-BOOTH (1913-1922)

SCRIPPS-BOOTH CO., DETROIT

(BECAME A G.M. PRODUCT IN 1918.)

SEVERIN 6 (1920-1922)

('20)

SEVERIN MOTOR CAR CO., KANSAS CITY, MO.

122" W.B., 6-CYL. CONTINENTAL
303.1 C.I.D. ENGINE

33 × 5 TIRES (33 × 4 ON LOWEST-PRICED MODELS.)

TOURING-SPORTSTER

SHAW (1920 - 1921)

('21)
V-12

WALDEN W. SHAW LIVERY CO., CHICAGO
(FORMERLY BUILT TAXIS)

WEIDELY V-12 ENGINE REPLACED 4-CYL. ROCHESTER-DUESENBERG ENGINE, 1921.
LATER BECAME "AMBASSADOR."

A PROJECT BEGUN UNDER G.M., SHERIDAN WAS ACQUIRED BY WM. C. DURANT WHEN HE LEFT G.M., AND IT EVOLVED DURING '21 INTO THE 4-CYL. and 6-CYL. DURANT CARS.

SHERIDAN

SHERIDAN MOTOR CAR CO., MUNCIE, IND.
(1920-1921)

116 or 132" W.B., 4-CYL. OR V-8 NORTHWAY ENGINES

4 CYL. "B-41" 35 H.P.

B 41   4 CYL.

33 × 4

33 × 4 OR 33 × 5 TIRES

252

SINGER MOTOR CO., INC.,
MT. VERNON, N.Y.

SINGER
(1915 – 1920)
3.77 GEAR RATIO   33 × 5 TIRES

('20)
V-12
389.5 C.I.D.
WEIDELY
ENGINE
138" W.B.

(REPLACED THE PALMER-SINGER CAR)

ROADSTER ALSO AVAIL.

"35" SERIES ('21)

CONNECTICUT IGN. CARTER CARB.

SKELTON 4
SKELTON MOTOR CAR CO., ST. LOUIS, MO.
(1920 – 1922)
112" W.B.   192.4 C.I.D., L-HEAD LYCOMING ENGINE
32 × 3½ TIRES

4-CYLINDER

STANDARD EIGHT

STANDARD STEEL CAR COMPANY
Automotive Dept.   *Pittsburgh, Pa*

(1912 – 1923)

(V-8)
OWN L-HEAD, 331.8 C.I.D. ENGINE (THROUGH '23)

('20)

127" W.B.
4.45 G.R.
ZENITH CARB and
34 × 4½ TIRES
(THROUGH '23)

SPLITDORF IGNITION REPLACES CONNECTICUT FOR '22 and '23.

('22)

STANLEY
STEAM CAR
(1897 – 1927)
MANUFACTURER, IN 1924, CHANGED NAME FROM STANLEY MOTOR CARRIAGE CO. TO STANLEY VEHICLE CORP. OF AMERICA NEWTON, MASS.

130" W.B.

('21)

32 × 4½ TIRES
1.50 GEAR RATIO ON '23 "740" SERIES;
32 × 5.77 TIRES, 122" W.B. and HYDRAULIC BRAKES ON FINAL "252" SERIES

34 × 4½ TIRES ('21)

2 CYL. STEAM ENGINE (4" × 5" CYLINDERS)

(1920 – 1922)
STANWOOD MOTOR CAR CO., ST. LOUIS, MO.

STANWOOD 6
6-CYLINDER CONTINENTAL ENGINE
224 C.I.D.

"A" TOURING CAR
118" W.B.
ATW. KENT IGN.
STROMBERG CARB.
33 × 4 TIRES   4.5 G.R.

('21)

253

Low-cost Transportation
Star ⬟ Cars

DURANT MOTORS, Inc., NEW YORK CITY

(SHOWN WITH WM. C. DURANT, FOUNDER OF DURANT MOTORS)

22-23

(STARTS 6-22)

30 x 3½ TIRES

102" W.B. and 4-CYLINDER CONTINENTAL 130.4 C.I.D. ENGINE (THROUGH '25)

WAGON ('23)

FOUR GREAT PLANTS AT ELIZABETH, N.J. o LANSING, MICH. o OAKLAND, CAL. o TORONTO, ONT.

24

For Your All-Weather Car
Get a Sedan STAR

"SPECIAL" MODELS HAVE NICKEL TRIM and OPTIONAL DISC WHEELS.

Low-cost Transportation
Star ★ Cars

25

(LEFT SIDE)
ENGINE
(RIGHT SIDE)

The Coupster
TRADE MARK

"4-M" (158 C.I.D.) 103" W.B.
30 H.P. @ 2200 RPM
"6-R" (169.2 C.I.D.) 107" W.B.
40 H.P. @ 2400 RPM

IMPROVED 4

26-27

NEW 6-CYL. MODEL

('27 HAS BOWL-
SHAPED LAMPS.)

CABRIOLET

COUPE
(6 CYL.)

1928 MODEL KNOWN TEMPORARILY AS
"DURANT-STAR," LATER AS DURANT 4.

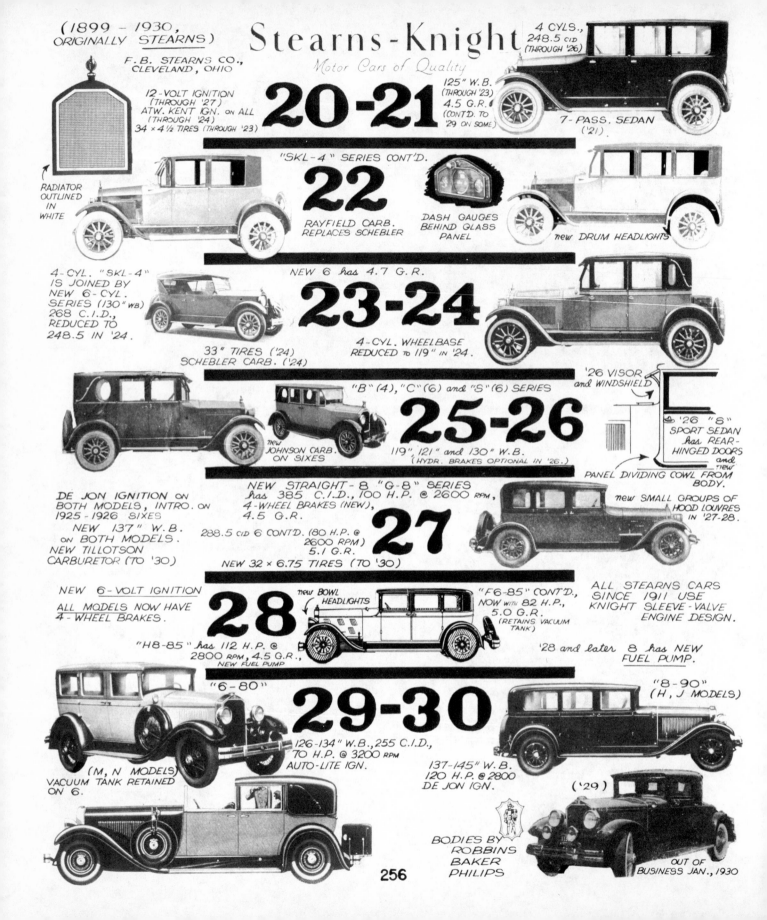

(1899 – 1930, ORIGINALLY STEARNS)

F.B. STEARNS CO., CLEVELAND, OHIO

Stearns-Knight
Motor Cars of Quality

4 CYLS., 248.5 CID (THROUGH '26)

12-VOLT IGNITION (THROUGH '27) ATW. KENT IGN. ON ALL (THROUGH '24) 34 × 4½ TIRES (THROUGH '23)

20-21

125" W.B. (THROUGH '23) 4.5 G.R. (CONT'D. TO '29 ON SOME)

7-PASS. SEDAN ('21).

RADIATOR OUTLINED IN WHITE

"SKL-4" SERIES CONT'D.

22

RAYFIELD CARB. REPLACES SCHEBLER

DASH GAUGES BEHIND GLASS PANEL

new DRUM HEADLIGHTS

4-CYL. "SKL-4" IS JOINED BY NEW 6-CYL. SERIES (130" WB) 268 C.I.D., REDUCED TO 248.5 IN '24.

NEW 6 has 4.7 G.R.

23-24

33" TIRES ('24) SCHEBLER CARB. ('24)

4-CYL. WHEELBASE REDUCED TO 119" IN '24.

'26 VISOR and WINDSHIELD

"B" (4), "C" (6) and "S" (6) SERIES

25-26

new JOHNSON CARB. ON SIXES

119", 121" and 130" W.B. (HYDR. BRAKES OPTIONAL IN '26.)

'26 "S" SPORT SEDAN has REAR-HINGED DOORS and new PANEL DIVIDING COWL FROM BODY.

DE JON IGNITION ON BOTH MODELS, INTRO. ON 1925-1926 SIXES

NEW 137" W.B. ON BOTH MODELS. NEW TILLOTSON CARBURETOR (TO '30)

NEW STRAIGHT-8 "G-8" SERIES has 385 C.I.D., 100 H.P. @ 2600 RPM, 4-WHEEL BRAKES (NEW), 4.5 G.R.

288.5 CID 6 CONT'D. (80 H.P. @ 2600 RPM) 5.1 G.R.

NEW 32 × 6.75 TIRES (TO '30)

27

new SMALL GROUPS OF HOOD LOUVRES IN '27-28.

NEW 6-VOLT IGNITION ALL MODELS NOW HAVE 4-WHEEL BRAKES.

28

new BOWL HEADLIGHTS

"F6-85" CONT'D. NOW with 82 H.P., 5.0 G.R. (RETAINS VACUUM TANK)

"H8-85" has 112 H.P. @ 2800 RPM, 4.5 G.R. NEW FUEL PUMP

ALL STEARNS CARS SINCE 1911 USE KNIGHT SLEEVE-VALVE ENGINE DESIGN.

'28 and later 8 has NEW FUEL PUMP.

"6-80"

29-30

126-134" W.B., 255 C.I.D., 70 H.P. @ 3200 RPM AUTO-LITE IGN.

"8-90" (H, J MODELS)

(M, N MODELS) VACUUM TANK RETAINED ON 6.

137-145" W.B. 120 H.P. @ 2800 DE JON IGN.

('29)

BODIES BY ROBBINS BAKER PHILIPS

OUT OF BUSINESS JAN., 1930

256

STEPHENS *Salient Six*

STEPHENS MOTOR WORKS *of Moline Plow Company* · Freeport, Illinois
(1916-1924)

Salient
"That which is strikingly manifest or catches the attention at once."
—Webster

17-22

6 CYL.
O.H.V.
224 C.I.D.
ENGINE
(THROUGH '24)

122" W.B.
(THROUGH '22)

('20)

('21) CONNECTICUT IGNITION REPLACES Auto-Lite.

33 × 4½ TIRES
(THROUGH '24,
EXC. '23-24 117"
W.B. MODELS,
('22)

WITH Artcraft Top

57 H.P. IN 1922

STEPHENS

NO MAJOR CHANGES BETWEEN 1917 AND 1922.

23-24

'23 RESTYLED, with MODERN "LIGHTNING" INSIGNIA.

STEPHENS

FOR '23, DELCO IGN. REPLACES CONNECTICUT IGN., and STROMBERG CARB. REPLACES TILLOTSON.

32 × 4 TIRES, 4.66, 5.1 G.R. ON 117"-W.B. "10."

NEW 117" and 124" W.B. "10," "20" models

STERLING - KNIGHT 6

6-CYL., 230.2 C.I.D. SLEEVE-VALVE ENGINE

B-6   125" W.B.

(1923-1925)
STERLING-KNIGHT MOTORS CO.,
CLEVELAND and
WARREN, OHIO

56 H.P. @2400 RPM and 5.09 G.R. ('25)

WESTINGHOUSE IGN.
32 × 4½ TIRES

STROMBERG CARB.
4.66 G.R. (TO '24)

STEVENS-DURYEA

138" W.B. (TO '27)

('21)

"E-6"
6-PASS.
3.94 G.R. (TO '24)

(1902-1927)
STEVENS-DURYEA (MOTORS) CO.
CHICOPEE FALLS, MASS.
6-CYL., 510.4 CID, L-HEAD ENGINE (TO '27)

VESTIBULE LIMO.

35 × 5

('22)

35 × 5

BOSCH IGNITION REPLACES BERLING IGNITION (AFTER '24)

90 H.P. @ 2000 RPM

33 × 5 TIRES ('23 ON)

STOUT "SCARAB" (1934-1939)

WM. B. STOUT ENGINEERING CO.,
DEARBORN, MICH.

FORD V-8 ENGINE (AT REAR)

('35-'36)

257

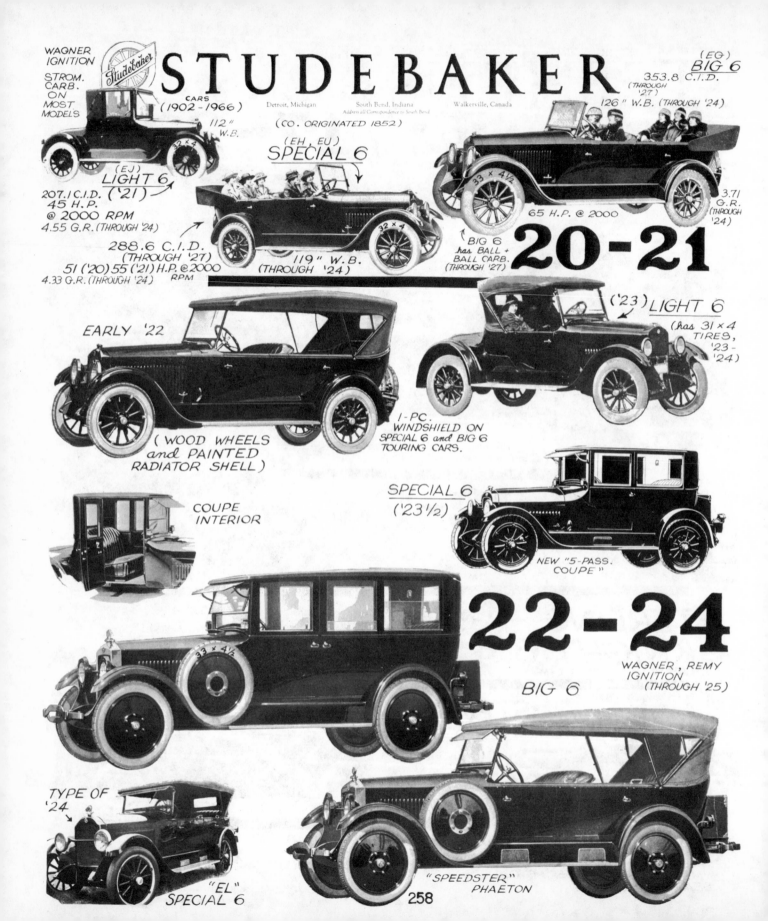

STUDEBAKER

WAGNER
IGNITION

STROM.
CARB.
ON
MOST
MODELS

CARS
(1902 - 1966)

Detroit, Michigan

South Bend, Indiana
Address all Correspondence to South Bend

Walkerville, Canada

(CO. ORIGINATED 1852)

(EG) BIG 6
353.8 C.I.D.
(THROUGH '27)
126" W.B. (THROUGH '24)

112" W.B.

(EH, EU)
SPECIAL 6

(EJ)
LIGHT 6 ('21)
207.1 C.I.D.
45 H.P.
@ 2000 RPM
4.55 G.R. (THROUGH '24)

288.6 C.I.D.
(THROUGH '27)
51 ('20) 55 ('21) H.P. @ 2000 RPM
4.33 G.R. (THROUGH '24)

119" W.B.
(THROUGH '24)

BIG 6
has BALL +
BALL CARB.
(THROUGH '27)

65 H.P. @ 2000

3.71
G.R.
(THROUGH
'24)

20-21

EARLY '22

('23) LIGHT 6
(has 31 x 4
TIRES,
'23 -
'24)

(WOOD WHEELS
and PAINTED
RADIATOR SHELL)

1-PC.
WINDSHIELD ON
SPECIAL 6 and BIG 6
TOURING CARS.

COUPE
INTERIOR

SPECIAL 6
('23½)

NEW "5-PASS.
COUPE"

22-24

WAGNER, REMY
IGNITION
(THROUGH '25)

BIG 6

TYPE OF
'24

"EL"
SPECIAL 6

"SPEEDSTER"
PHAETON

258

STUDEBAKER

new STANDARD 6
has 241.6 C.I.D.,
50 H.P. @ 2200 RPM
(TO '28) new 113" W.B. (THROUGH '29 "DICTATOR")
new 4.18 G.R.

(STD. 6 REPLACES LIGHT 6)

STD. 6 "DUPLEX" →

25

COMPLETELY
RESTYLED

(INTRO. FALL, '24)

31 × 5.25

← STANDARD 6
FRONT VIEW

new *Duplex*

OPEN MODELS WITH
RIGID, STEEL-REINFORCED
TOPS.

("DUPLEX" MODELS AVAIL. THROUGH '27.
1928 "DICTATOR" SERIES INCLUDES
"DUPLEX" PHAETON.)

2-WHEEL MECHANICAL
BRAKES ON ALL 3
SERIES, with 4-WH.
HYDRAULIC BRAKES
OPTIONAL
(THROUGH '26)

STD. 6

"DUPLEX"
ROADSTER,
WITH DETAILS OF
PULL-DOWN
CURTAINS

SPECIAL 6 "DUPLEX" →

WITH CURTAINS
OPEN →

SPECIAL 6
has new 4.36 G.R. (THROUGH '27)
65 H.P. @ 2400 RPM
(THROUGH '27)
32 × 6.20 TIRES (THROUGH '26)
120" W.B. (THROUGH '28,'30
"COMMANDER")

WITH
SIDE CURTAINS CLOSED

SPECIAL 6 CONTINUES ITS UNIQUE
FLUTED RADIATOR SHELL

BIG 6
"5-PASS.
COUPE"
(COACH-STYLE,
UNLIKE
STUDEBAKER
4-PASS.
VICTORIA CPES.
WHICH HAVE
REAR DECK.)

BIG 6
has 75 H.P. @ 2400 RPM (THROUGH '27)
34 × 7.30 TIRES (THROUGH '26)
127" W.B. (THROUGH '27)   4.36 G.R.

259

STUDEBAKER

25 ½

STANDARD 6 "DUPLEX"

STANDARD 6 BROUGHAM

BIG 6

BROUGHAM

A NEW, CAPPED VISOR IDENTIFIES THESE TRANSITIONAL MODELS OF SPRING, 1925.

31 × 5.25 TIRES CONT'D. ON STD. 6 (THROUGH '27)

COUPE TOP

LE BARON "PRINCE OF WALES" SEDAN

(ONE OF A GROUP OF NEW CUSTOM-BODY TYPES.)

26

STD. 6 (NEW RADIATOR DESIGN and PAINT, 6-25)

NEW FRENCH-STYLE ROOF-VISOR (TO EARLY '28)

KEYS SOMETIMES PRESENTED IN GIFT-STYLE BOX, DURING 1920s.

DELCO-REMY IGNITION ON ALL MODELS (THROUGH '33)

BIG SIX SEDAN

(new 32 × 6.20 TIRES AVAIL.)

STD. 6 and BIG 6 have 4-WH. MECH. BRAKES. (SPEC. 6 has 2-WH. MECH. BRAKES with 4-WH. HYDRAULICS OPTIONAL.

STD. 6

BIG 6

27

FINAL YEAR FOR VACUUM-TANK FUEL FEED.

32 × 6.75

PRESIDENT IS A DELUXE SEDAN IN '27 BIG 6 LINE, REPLACES BIG 6 WITH NEW LINE FOR '28.

260

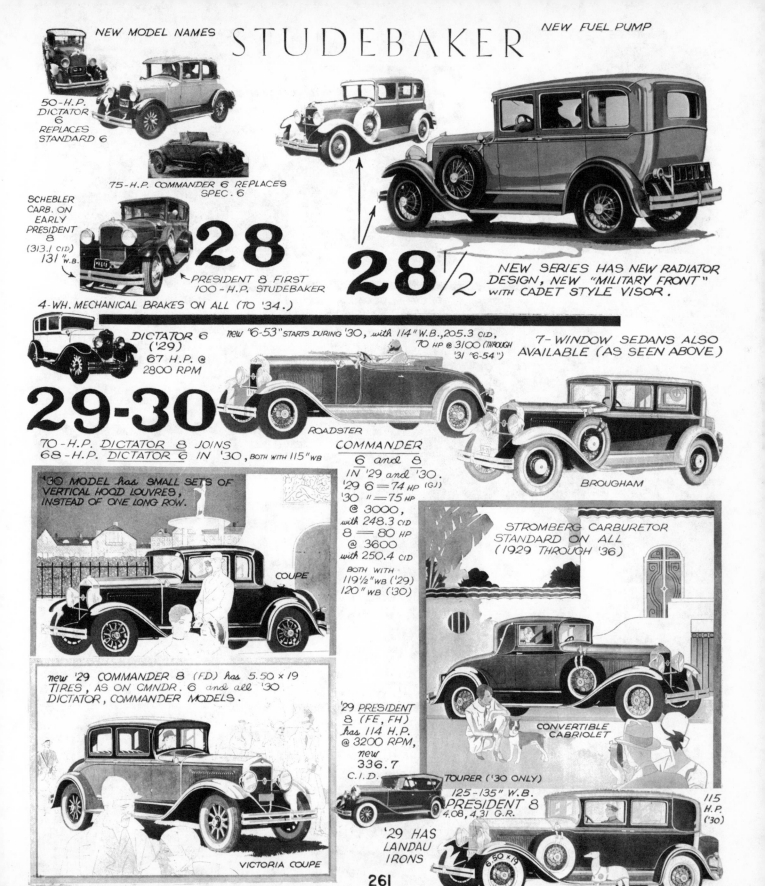

NEW MODEL NAMES

STUDEBAKER

NEW FUEL PUMP

50-H.P. DICTATOR 6 REPLACES STANDARD 6

75-H.P. COMMANDER 6 REPLACES SPEC. 6

SCHEBLER CARB. ON EARLY PRESIDENT 8 (313.1 CID) 131" W.B.

28

PRESIDENT 8 FIRST 100-H.P. STUDEBAKER

28½

NEW SERIES HAS NEW RADIATOR DESIGN, NEW "MILITARY FRONT" WITH CADET STYLE VISOR.

4-WH. MECHANICAL BRAKES ON ALL (TO '34.)

DICTATOR 6 ('29) 67 H.P. @ 2800 RPM

new "6-53" starts during '30, with 114" W.B., 205.3 CID, 70 HP @ 3100 (THROUGH '31 "6-54")

7-WINDOW SEDANS ALSO AVAILABLE (AS SEEN ABOVE)

29-30

70-H.P. DICTATOR 8 JOINS 68-H.P. DICTATOR 6 IN '30, BOTH WITH 115"WB

ROADSTER

COMMANDER 6 and 8 IN '29 and '30. '29 6 = 74 HP (GJ) '30 " = 75 HP @ 3000, with 248.3 CID 8 = 80 HP @ 3600 with 250.4 CID BOTH WITH 119½"WB ('29) 120"WB ('30)

BROUGHAM

'30 MODEL has SMALL SETS of VERTICAL HOOD LOUVRES, INSTEAD OF ONE LONG ROW.

COUPE

STROMBERG CARBURETOR STANDARD ON ALL (1929 THROUGH '36)

new '29 COMMANDER 8 (FD) has 5.50 x 19 TIRES, AS ON CMNDR. 6 and all '30 DICTATOR, COMMANDER MODELS.

'29 PRESIDENT 8 (FE, FH) has 114 H.P. @ 3200 RPM, new 336.7 C.I.D.

CONVERTIBLE CABRIOLET

TOURER ('30 ONLY)

125-135" W.B. PRESIDENT 8 4.08, 4.31 G.R.

115 H.P. ('30)

'29 HAS LANDAU IRONS

6.50 x 19

VICTORIA COUPE

261

STUDEBAKER

31

6 (6-54)

205.3 C.I.D. SIX (114" W.B.) HAS 70 H.P. @ 3200

114"-W.B. DICTATOR IS 8 ONLY, IN '31.

new = "FREE WHEELING" (AVAIL. TO '35)

1931 MODELS HAVE NEW GRILLE, "OVALOID" HEAD-LIGHTS

ROLL-UP WINDOWS

COMMANDER 8 BROUGHAM 124" W.B.

101 H.P.

PRESIDENT 8 CONVERTIBLE RDSTR.

122 H.P. @ 3200 RPM (THROUGH '32)

32

1932 MODELS : SIX DICTATOR 8 (62) COMMANDER 8 (71) PRESIDENT 8 (91)

NEW CIRCULAR GAUGES IN OVAL PANEL (REPLACE FORMER UPRIGHT-RECTANGULAR GAUGES IN HORIZONTAL RECTANG. PANEL.

new ST. REGIS COUPE

'32 6 (6-55) has 117" W.B. (THROUGH '33) 230 C.I.D. (THROUGH '33) 80 H.P. @ 3200 RPM

DICT. 8 has 117" W.B. 81-85 H.P. @ 3200 (221 CID AS IN '31)

CMDR. 8 has new 125" WB BUT 101 HP @ 3200 and 250.4 CID AS BEFORE.

Studebaker Free Wheeling is controlled by a touch of a lever on the dash. There is no necessity for keeping your foot constantly on a button.

To start the Triumphant New Studebakers you simply switch on the ignition with a key. The engine instantly responds —and ever should it stall at any time, it automatically starts again.

PRES. 8 has 135" WB 4.31 G.R.

'32 tire sizes = 5.50 × 18 (6 and DICT. 8)   6.00 × 18 (CMNDR. 8)   6.50 × 18 (PRES. 8)

33

MODELS : SIX, COMMANDER 8, (117" WB) PRESIDENT 8 and SPEEDWAY PRESIDENT 8 (125", 135" WB)

110-H.P. PRES. 8 (82) USES 250.4 CID STR.-8 ENGINE FORMERLY IN '32 CMNDR.

6 (56) has 85 HP @ 3200 RPM

CMR. 8 (73) has 236 CID, 100 HP @ 3800 RPM

"DICTATOR" MODEL SUSPENDED, RESUMED '34.

SPDWY. PRES. 8 (92) IS FINAL USER OF THE 336.7 CID STR. 8 (132 HP @ 3400)

17" WHEELS ('33-'34)

117, 117, 125, 135" WHEELBASES, AS IN 1932.

STUDEBAKER

34

CMNDR. 8 has 221 CID, 103 HP @ 4000 RPM 119" WB

SEDAN REAR

BENDIX POWER BRAKES
(MECH. BRAKES ON DICTATOR 6)

'34 DICT. 6 has 205.3 CID (THROUGH '35) 87 H.P. @ 3600 RPM 113" W.B. 4.55 G.R.

new STREAMLINED "LAND CRUISER" REAR ('34)

NARROW GRILLE FOR 1935

PRESIDENT LAND CRUISER ('35)

35

88-H.P. DICTATOR new 6 114" WB

HYDRAULIC BRAKES (ALL)

120"-W.B. CMNDR. 8 has 107 HP @ 3800 RPM

"REGAL" has FENDERWELLS

DICTATOR 6

new 116" WB (THROUGH '37)

6.00 x 16

217.8 CID, 90 HP @ 3400 (THROUGH '40 CMNDR.)

(4.55 G.R. BECOMES STANDARD ON ALL.)

PRESIDENT 8

new 125" WB (THROUGH '37) 250.4 CID ('33 THROUGH '42) 115 H.P. @ 3600 (THROUGH '37)

36

6.50 x 16

'36-'37 COUPE REAR WINDOW.

STATE PRESIDENT 8

37

DICTATOR 6 USES CARTER CARB. DURING 1937.

new 1-PIECE HOOD is HINGED AT BACK. VENT PANES IN FRONT DOORS. EMERGENCY BRAKE LEVER HUNG AT LEFT.

COMMANDER 6
8-A

2-PIECE REAR WINDOW →

STUDEBAKER
DRIVE IT AND YOU'LL BUY IT!

PRESIDENT
4-C 8

FIRST COMMANDER SINCE '35 "8"

"DICTATOR"
MODEL NAME
ABANDONED, IN FAVOR
OF "7-A" SIX
(SAME SPECS. AS CMNDR.)

38

INTERIOR

STATE
PRESIDENT 8
CLUB
SEDAN

NOTE FENDER PARKING LIGHTS

(OPTIONAL)
"MIRACLE SHIFT"
BELOW DASH

STROMBERG CARB. ON ALL '38s, AND ON '39s EXCEPT CHAMPION

COMMANDER 6 (9-A)
226.2 C.I.D., 90 H.P.
@ 3400 RPM, 116½" W.B.
(SINCE '38)
6.00 × 16 TIRES (SINCE '38)

AUTO-LITE IGN.
ON SIXES,
DELCO-REMY IGN.
ON EIGHTS
(SINCE '33)

CHAMPION →

PRES. INTERIOR

EXCLUSIVE! REVOLUTIONARY!
Studebaker's new Central
CLIMATIZER

PRESIDENT 8 (5-C)
250.4 C.I.D. ENGINE
(INTRO. '29 IN CMNDR.)
110 H.P. @ 3600 RPM
(SINCE '33)
122" W.B.
(SINCE '38)
6.50 ×16 TIRES
(SINCE '36)

39

CHAMPION 6 (G)
(NEW)

110" WB

164.3
C.I.D.
78
H.P.

PRESIDENT 8
(COMMANDER 6 SIMILAR)

DASH
(CHAMPION)

264

5.50 × 16
TIRES

"CHAMPION" INTRODUCED
THURS., APRIL 20, 1939.
(CARTER CARB.)

19-20

THE CAR THAT MADE
STUTZ
GOOD IN A DAY

(1912 - 1934)

STUTZ MOTOR CAR CO. OF AMERICA, INC., Indianapolis, U.S.A.

130" WHEELBASE
(4-CYL. MODELS
and '25 "6 95")

STROMBERG
CARB. (THROUGH
'25)

PRESSURE
FUEL FEED (ON
4-CYL. MODELS
THROUGH '24)

"H" SERIES

AVAIL. IN
VARIOUS
BODY TYPES.

3.5
GEAR RATIO

↑ STUTZ factory

"BEARCAT"
STUTZ' MOST FAMOUS
SPORTS MODEL.
(AVAIL. AS "SUPER BEARCAT" ON
SHORT WHEELBASE, IN EARLY 1930s.)

IGNITION: DELCO (4-CYL.)
REMY (6-CYL., 23-25)
DELCO - REMY (AFTER '25)

4 CYL., 360.8 C.I.D. T-HEAD ENGINE (TO '24)

BEARCAT

(LEFT-HAND DRIVE)

21-22

"K" and "H"
MODELS

FINER HOOD LOUVRES;
HORN REMOVED FROM RT. SIDE

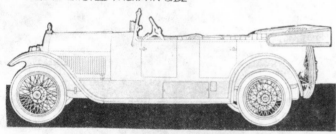

"KLDH" 1922 MODEL HAS NEW
"DH" ENGINE and COMPENSATING
SPRINGS.

KLDH
"SPEEDWAY
4"
2 - PASS.
ROADSTER
(3.75 G.R.)

268 C.I.D.
NEW VACUUM
FUEL FEED
ON 6.

23

"690" 6 CYLINDER (NEW)
5 - PASS.
SEDAN

120" W.B.
(ALSO ON '24 "690" and '25
"693," "694" "694-HB" SERIES

"SPEEDWAY 4"
(FINAL YEAR FOR
4-CYL. MODEL WAS
1924.)

SPEEDWAY 6 "695"

24-25

1925 IS FINAL YEAR FOR STUTZ 6
(BOTH THE 130"- W.B. SPEEDWAY 6
AND 120"- W.B. SPECIAL 6 [694-HB
LATE MODELS AVAIL. WITH LOCKHEED HYD. BRAKE SYSTEM.])

SAFETY STUTZ

32 × 6.20 TIRES (THROUGH '28)
NEW HYDRAULIC BRAKES

Six body styles, designed and constructed under the supervision of Brewster of New York. All closed bodies automatically ventilated.

TOP
50"
70"
20"

131" W.B. (THROUGH '28)

The symbol of Safety

SAFETY *New* CHASSIS

NEW ZENITH CARB.
92 H.P. @ 3200 RPM

The first and only automobile to provide safety-glass all around without extra charge to the buyer ✱

✱ = STUTZ' EARLY SAFETY GLASS RE-INFORCED BY FINE HORIZONTAL WIRES, VISIBLE TO THE EYE. ILCO-RYAN THICK-LENSED HEADLIGHTS ADOPTED, 1927 →

WORM DRIVE

287.3 C.I.D. STRAIGHT-8 (NEW)
(298.6 C.I.D. IN '27 and '28)

STUTZ 8
SAFETY CHASSIS

26-27

5.0 G.R. (THROUGH '28)

MODEL "AA"
"AA" SERIES

28

"BB"
115 H.P. @ 3600 RPM

32 × 6.20
OR
32 × 6.75
TIRES

VACUUM and OTHER FUEL FEEDS AVAIL.

266

STUTZ

'29-30 BLACKHAWK L-8 has FUEL PUMP

BODIES BY HALE KILBURN LE BARON WEYMANN

WITH WEYMANN FABRIC-PANELED LIGHTWT. BODY

BLACKHAWK "L-6" has 6 CYLS., 241.5 C.I.D. 85 H.P. @3200

"L-8" has STRAIGHT-8 ENG., 268.5 C.I.D. 88-90 H.P. @ 3100-3200 RPM

BLACKHAWK ('29)

"MONACO"

SOME EARLY '29 BLACKHAWKS HAVE DART LOUVRES AT REAR OF HOOD.
127½" W.B. ON ALL BLACKHAWKS. 4.75 G.R. ('29)

"M" SERIES

All engines have overhead camshaft.

'29 FLEETWOOD TOWN CAR ALSO AVAIL.

6.50 x 20

134½-145" W.B. (TO '34)
STRAIGHT-8, 322 CID ENG. (TO '34)

115 H.P. @ 3600 RPM

4.5 G.R., EXCEPT ON '29 BLACKHAWK

29-30

FRONT DETAILS

BODIES BY Le BARON, WEYMANN, ROLLSTON, BRUNN, ETC.

STRAIGHT-8
6-CYL. "LA, LAA" SERIES (THROUGH '33) CONTINUES BLACKHAWK 6 SPECS.)

VENT DOORS ON HOOD

DASH

('31)

31-34

NEW "CHALLENGER" SERIES JOINS "CUSTOM" IN 1933.

"SV-16", "DV-32"

SOME 1933-1934 STUTZES HAVE NEW STREAMLINING BUT RETAIN FLAT RADIATOR.

7.00 x 18

267

AUTO. CHOKE and CLUTCH, LARGER COWL VENTS IN '33

TEMPLAR (1917-1924)

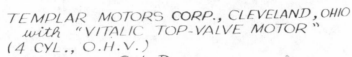

TEMPLAR MOTORS CORP., CLEVELAND, OHIO
with "VITALIC TOP-VALVE MOTOR"
(4 CYL., O.H.V.)
C.I.D.
43 H.P. @ 2100 RPM
118" W.B.

SPOTLIGHT MOVED LOWER DURING 1919.

ONLY 3 LUG-BOLTS BEFORE 1920.

TEMPLAR "SPORTETTE" ('21)

ROADSTER ('22)

6-CYL. AVAIL. BEFORE TEMPLAR DISC○

('24)

(THE FINAL TEMPLAR)

TERRAPLANE
(1933-1938)

BUILT BY HUDSON
(REPLACES THE 1932
ESSEX. TRANSITIONAL
MODELS OF 1932-1933 NAMED
"ESSEX-TERRAPLANE.")

33

106"(6) OR 113"(8) W.B.

8
HAS HOOD
VENT DOORS

6 CYL.
193.1 C.I.D.
70 H.P. @ 3200
8 CYL.
244 C.I.D.
94 H.P. @ 3200

TERRAPLANE

6 CYL.
212 C.I.D. (THROUGH '40 HUDSON)
80 H.P. @ 3600
4.11 GEAR RATIO

HOOD DOORS ON SOME MODELS.

112 OR 116" W.B.
34
"K" and "KU"

5.25 x 17 TIRES

6.00 x 16 TIRES ON "KU" (DELUXE)

6.00 x 16 TIRES (THROUGH '38)
"G" SPECIAL
"GU" DE LUXE

TRUNK

112" W.B.

35
88 H.P. @ 3800 (THROUGH '36)

DE LUXE EQUIP.: DUAL HORNS and TAIL-LIGHTS, 15½-GAL. FUEL TANK, AUTOMATIC CHOKE.

"61" DE LUXE
"62" CUSTOM
115" W.B.
NEW HYDRAULIC BRAKES

36

STATION WAGON (NEW)

37
96 H.P. @ 3900 RPM
117" W.B.
"71" DE LUXE
"72" SUPER (WITH DUAL CARB.)

INTERIOR

(FOR 1938, BECAME THE "HUDSON-TERRAPLANE")

269

TEXAN

TEXAS MOTOR CAR ASSN.,
FORT WORTH, TEXAS

(1918-1922)

4 CYLS.   115" W.B.
"A-38" has LYCOMING ENGINE
"C-12" has HERSCH.-SPLMN. ENGINE
3½ x 5" is BORE and STROKE of EACH
(192.4 C.I.D.)

33 x 4 TIRES

TULSA 4   ← EMBLEM

33 x 4 TIRES
('20-22)

TULSA AUTO MFG. CO., TULSA, OKLA. (1917-1922)

MODEL "E"
('20-22)
117½" W.B.
4 CYL.
192.4 C.I.D.
HERSCHELL-
SPILLMAN
ENGINE
4.5 GEAR RATIO

ZENITH CARB.
CONNECTICUT
IGN.

VELIE

(1908 TO 1928)

VELIE MOTORS CORPORATION.
Moline, Illinois

MODEL "48" →

6 CYLINDERS (ALL BUT '28 "8-88")

MODEL "34"
112" W.B.
(THROUGH '22)

195.6 C.I.D. O.H.V.
FALLS ENGINE

20-21

ATWATER KENT IGN.
(TO '24)

115" W.B. (THROUGH '23)

(224 C.I.D. CONTINENTAL L-HEAD ENGINE)
(THROUGH '22)

RAYFIELD CARB. ('20)   STROMBERG CARB. ('21-'29)

"34" and "48"
MODELS AVAILABLE ALSO

22

(WITH VELIE-BUILT 195.6 C.I.D.
ENGINE IN NEW 115"-W.B. "58")
(OVERHEAD VALVES)   4.66 G.R. (THROUGH '23)
32 x 4 TIRES (THROUGH '23,
AND ON '24 "56")

FINAL YEAR FOR
FALLS ENGINE
(ON MODEL "34")

FINAL YEAR FOR
CONTINENTAL ENGINE
(ON MODEL "48")

new MODEL "58"

"SPORT CAR"

270

Velie

Velie Model 58, five-passenger Touring; beautifully finished and equipped; all Velie cars are powered with the remarkable vibrationless six-cylinder, valve-in-head Velie-built motor.

Velie Silver Swallow, five-passenger Sport with satin-aluminum body; equipment includes two extra cord tires, disc wheels, bumpers, spotlights, trunk, two suitcases, hat box, and many other items.

Velie Model 58, three-passenger Sport Roadster; specially painted; extra cord tire, disc wheels, bumpers, spotlights. We also furnish a similar roadster with standard equipment.

4.66 GEAR RATIO IN 1923

115" W. B. (THROUGH '23) 118" W. B. ON BOTH "56" and "58" MODELS, 1924.

WESTINGHOUSE IGNITION (LATE '24 THROUGH '25)

2 - WHEEL MECHANICAL BRAKES

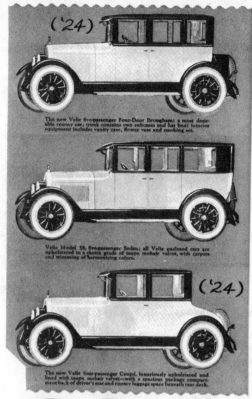

('24)

The new Velie five-passenger Four-Door Brougham; a most desirable roomy car; trunk contains two suitcases and hat box; interior equipment includes vanity case, flower vase and smoking set.

Velie Model 58, five-passenger Sedan; all Velie enclosed cars are upholstered in a choice grade of taupe mohair velvet, with carpets and trimming of harmonizing colors.

('24)

The new Velie four-passenger Coupé, luxuriously upholstered and lined with taupe mohair velvet—with a spacious package compartment back of driver's seat and roomy luggage space beneath rear deck.

23-24

NEW 118" W. B. IN 1924 ; NEW ('24)
203.5 C.I.D.; 4.7 OR 5.1 GEAR RATIO

"60" IS ONLY SERIES OF VELIE FOR 1925 and 1926.

25

MODEL "60"   6 CYLINDERS
OVERHEAD VALVES   204 C.I.D.
48 H.P. @ 2600 RPM

5.10 GEAR RATIO
118" WHEELBASE

new HYDRAULIC 4 - WHEEL BRAKES (TO '29)

THE SMARTEST CAR ON THE HIGHWAY

Four Door Coach

VELIE ROADSTER

VELIE

"60" has new REMY IGNITION (DELCO-REMY ON '27 "60," '28 "77," "88")

30 × 5.25 TIRES

'26 "60" has new 221.3 C.I.D., 58 H.P. @ 3000 RPM

FOR 1927 and 1928, new "STANDARD 50" SERIES JOINS VELIE LINE, with AUTO-LITE IGNITION, OWN 196 C.I.D., 6-CYL. O.H.V. ENGINE, 48 H.P. @ 2600 RPM
29 × 5.00 TIRES ('27) (30 × 5.25 ON '28 "STD. 50" and also "6-66";) also Auto Lite IGN.)

VELIE-BLT. ENGINES CONTINUE THERMO-SYPHON COOLING SYSTEM.

26-28

KNOWN IN '26 AS "SEDAN DE LUXE," AFTERWARDS AS THE "ROYAL SEDAN" (FRONT DOOR SLANTS TO ANGLE OF WINDSHIELD.)

('26)

DASH ('28)

VELIE O.H.V. ENGINE

BOWL-SHAPED HEADLAMPS APPEAR ON 1927 VELIES.

STRAIGHT-8 (298.6 CID) LYCOMING-ENGINED, 125" WB "8-88" VELIE ALSO, IN 1928 (FINAL YEAR.)

1928 "77" and "88" MODELS HAVE SURCINGLE PARKING LIGHTS; ON REAR OF COWL ON "66." 4.9 GEAR RATIO, EXCEPT 4.6 ON "8-88" (ONLY MODEL WITH SCHEBLER CARB.) "1929" MODELS BUILT DURING 1928.

"6-66" ('28) 112" WB, 203.5 CID, 56 HP @ 2800 RPM
"6-77" ('28-9) 118" WB, 221 CID, 60 HP @ 2900 RPM, 32 × 6.00 TIRES

29

"6-77" ROYAL SEDAN (SAME AS '28 MODEL

AUTO PRODUCTION CEASED BY 1-29.

(LENGTH EXAGGERATED)

VIKING

P R O D U C T   O F   G E N E R A L   M O T O R S

BUILT
1929 – 1930
BY GM's
OLDSMOBILE
DIVISION

29

(INTRODUCED
APRIL, 1929)

EMBLEM

V-8 ENGINE
259.4 C.I.D.

80 H.P. @
3200 RPM

125" WHEELBASE
(THROUGH '30)

30 × 6.00 TIRES

30

81 H.P. @ 3200 RPM

6.00 × 18 TIRES

WALTHAM

6 CYLS.
45 H.P.

WALTHAM
MOTOR MFRS., INC.,
WALTHAM,
MASS.

REPLACES
"METZ" CAR
(1922 ONLY)

22

WASP

('20)

MARTIN-WASP CORP.,
BENNINGTON., VT. (1919-1925)
4 AND 6 CYL.

"2611" ('21) has 132" W.B., 4-CYL., 389.9 C.I.D.
WISCONSIN T-III AD ENGINE
BOSCH IGNITION   3.70 G.R.
STROMBERG CARB.   33 × 5 TIRES

WESTCOTT

The Car with a Longer Life

(1912 - 1925)

THE WESTCOTT MOTOR CAR CO.
SPRINGFIELD, OHIO

TWIN OVAL REAR
WINDOWS IN TOP
CONTINENTAL ENGINES (ON
ALL BUT
'24
"60")

C-"38" (224 CID THROUGH '22)
LIGHTER 6 (5.09 G.R.)
(118" W.B.)

C-"48" (303.1 CID THROUGH '24) (A)
(4.45 GR) LARGER 6
(125" W.B.)

19-20

(C)

(38)   (48)
33 × 4 OR 32 × 4½
TIRES
(THROUGH
'22)

"C-38"

'19 MODEL
SHOWN. '20 HAS FULL-LENGTH
BODY-HOOD BELT CREASE JUST
ABOVE DOOR HANDLES, ALSO A
NEW COWL VENT.

DELCO IGNITION ON ALL
RAYFIELD CARB.
(THROUGH '24)

"C-48"

21

1922 "A-44" LIKE '21 "C-38," BUT
HAS 120" W.B., 4.66 G.R.

The Closure			$1795
Special Closure			1998
Brougham (including trunk)			2490
Sedan			2490
Special Sedan			2690

23

NON-REMOVABLE CYLINDER-HEAD ON 303.1 CID ENG. → "C-44 and
                                                    "D-48" for '23)

"CLOSURE" IS NEW ENCLOSED TOURING CAR
FOR 1923

32 × 4½
TIRES ON ALL
'23-'24
WESTCOTTS

C-44-241.5 CID, 4.9 GR
D-48-303.1 CID,
4.45 GR

The Car with a Longer Life

"6-60"
5-PASS.
SEDAN
('24)
("OWN"
ENGINE)

24

Interior of The New Westcott Model
The Closure

274

('25 has
4-W. BRKS.,   32 × 6.20 TIRES,
                 STROMBERG CARB., 56 H.P. @   2300 RPM)

OVERLAND
Whippet
FOURS SIXES

4-CYL. "96" (INTRO. 7-26)
134.2 C.I.D.
(THROUGH '29)
30 H.P. @ 2800 RPM
4.5 G.R.
100 1/4" W.B. (THROUGH '28)

28 x 4.75 TIRES (19") (THROUGH '29)

27

6-CYL. "93-A"
169.6 C.I.D. (THROUGH '28)
40 H.P. @ 2800 RPM

6-CYL. LANDAU →

109 1/2" W.B. (THROUGH '28)

29 x 4.75 TIRES (6 INTRO. 1-27)

VACUUM FUEL FEED, TILLOTSON CARB. and AUTO-LITE IGN. (THROUGH '30)

WHIPPET MASCOT →

BOTH SERIES have 4-WHEEL MECHANICAL BRAKES.
RAISED PANEL ON '27 FENDERS ↓

FISK

275

Whippet
FOURS   SIXES

John N. Willys
President,
The Willys-Overland Company

$455

The Touring

6

COACH
$535
F. O. B. Factory

4

$535

The Coupe

$525

The Roadster

$545

The Cabriolet Coupe

4-Door Sedan

28

4-CYL. "96"

32 H.P. @ 2800 RPM

6-CYL. "98"

new 178.3 C.I.D. (THROUGH '30)
43 H.P. @ 2800 RPM

new CADET-STYLE VISOR ON SEDANS

28 x 4.75 TIRES ON BOTH MODELS.

4-CYL. "96-A"
new 103¼" W.B.
new 145.7 C.I.D.
40 H.P. @ 3200 RPM
4.75 x 19 TIRES

6-CYL. "98-A"
new 112½" W.B.
50 H.P. @ 3200 RPM
5.00 x 19 TIRES

NEW "SUPERIOR" MODEL

INTRODUCING THE NEW
"FINGER·TIP CONTROL"

ROADSTER

6

PULL UP TO START MOTOR

PRESS DOWN TO SOUND HORN

SHORT RIGHT TURN FOR PARKING LIGHTS

FULL RIGHT TURN FOR BRIGHT LIGHTS

TURN HALF RIGHT FOR DIM LIGHTS

NEW RADIATOR DESIGN

← DASH

NEW BELT MOLDINGS

4

29-30
4.56 G.R. (4 and 6 CYL.)

4

WHITE

CLEVELAND, OHIO
(SINCE 1900)

BETWEEN 1918 and 1936, CARS ON SPECIAL ORDER ONLY. TRUCK PRODUCTION CONTINUES.

1922 MODEL "15-A" 4 CYL.
"UTILITY" MODEL ("BUSINESS CAR," ANNOUNCED 11-21)

WILLS SAINTE CLAIRE

(1921-1927) DELCO IGN. (THROUGH '27) 65 H.P. @ 2700 RPM ('22) 4 TO 1 STD. GEAR RATIO

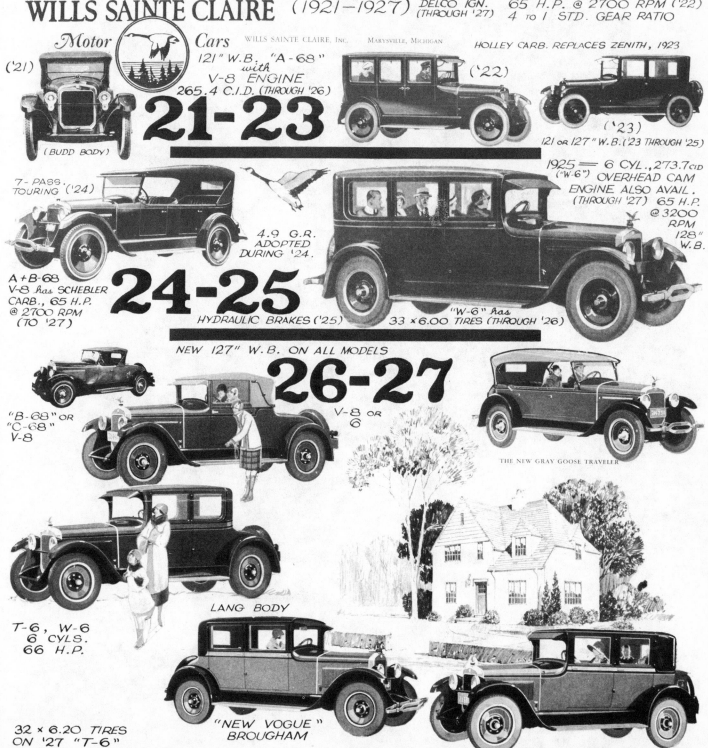

Motor ✈ *Cars*   WILLS SAINTE CLAIRE, INC.   MARYSVILLE, MICHIGAN

HOLLEY CARB. REPLACES ZENITH, 1923

('21)   121" W.B. "A-68" *with* V-8 ENGINE 265.4 C.I.D. (THROUGH '26)

(BUDD BODY)

21-23

('22)

('23)
121 or 127" W.B. ('23 THROUGH '25)

7-PASS. TOURING ('24)

1925 = 6 CYL., 273.7 CID ("W-6") OVERHEAD CAM ENGINE ALSO AVAIL. (THROUGH '27) 65 H.P. @ 3200 RPM 128" W.B.

4.9 G.R. ADOPTED DURING '24.

A+B-68 V-8 has SCHEBLER CARB., 65 H.P. @ 2700 RPM (TO '27)

24-25

HYDRAULIC BRAKES ('25)

"W-6" has 33 x 6.00 TIRES (THROUGH '26)

NEW 127" W.B. ON ALL MODELS

26-27

V-8 OR 6

"B-68" OR "C-68" V-8

THE NEW GRAY GOOSE TRAVELER

T-6, W-6 6 CYLS. 66 H.P.

LANG BODY

32 x 6.20 TIRES ON '27 "T-6" 4.9 G.R. ('27)

"NEW VOGUE" BROUGHAM

277

DISCONTINUED 1927

SIXES AND EIGHTS

WILLYS

WILLYS-OVERLAND, INC., TOLEDO, OHIO

Eight

WILLYS 8 SEDAN DE LUXE

8 HAS 120" W.B., 245.4 C.I.D., 80 H.P. @ 3200 RPM, 5.50 × 19 TIRES (THROUGH '31)

Six **30**

6 HAS 110" W.B., 192.9 C.I.D., 65 H.P. @ 3400 RPM, 5.00 × 19 TIRES (THROUGH '31)

REPLACES "WHIPPET" 6

"6-97" and 113"-WB "6-98-D" SHARE '30 "6" SPECS.

NEW NAME USED FOR 1931

HORIZONTAL HOOD LOUVRES ON SIX

"6-97," "6-98-D," and "8-80-D"

INSTRUMENT PANEL (6)

"8-80-D" SAME SPECS. AS '30, BUT 121" W.B.

HOOD VENT DOORS ON EIGHT

WILLYS·OVERLAND

31

SIDE VIEW SIMILAR TO 1931-1932 WILLYS-KNIGHT "95." (SEE "WILLYS-KNIGHT.")

70-80 M.P.H.

WILLYS 8 and WILLYS-KNIGHT INSTRUMENT PANEL

278

WILLYS

1932 "SILVER ANNIVERSARY" MODELS with "SILVER STREAK" ENGINES

('32 6 DASH IS SAME DESIGN AS '31 6, BUT HAS WOOD-GRAIN EFFECTS)

32

('32 HAS RADIATOR FILLER UNDER 2" LONGER HOOD, AND TRUMPET HORN IN PLACE OF 1931 DISC-SHAPED VIBRATOR HORN.) "6-90-A" and "8-88-A "(AFTER 6-32) IS "1933" MODEL.

The Six Coach, $530

'32 "8-88" and "6-90" have SAME SPECS. AS CORRESPONDING '30-'31 MODELS, BUT 5.50×18 and 5.25×18 TIRES

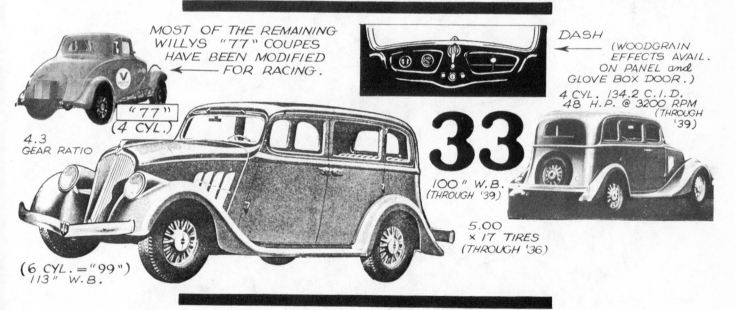

MOST OF THE REMAINING WILLYS "77" COUPES HAVE BEEN MODIFIED — FOR RACING.

DASH ← (WOODGRAIN EFFECTS AVAIL. ON PANEL and GLOVE BOX DOOR.)

4 CYL. 134.2 C.I.D. 48 H.P. @ 3200 RPM (THROUGH '39)

"77" (4 CYL.)

4.3 GEAR RATIO

33

100" W.B. (THROUGH '39)

5.00 × 17 TIRES (THROUGH '36)

(6 CYL. = "99") 113" W.B.

34

NEW WIRE WHEELS

NEW SEMI-HORIZONTAL LOUVRES

WILLYS

35

(BUBBLE-SHAPED HOOD VENT PORTS)
'35 HAS WIRE WHEELS.

36

'36 HAS STEEL-SPOKE ARTILLERY WHEELS.

INTERIOR

EARLIEST '37 MODELS (BUILT FALL, 1936,) HAVE NO VERTICAL BUMPER GUARDS.

37-38

5.50 x 16 TIRES

39

THIS NEW MODEL "61" DEVELOPS 61 H.P. @ 3600 RPM, HAS HYDRAULIC BRAKES, 4.3 - 4.55 GEAR RATIO, 102" WHEELBASE.

DASH (61)

MODEL "48" WILLYS HAS 100" W.B., MECHANICAL BRAKES, 4.1 GEAR RATIO, 5.00 x 16 TIRES, 1938 STYLING.

5.50 x 16 TIRES ON "61"

Slip-stream
A DESIGN OF SUPERB BEAUTY

SHELL

DURING 1939, WILLYS "61" KNOWN AS OVERLAND (4 CYL.)

WILLYS-KNIGHT

4-CYLINDER SLEEVE-VALVE ENGINE

(1914–1932)

185.8 C.I.D. (THROUGH '25)

40 H.P. @ 2600 RPM ('21-'22)

118" W.B. (THROUGH '25)

WILLYS-OVERLAND, INC., *Toledo, Ohio*
WILLYS-OVERLAND, LIMITED, *Toronto, Canada*

20-21

5.00 GEAR RATIO (THROUGH '22)

DIAGRAM OF A CYLINDER, ILLUSTRATING THE SLEEVE-VALVE MECHANISM →

22

23-24

40 H.P. @ 2400 RPM MODEL "64" 118" W.B. and 32×4 TIRES

'23 MODEL "67" HAS 124" W.B. and 32×4½ TIRES

"COUNTRY CLUB" TOURING

4.44 GEAR RATIO ('23)

4.44 and 5.12 ('24)

Coupe-Sedan Standard

281

WILLYS-KNIGHT

33 × 4.95

42 H.P. @ 2200 RPM

4

4

25

"66"

NEW 6 HAS 236.4 C.I.D. (THROUGH '27) and 60 H.P. @ 2800 RPM

126" W.B. (UNTIL '28)

32 × 6.20

6 (NEW)

282

WILLYS-KNIGHT

113¼" W.B. (THROUGH '28)

"70" (6 CYL.)
177.9 C.I.D. (THROUGH '32)
53 H.P. @ 3000 RPM

26

GREAT 6
60 H.P. @ 3000 RPM

27-28

ROADSTER

WITH TOP UP

TOP DOWN

CABRIOLET

"70" SIX
The Only Motor-Car Engine That Improves With Use.

53 H.P. @
3100 RPM (3000 RPM, '28-9)

1928 "70"
KNOWN AS
"SPECIAL 6"

WILLYS-KNIGHT

27-28
(CONT'D.)

MASCOT

109½" New
W.B. Standard Six
157.6 ("56")
C.I.D. ("56") ('28)

("56")

45 H.P. @ 3000 RPM

"GREAT 6"
"66" (1927)
"66-A" (1928)
NEW HORIZONTAL HOOD LOUVRES
('27½-'28)

DASH

One of the many new beautiful color combinations now available on the Willys-Knight Great Six. Upper body, black; lower body and wheels, spruce-green. Striping, ivory and red. Upholstered in fine quality gray-green mohair.

'28 "66-A" HAS
255 C.I.D.
(ENGINE SIZE RETAINED
THROUGH '32)

INSTR.
PANEL
('29)

29-30

"70-B"
6 CYLS., 177.9 C.I.D.
53 H.P. @
3000 RPM
4.89 G.R.
29 x 5.50
TIRES (5.50
x 19 IN '30)

('29)

112½" W.B.

284

29-30
(CONT'D.)

WILLYS·KNIGHT

GREAT SIX
"66-B" 6 CYLS., 255 C.I.D.

72 ('29)
87 ('30)
H.P. @
3200 RPM

120" WHEELBASE
"GREAT 6" CAB. CPE., 7-PASS.
SEDAN AND LIMOUSINE have
ROBBINS BODIES.
WILLYS-OVERLAND BODIES
ON OTHERS.

GREAT
SIX →

The artistically designed instrument panel, with instruments grouped in a setting of beauty and dignity.

('30)

"87" (/1930)

The door interiors are upholstered in broadcloth, with a center strip of Bedford Cord, topped by an artistic panel in needlepoint.

31-32
(FINAL WILLYS-KNIGHT IS 1932 MODEL.)
"66-D"   87 H.P.
@ 3200

"95"
(1932)
177.9
C.I.D.
60 H.P. @ 3400
(SINCE '31)

285

(1929-1930) WINDSOR 8

MOON MOTOR CAR CO., ST. LOUIS, MO.

1929 "WHITE PRINCE" has STRAIGHT-8 CONTINENTAL "15-S" ENGINE (268.6 C.I.D.) 88 H.P. @ 3100 RPM 125½" W.B.
('29)
* 4.8 and other GEAR RATIOS
31 × 6.00 TIRES ("8-82")
31 × 6.50 " ("8-92")
* 4.88 GEAR RATIO ("8-82")
3.93 " " ("8-92")

'29 DASH

6-CYL.'30 MODELS ALSO

"6-75" ('30)
1930

1930 "6-69" has 6-CYL. CONT. "37-L" ENGINE (185 C.I.D.) 47 H.P. @ 2600 RPM, 5.25 × 19 TIRES

1930 6-CYL. "6-69" and "6-75" have 120" W.B., 4.9 GEAR RATIO

"6-75" has 6-CYL. CONT. "11-E" ENG.(214.7 C.I.D.) 66 H.P. @ 3100 RPM, 5.50 ×19 TIRES

('29)

WINDSOR HAS MOON-STYLE **RADIATOR** (PAINTED, ON MOST TYPES) "8-82" BECOMES "8-85" FOR 1930, has 4.63 G.R., 6.00 × 19 TIRES

"8-92" CONT'D. 1930, with 6.50 × 19 TIRES, 3.9 G.R.

WINTHER 6 (1920-1923)

WINTHER MOTORS, INC., KENOSHA, WIS.

MODEL "61" ('21) has 120" W.B., 4.45 GEAR RATIO

RADIATOR DESIGN

HERSCHELL-SPILLMAN ENGINE (248.9 C.I.D.) (TRUCKS ALSO)

(DISC WHEELS ALSO AVAIL.

WINTON SIX (1897—1924)

THE WINTON COMPANY   CLEVELAND

DURING 1922, MODEL "25" REPLACED BY MODEL "40"

has 132" W.B., OWN 6-CYL. L-HEAD ENGINE (347.9 C.I.D.) 4.90 G.R. (THROUGH '21)

('22)

NEW "40" 4-PASS. SPORT CAR

WINTON-BUILT BODY

('23)

('23)

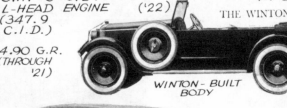

"40" 7-PASS. SEDAN

STROMBERG CARB. REPLACED BY RAYFIELD CARB., and NEW 4.58 G.R. FOR 1923 and 1924.

('24) 5-PASS. COUPE

YELLOW CAB (1921-1936)

Manufacturing Co.
Chicago, U.S.A.

'21

BUILT BY GENERAL MOTORS AFTER MID-1920s. KNOWN AS GENERAL CAB FROM 1936 TO 1938)

APPENDIX

The following names, listed alphabetically, represent makes of automobiles which were not in regular production or those which are not illustrated in this book.

Certain *model names* are also listed here, and reference is made to where they may be found in the illustrated portion. For example, **BEARCAT** is not a make of car, but a model of **STUTZ**, etc.

A.B.C. (1922-1939)

ACE (See *CONTINENTAL*, 1933)

A.C.F. (1926)

ADAMS (1924)

ADELPHIA (1920-1921)

ADRIA (1921-1922) Adria Motor Car Co., Batavia, N.Y. 4-cyl. Supreme engine. Not in full production.

ADVANCED 6 (See *NASH*)

AERO; AERO CAR (1921)

AERODYNAMIC (See *HUPMOBILE*, 1934-1936)

AERO TYPE (1921) (See also *MOON*, 1929)

AETNA (1922)

AIRFLOW (See *CHRYSLER*, 1934-1937; see also *DE SOTO*, 1934-1936)

AIR LINE 8 (See *JORDAN*, 1928)

AIRSTREAM (See *CHRYSLER*, 1935-1936; see also *DE SOTO*, 1935-1936)

AJAX (1920-1921) (See also *NASH*, 1925)

ALENA (1922)

ALL-AMERICAN (1923)

ALL-AMERICAN 6 (See *OAKLAND*, 1928-1929)

ALL-POWER (1917-1921)

ALSACE (1920-1921) Automotive Products Co., N.Y.C. Produced by *PIEDMONT*, for export. Peaked radiator, 4-cyl. Herschell-Spillman engine.

AMBASSADOR (See *NASH*)

AMBASSADOR 6 (1922-1926) Yellow Cab Mfg. Co., Chicago. Replaces *SHAW* car. Large 1922-23 models were Shaws with Continental 6-cyl. engines. Smaller "D-1" 1924-1926 series became the *HERTZ* car. 4-cyl. model R-2 listed 1921.

AMERICAN BANTAM (See *AUSTIN*, 1936-1940)

AMERICAN BEAUTY (1920-1921) 6-cyl. Continental engine (see *PAN-AMERICAN*).

AMERICAN JUNIOR (1916-1920) American Motor Vehicle Co., Lafayette, Ind. 1-cylinder juvenile cycle car.

AMERICAN SOUTHERN (1921)

AMERICAN STEAM CAR (1929-1932) American Steam Automobile Co., West Newton, Mass. Hudson body & chassis parts used.

ANSTED (1926-1927) Ansted Motors, Connersville, Ind. Leftover *LEXINGTON* cars, with new radiator emblem and new hubcaps.

APEX (1920-1921)

APEX (1920-1921)

APPLETON (1922)

ASTOR (1925)

ASTRA (1920)

ATCO (1920-1922)

AUSTIN (1901-1921) Austin Automobile Co., Grand Rapids, Mich. Not related to 1930-1940 *AMERICAN AUSTIN* or *AMERICAN BANTAM* cars.

AUTOHORSE (1917-1921)

AUTOMATIC ELECTRIC (1921-1925) Automatic Electric Transmission Co., Buffalo, N.Y. Electric car; 65" wheelbase.

AUTO RED BUG (See *RED BUG*)

AVERY (1921)

BACKHUS (1925)

BACON (1920) New Castle, Pa.

BAKER (steam) (1917-1924) Baker Steam Motor Car and Mfg. Co., Pueblo and Denver, Colorado. Also built replacement boilers for *STANLEY*.

BAKER R & L (1915-1920) (See *RAUCH & LANG*)

BARBARINO (1923-1925) Barbarino Motor Car Corp., N.Y.C. and Port Jefferson, N.Y. Replaced *RICHELIEU* car, but used 4-cyl. Le Roi engine.

BARLEY (1922-1924) (See *ROAMER*)

BARLOW (1922)

BARTLETT (1921)

BARVER (1925)

BAUER (1925)

BEACON (See *CONTINENTAL*, 1933)

BEARCAT (See *STUTZ*)

BEAVER (1916-1923) Beaver State Motor Co., Gresham, Oregon. 6 cylinders; worm drive.

BECK (1921)

B.E.L. (1921) Consolidated Motor Car Co., New London, Conn. Successor to *STERLING* car. 101" wheelbase, own 4-cylinder engine.

BERWICK ELECTRIC (1926)

BIDDLE-CRANE (1922-1923)

BLACKHAWK (See *STUTZ*, 1929-1930)

BLUE BOY (See *JORDAN*)

BLUE STREAK (See *GRAHAM*, 1932)

BOLLSTROM (1920)

BOURONVILLE (1921-1922)

BOWMAN (1921-1922)

BOYNTON (1922)

BRADFIELD (1929) (See *KISSEL*)

BRADFORD (1920)

BRADLEY (1920-1921) Bradley Motor Car Co., Cicero, Illinois. Lycoming engines; 4-cyl. 1920 Model H, 6-cyl. 1921 Model F, 116" wheelbase.

BREMAC (1932) Bremac Motor Car Corp., Sydney, Ohio. With 8-cyl., 80 hp rear engine; experimental.

BRIDGEPORT (1922)

BRIGGS (1933) Experimental.

BROCK (1920-1921)

BROWN (1922)

BUCK (1925)

BUDDIE (1921)

BUDDY (1925)

CALIFORNIAN (1920-1921) California Motor Car Corp., Los Angeles.

CALVERT (1927) Calvert Motor Associates, Baltimore; own 6-cyl. engine.

CAMERON (1902-1920) Cameron Motors Corp., Stamford, Conn. 1919-20 Model "55" has own 6-cyl. engine, 118" wheelbase, 32"x4" tires.

CAPITOL (1920) (See also *CHEVROLET*, 1927)

CARRILOE (See *NASH*, 1923)

CARROLL (1912-1920) Carroll Motor Car Co., Strasburg, Pa.; 4-cyl. and 6-cyl. models.

CARROLL 6 (1920-1922) Carroll Automobile Co., Lorraine, Ohio. 6-cyl. Beaver engine; open cars only.

CARTERMOBILE (1924-1925) Carter Motor Car Co., Washington, D.C.; 4-cyl. Herschell-Spillman engine.

CARTHAGE (1924)

CASCO (1926)

CAWARD-DART (1924)

CELT (1927)

CENTURY (See *BUICK*, also *HUPMOBILE*)

CHAMPION (1917-1923) Direct Drive Motor Co., Pottstown, Pa.; Champion Motors Co., Philadelphia. Tourist has 4-cyl. Lycoming engine; Special has 4-cyl. Herschell-Spillman engine. (See also *OVERLAND*, 1924, and *STUDEBAKER*, 1939)

CLINTON (1923)

CLOSURE (See *WESTCOTT*, 1923)

COLLINET (1921)

COLLINS (1920) Collins Motors, Inc., Huntington, L.I., N.Y. 6-cyl. Country Club model.

COLONIAL Four different makes with this name in 1920's: Indianapolis (1917-1921), San Francisco (1920), Boston (1921 1922) and Chicago (1922: by *SHAW*).

COMET ELECTRIC (1921)

COMMANDER (1921, 1922) (See also *STUDEBAKER*)

COMMERCE (1924)

COMMERCIAL (1927)

COMMODORE (1921-1922)

CONCORD (See *LEXINGTON*)

CONFEDERATE (See *CHEVROLET*, 1932)

COOK (1921)

CORINTHIAN (1922-1923)

CORTLAND (1916-1924)

COTAY (or CO-TAY) (1920-1921)

COUPSTER (See *STAR*, 1925)

COVIC (1930)

CRAIG-HUNT (1920) No actual production known.

CRESCENT (1923)

CROWN; CROWN-MAGNETIC (See OWEN)

CRUSADER (1923) (See also CRAHAM, 1936-1937)

CUMMINS (1930)

CURRAN (1928)

CURTIS (1921) Curtis Motor Car Co., Little Rock, Ark.; 4-cyl. Herschell-Spillman engine.

CUSTER (1921)

CYCLOMOBILE (1920) Cyclomobile Mfg. Co., Toledo, Ohio; air-cooled V-2 Spacke engine.

CYCLONE (1921)

D.A.C. (1922-1923; See DETROIT AIR COOLED)

DARTMOBILE (1922)

DA VINCI (1925)

DEEMOTOR (1923)

DELMORE (1923)

DELTA (1923-1925) Only 1 car known to exist. Had 6-cyl. Continental engine.

DENEGRE (1920)

DERBY (1924)

DIAL (1923)

DICTATOR (See STUDEBAKER)

DIEHL (1923)

DIFFERENTIAL (1921)

DILLON STEAM (1920)

DISPATCH (1911-1922) Dispatch Motor Co., Minneapolis, Minn. (See also CHANDLER, 1921)

DIXON (1922)

DODGESON 8 (1926) Dodgeson Motors, Detoit. Pilot models only, with straight-8, rotary-valve engine; 72 hp at 3000 rpm.

D'OLT (1921-1926)

DOUGLAS (1918-1922) Douglas Motors Corp., Omaha; with V-8 Herschell-Spillman engine (replaced the DRUMMOND car).

DRAGON (1921) Dragon Motors Corp., Chicago. Styling generally resembles REVERE car.

DRAKE (1921)

DUER (1925)

DUPLEX (See STUDEBAKER)

EAGLE (See CHEVROLET, 1933)

ECONOMY 6 (1917-1921) Economy Motor Co., Tiffin, Ohio. 6-cyl., 224 cid Continental engine, 115" wheelbase, 4.5 gear ratio, 33"x4" tires on model "6-46".

EL CURTO (1921)

ELECTROCAR (1922) Electrocar Corp., N.Y.C.; taxicab.

ELKHART (1922)

ELMIRA (1920)

ELYSEE (1926)

ENDURANCE (steam) (1923-1924) Endurance Steam Car Co., Los Angeles; touring cars only.

EUGOL (1921)

FACTO (1920)

FALCAR (1922)

FALCON (1938-1943)

FARNER 6 (1922-1923) Farner Motor Car Co., Streator, Ill.; 6-cyl. Falls engine.

FAST 4 (See DODGE, 1927-1928)

FERGUS 6 (1921-1922) Fergus Motors of America, Newark, N.J. Pilot model built in Ireland. Irish-American venture, begun a few years previously.

FISHER (1924)

FLEETWOOD (See CADILLAC)

FLEXIBLE (1932)

FLYER (See CONTINENTAL, 1933)

FLYING CLOUD (See REO)

FRANKFORT (1922)

FREEMAN (1931)

FREEMONT (1923)

FREMONT (1921-1922)

FRIEND 4 (1920-1921) Friend Motors Corp., Pontiac, Mich.; own 4-cyl. engine.

FRISBEE (1921)

FRITCHLE ELECTRIC (1907-1922)

FRONT DRIVE (1921)

FRONTENAC (1922) (1924) Name also used in Canada.

GENERAL CAB (1929)

GLIDE (1903-1920) The Bartholomew Co., Peoria, Illinois.

GLOVER (1920-1921) U.S.-assembled for export to England; 4 cylinders.

GOLD BUG (See KISSEL)

GOLDEN STATE (1928)

GOODSPEED (1922) Commonwealth Motors Corp., Chicago. Intended successor to the COMMONWEALTH car, only 2 phaetons built; aluminum bodies.

GOODWIN (1923)

GOVE (1921)

GRASS-PREMIER (1923)

GREAT 6 (See WILLYS-KNIGHT, 1926-1930)

GREATER 6, 8 (See HUDSON)

GREENVILLE (1925)

GREGORY (front-drive) (1922) 1922 title — Front Drive Motor Co., Kansas City, Mo. 4 cylinders, pilot models only.

GREYHOUND (1920)

GROWLER COUPE (See LOCOMOBILE)

GUNBOAT ROADSTER (See LOCOMOBILE)

HACKETT (1915-1920) Hackett Motor Car Co., Jackson and Grand Rapids, Mich. 1920 model had 4-cyl., 192.4 cid Herschell-Spillman engine; 114" wheelbase, 4.75 gear ratio, 32"x4" tires.

HAMILTON (1917-1922)

HAMLIN-HOLMES (1919-1930) Hamlin-Holmes Motor Co., Chicago. Various front-wheel-drive experimental models, never in full production. A Hamlin car proposed for 1930.

HANOVER (1921-1924) Hanover Motor Car Co., Hanover, Pa. Air-cooled, 2-cyl. cycle car. Many exported to Japan.

HARRIE (1925)

HARRIGAN (1922)

HARRISBURG (1922)

HARROUN (1917-1922) Harroun Motor Sales Corp., Wayne, Mich. 4-cylinder open cars.

HARVARD (1915-1920) Harvard Motor Car Co., Hyattsville, Md., was builder of the final models. Right-hand drive, 4-cylinder engine model was exported to New Zealand. (See also DORT)

HATFIELD (1917-1924) Cortland Car & Carriage Co., Sydney, N.Y. 1920 model similar to 1919, with 4-cyl. Herschell-Spillman engine, 115" wheelbase. "A-42" model cont'd. through '22 season, then replaced by 1923 "6-55" with new 6-cyl. Herschell-Spillman engine — 248.9 cid, instead of 192.4 as on 4-cyl. model; 121" wheelbase.

HATHAWAY (1924)

HAYES-ANDERSON (1928)

HEIFNER (1921)

HENNEY (1921-1931) Henney Motor Car Co., Freeport, Illinois. Frequently used Continental 6 or Lycoming straight-8 engines. Also built ambulances and hearses, even after 1931.

HERMES (1920) Tsacomas Desmos, N.Y.C. 4 cylinders; for export to Greece. At least 2 cars known to have been built.

HIGHLANDER (1921) Midwest Motor Co., Kansas City, Mo. 6-cyl. Continental engine; sometimes referred to as Hylander car.

HIGHWAY KNIGHT (1920)

HILTON (1921) Motor Sales and Service Corp., Philadelphia. Factory in Riverton, N.J. 4-cyl. Herschell-Spillman engine; coupes only.

HINKEL (1925)

HOFFMAN (1931) R.C. Hoffman, Detroit, Mich. Two front-drive cars with straight-8 Lycoming engines.

HOLLIER (1915-1921) Lewis Spring & Axle Co., Chelsea and Jackson, Mich. 1920 model "206-B" has same styling and nickeled radiator as 1919 model.

HOLTON (1921)

HOSKINS (1921)

HOUSE (1920)

HOWARD (1929-1930) Howard Motor Intl. Corp., N.Y.C. 6-cylinder Continental engine, hydraulic brakes; also know as Howard Silver Morn.

H.R.L. (1921)

HURLBURT (1922)

HURON (1921)

HURRYTON (1922)

HYLANDER Another spelling of HIGHLANDER car.

IMPERIAL (See CHRYSLER, 1926-1939)

INDEPENDENCE (See CHEVROLET, 1931)

INDEPENDENT (1920; 1927)

INDIAN (1928-1929) Indian Motorcycle Co., Springfield, Mass.; experimental small cars.

INDIANA (1921)

INGERSOLL-RAND (1921)

INLAND (1920)

INTERNATIONAL (See CHEVROLET, 1929)

JACQUET FLYER (1921) Jacquet Motors Corp. of America, Belding, Mich.; 4 cylinders.

JAY-EYE-CEE (See CASE)

JEM SPECIAL (1922)

JUNIOR 8 (See LOCOMOBILE, 1925)

KALAMAZOO (1922)

KAWS (1922)

KEASLER (1922)

KELDON (1920)

KENILWORTH (1923)

KENTUCKY (1915-1924)

KESSLER (1921-1922) Kessler Motor Car Co., Detroit. Own 4-cyl. engine, touring cars only. Later developed Kess-Line 8.

KESS-LINE 8 Later development of *Kessler*.

KIMBALL (1922)

KINNEY (1922)

KNOX (1922)

K.O. (1921)

KURTZ AUTOMATIC (1921-1923) Kurtz Motor Car Co., Cleveland, Ohio. 6-cyl. Herschell-Spillman engine; pre-selector gearshift control on steering column.

LA FRANCE-REPUBLIC (1925)

LA MARNE (1920-1921) La Marne Motor Co., Cleveland, Ohio; straight-8, ohc, 85 hp.

LAND CRUISER (See *STUDEBAKER*)

L and E (1922-1931) Lundelius & Eccleston, Los Angeles. 6-cylinder, air-cooled engine; various experimental models.

LANE (1920)

LARK (See *LEXINGTON*)

LARRE-BEE-DEYO (1920) Primarily commercial vehicles.

LAUREL (1916-1920) Laurel Motors Corp., Anderson, Indiana. 4-cylinder G.B.&S. engine; name of car in small script above hood louvres.

LEHIGH (1926)

LENOT (1912-1922)

LEVER (See *ELCAR*)

LEWIS AIRMOBILE (1937)

LIMITED (See *BUICK*)

LITTLE (1921)

LITTLEMAC (1930-1931) Thompson Motor Corp., Muscatine, Iowa; small cars with 4-cyl. Durant-Star engines.

LITTLE TOMBOY (See *JORDAN*, 1928)

LOMGARD (1921)

LONE STAR (1920-1922) Lone Star Motor Truck and Tractor Corp., San Antonio, Texas. Assembled by *Piedmont*: Model "4-30" with 4-cyl. Lycoming engine, model "6-40" with 6-cyl. Lycoming engine.

LONG (1923)

LOYAL (1920)

LUXOR CAB (1920-1926)

MacDONALD (1923)

MAGIC (1922)

MAJESTIC (1925)

MANEXALL (1921) Manufacturers and Exporters Alliance, N.Y.C. Small car with 2-cyl. De Luxe air-cooled engine; 13 hp at 2500 rpm.

MANHATTAN (1921)

MARLAN (1920)

MARSH (1919-1921) Marsh Motors Co., Cleveland, Ohio; 6 cylinders.

MARSHALL (1919-1921) Marshall Mfg. Co., Chicago. 4-cyl. Lycoming engine; touring cars only.

MARTIN (1920; 1926) **MARTIN SCOOTMOBILE** (1920-1922) **MARTIN AERODYNAMIC** (1928-1932)

MARTIN DART (1929-1932) Martin Motors, Inc., Washington, D.C. Martin Aeroplane factory, Hagerstown, Md. and Garden City, L.I., N.Y. 4-cylinder Cleveland motorcycle engine; 60" wheelbase.

MARTIN-WASP (See *WASP*)

MASON (1922)

MASTER (See *BUICK, CHEVROLET,* and *REO*)

MATE (See *REO*, 1929)

MATHIS (1930-1931)

MAXIM (1920; 1928)

MAYFAIR (1925)

McCARRON (1929)

McCURDY (1922)

McGEE STEAMER (1937)

McGILL (1922) McGill Motor Car Co., Fort Worth, Texas; 6 cylinders.

MECHANICS (1925)

MEECH-STODDARD (1924)

MEL SPECIAL (1921)

MENARD (1921)

MERCU (1909-1929)

MERIT (1920-1923) Merit Motor Co., Cleveland; 6-cyl. Continental engine.

METEOR (1919-1922) Meteor Motors, Inc., Philadelphia. 4-cyl. Rochester-Duesenberg engine; 129" wheelbase, 4.41 gear ratio.

METROPOLITAN (1922-1923) Metropolitan Motors, Inc., Kansas City, Mo. Late in 1922, own 4-cylinder engine replaced Continental engine formerly used.

METZ (1908-1922) Metz Co., Waltham, Mass. Master 6 had 6 cylinders, 230.1 cid, 45 hp; replaced in 1922 by *WALTHAM* car. Rutenber engine, 120" wheelbase, 32"x4" tires; gear ratios were 4.63 (1920) and 4.67 (1921).

MEYER (1922)

MICHELET (1921)

MILWAUKEE (1925)

MINUTE MAN 6 (See *LEXINGTON*)

MOLIGAN (1920)

MOLINE-KNIGHT (See *R & V KNIGHT*)

MOLLER (1920-1921) Moller Motor Car Co., Lewistown, Pa. 4 cylinders, right-hand drive, designed for export; taxicabs also.

MOR-POWER (1920)

MORRISSEY (1925)

M.P.C. (1925)

MURRAY 6 (MURRAY-MAC) (1921-1928) Murray Motor Car Co., Atlantic, Mass.

NATIONAL (See *CHEVROLET*, 1928)

NAVARRE 6 (1921) A.C. Schulz, Springfield, Mass.; pilot models only.

NEVIN (1927)

NEWCOMB (1921)

NEW ORLEANS (1920)

NEW VOGUE (See *WILLS SAINTE CLAIRE*)

NEW YORK (1926)

NEW YORK 6 (1929) Automotive Corp. of America; New York Motors Co., Moline, Illinois — built by *Davis*. Unique "Parkmobile" device allowed car to move sideways into tight parking space.

NEW YORK SPECIAL (See *CHRYSLER*, 1938)

NEW YORKER (See *CHRYSLER*, 1939)

NILES (1921)

NOLAN (1924)

NORTHWAY 6 (1921) Northway Motor Sales Co., Natick, Mass.; Northway engine.

NORWALK (1910-1922) Norwalk Motor Car Co., Martinsburg, W. Va.; 6-cyl.

NUCAR (1929)

O'CONNELL (1928)

OFFENHAUSER (1934)

OLDFIELD (1924)

OLD RELIABLE (1926)

OLIVER (1935)

OLYMPIAN (1917-1921) Olympian Motors Co., Pontiac, Michigan. 4 cylinders. Tourist touring car and Gypsy roadster.

OLYMPIC (1920)

OMORT (1927)

ORIOLE (1927)

ORLEANS (1920)

OSHKOSH (1926)

PAGÉ (1921-1924) Victor W. Page Motors Corp., East Stamford, Conn. 4-cyl. aircraft-type engine; roadsters and coupes. Utility model, 1921-22.

PALMER-SINGER (See *SINGER*)

PAN-AMERICAN (1917-1922) Pan-American Motor Corp., Chicago & Decatur, Illinois. 6-cyl. Continental engine; American Beauty model, 1920-1921.

PARAGON 6 (1921-1922) Paragon Motor Car Co., Connellsville, Pa.; phaetons with disc wheels.

PARAMOUNT CAB (1924) Later models also known.

PATRIOT (1922)

PEDERSEN (1922) L.C. Pedersen Motor Car Co., Chicago. Had 2-cyl., 9 hp deluxe air-cooled engine, 70" wheelbase, 28"x3" tires, wire wheels, 5.0 gear ratio. Intended for mail-order sale.

PEET (1923-1926)

PENFORD (1924)

PENNANT (1923-1925) Barley Motor Car Co., Kalamazoo, Mich.; taxicabs.

PERU (1938)

PHANTOM (See *ROLLS-ROYCE*)

PHILADELPHIA (1924)

PICKWICK (1930)

PIONEER (1920)

PITCHER (1920)

PLAYBOY (See *JORDAN*)

POLO (1927)

POMEROY (1920-1924) Aluminum Co. of America, Cleveland. Six 4-cylinder cars built. After 1922, *Pierce-Arrow* built a 6-cyl.-model Pomeroy. Cars were primarily of aluminum, experimental, and not offered for sale to the public.

PONDER 6 (1923) Ponder Motor Mfg. Co., Shreveport, La. 6-cyl. Continental engine, successor to *Bour-Davis*.

POWER PLUS 6 (See *LEACH*)

PRADO 8 (1920-1922) Prado Motors Corp., N.Y.C. Had 8-cyl. converted Curtiss OX-5 aircraft engine, disc wheels, cycle-type fenders.

PREFERRED (1920)

PREMOCAR (1921-1923) Preston Motor Corp., Birmingham, Alabama; 6-cyl. Falls or 4-cyl. Rochester-Duesenberg engine.

PRESIDENT (See *STUDEBAKER*)

PRESTON (1921-1923) (See *PREMOCAR*)

PRINCETON (1923-1924) Durant Motors, Muncie, Indiana; 6-cyl. Ansted engine.

PROSPERITY 6 (See *GRAHAM*, 1931)

RADIO SPECIAL (See *GARDNER*)

RALEIGH 6 (1920-1922) Raleigh Motors, Inc., Reading, Pa.; Bridgeton, N.J. 6-cyl. Herschell-Spillman engine.

R & L ELECTRIC (1920) (See *RAUCH & LANG*)

RANGER 4 (1920-1922) Southern Motor Mfg. Assn., Houston. Own 4-cyl. engine; 6-cyl. available in 1922.

RED BALL (1924)

RED BUG (1923-1928) Automotive Electrical Service Co., Newark, N.J.; Standard Automobile Corp., North Bergen, N.J. Similar to *BRIGGS & STRATTON* buckboard auto, but with electric motor. Sometimes known as Auto Red Bug.

RED SEAL (See *CONTINENTAL*, 1934)

RED WING (1928)

REES (1921)

REGAL (1907-1920) Regal Motor Car Co., Detroit; 6 cylinders.

REILAND and BREE (1928)

REMEL-VINCENT STEAM (1923)

REYNOLDS (1920)

RIDDLE (1916-1926) Riddle Mfg. Co., Ravenna, Ohio; 6-cyl., 50 hp Continental engine.

RIESS-ROYAL (1922)

ROAD KING (1922) (see also *PLYMOUTH*, 1938-1939)

ROADMASTER (See *BUICK*, 1936-1939)

ROBE (1923)

ROCHE (1920; 1926)

ROCKET (1924)

ROCK FALLS (1919-1925) Rock Falls Mfg. Co., Sterling, Illinois; 6-cylinder Continental engine.

RODGERS (1923)

ROMER (1921-1922) Romer Motors Corp., Boston. 6-cyl. Continental engine. Trucks only after early 1922. Not to be confused with *Roamer*.

ROSS (1929)

ROTARIAN (1921)

ROTARY (1922-1923) Bournonville Motors Co., Hoboken, N.J.; 6-cyl. rotary-valve engine.

ROVENA FRONT-DRIVE (1926)

ROWE-STUART (1922)

ROYAL (See *CHANDLER*, also *CHRYSLER*)

ROYALE (See *REO*, 1931-1932)

RUBAY (See *LEON RUBAY*)

RUMLEY (1920)

SAFEWAY (1925)

SAF-T-CAB (1926-1932)

SALIENT 6 (See *STEPHENS*)

SAMSON (1922) Samson Tractor Co., Janesville, Wis., a division of General Motors Corp. Only one car known built, but trucks available until 1923.

SANDOW CAB (1925)

SARATOGA (See *CHRYSLER*, 1939)

SCARAB (See *STOUT*)

SCHWARTZ (1920)

SCIENTIFIC (1921)

SCOTT (1921)

SCOTT-NEWCOMB STEAM (1921) Standard Engineering Co., St. Louis.,

SEAGRAVE (1921)

SEKINE (1923) I. Sekine and Co., N.Y.C. Built for export to Japan; 4 cylinders.

SEMINOLE (1928)

SENECA (1917-1924) Seneca Motor Car Co., Fostoria, Ohio. Four cylinders — 138.1 cid Le Roi engine before 1922; 192.4 cid Lycoming engine used afterward. 108" wheelbase L model through 1921. New 1922 "50" had 112" wheelbase, but during 1923 the companion L-2 and O-2 had 108" wheelbase with same Lycoming engine as "50" and "51"; cid increased to 206.4 in 1924.

SENIOR 6 (See *DODGE*, 1927-1930)

SERRIFILE (1921)

SHAD-WYCK (1917-1923) Shadburne Bros., Chicago and Frankfort, Indiana. Starting in 1920, 4-cyl. Rochester-Duesenberg engine replaced 6-cyl. type.

SILVER ARROW (See *PIERCE-ARROW*, 1933-1934)

SILVER GHOST (See *ROLLS-ROYCE*)

SILVER MORN (See *HOWARD*)

SILVER STREAK (See *PONTIAC*, 1935-1939; see also *WILLYS*, 1932).

SIMMS (1920-1921) Simms Motor Car Co., Atlanta, Ga. Own 4-cyl. engine; touring cars only.

SIMPLICITY 6 (1921)

SINCLAIR (1921)

SKYLARK (See *HUPMOBILE*, 1939)

SMALL (1919-1922)

SMITH FLYER (1917-1920) A.O. Smith, Milwaukee; 1-cyl. buckboard-type with 5th, power, wheel.

S.N. (1921)

SOUTHERN (1921-1922) Southern Auto Mfg. Co., Memphis; 6-cyl. Herschell-Spillman engine.

SPACKE (See *BROOKE-SPACKE*)

SPEEDWAY ACE (See *JORDAN*, 1930)

SPEEDWAY 4; SPEEDWAY 6 (See *STUTZ*)

SPENCER (1921-1922) Research Engineering Co., Dayton, Ohio; with Spencer 4-cyl. engine.

SPERLING (1921-1923) Associated Motors Corp., Elkhart, Indiana (export).

SPORT (1921)

STANDARD (steam) (1920-1921) Standard Engineering Co., St. Louis; with Scott-Newcomb 2-cyl. steam engine.

STANDISH (1924-1925) Luxor Cab Mfg. Co., Framingham, Mass. (a subsidiary of *Dagmar*). 6-cyl. Continental engine; brass trim frequently used.

STATE PRESIDENT (See *STUDEBAKER*)

STATIC (1923) Static Motor Co., Philadelphia; Static Super-Cooled 6.

STEIN-KOENIG (1926)

STEINMETZ (1920)

STEWART-COATES (1922)

ST. CLOUD (1921)

ST. LOUIS (1922)

ST. REGIS (See *STUDEBAKER*, 1932-1933)

STORK-KAR (1919-1921) Affiliated with *PIEDMONT*; probably from Norwalk and Martinsburg, W. Va.

STRATTON 4 (1923) Stratton Motors Corp., Indianapolis; own 4-cylinder engine.

SUBMARINE SPEEDSTER (See *DANIELS*)

SUCCESS (1920)

SUN (1921-1924) The Automotive Corp., Toledo, Ohio; with 4-cyl., air-cooled Cameron engine.

SUPER-COOLED 6 (see *STATIC*)

SUPER TRACTION (1923)

SUPREME (1922; 1930)

TAIT (1923)

TARKINGTON 6 (1922-1923) Tarkington Motor Car Co., Rockford, Illinois. Own 6-cyl. engine; touring cars.

TAYLOR (1921)

TEMPLE-WESTCOTT 6 (1921-1922) Amesbury, Mass. Not affiliated with *WESTCOTT* car.

TEXMOBILE (1921-1922) Little Motors Kar Co., Dallas; 4-cylinder Texmobile engine.

THOMART (1921)

THORNE (1929)

TITAN VIM (1925)

TJAARDA (1934) Experimental.

TRABOLD (1921)

TRASK-DETROIT (1922) (See *DETROIT STEAM CAR*)

TRAVELER (1924)

TRAYLOR (1920)

TRIUMPH (1920)

TRUE BLUE 6 (See *OAKLAND*, 1924)

UNIVERSAL (See *CHEVROLET*, 1930)

ULTIMATE (1920)

UTILITY (1921-1922) Victor W. Page Motors Corp., Stamford, Conn.

VALLEY DISPATCH (1927)

VAUGHN (1923)

VERNON ABLE 8 (1915-1920) Vernon Automobile Corp., Mt. Vernon, N.Y.; V-8 engine.

VERSARE (1928)

VETERAN (1921)

VICTOR (1921)

VICTORS (1923)

VICTORY (1920)

VICTORY MOON (See *MOON*)

VICTORY SIX (See *DODGE*, 1928-1929)

VOGUE (1917-1923) Vogue Motor Car Co., Tiffin, Ohio. 6-cyl. Continental and Herschell-Spillman engines; 119" wheelbase.

VREELAND (1920)

VULCAN (1920)

WALTER (1921)

WARD (1921)

WASHINGTON 6 (1921-1923) Washington Motor Co., Middletown and Eaton, Ohio; 6-cyl. Continental engine.

WEBBERVILLE (1920)

WHARTON 8 (1921-1922) Wharton Motors Co., Dallas. Had Curtiss OX-5 aircraft engine (modified); 4 and 6-cyl. models also planned.

WHITCOMB (1928)

WHITE EAGLE (See *KISSEL*, 1929)

WHITE PRINCE (See *WINDSOR*, 1929)

WINDSOR (See *CHRYSLER*, 1939)

WINFIELD (1921)

WING MIDGET (1922) H.C. Wing & Sons, Greenfield, Mass.; small car with racing-type body.

WITT THOMPSON (1921-1923)

WIZARD (1921-1922) Wizard Auto. Co., Charlotte, N.C.; air-cooled V-2 engine.

WOLVERINE (1917-1920) Wolverine Motors, Inc., Kalamazoo, Mich.; 4-cyl. Rochester-Duesenberg engine. (See also *REO*, 1928-1929)

WRIGHT (1925)

YALE (1921) (See also *DORT*)

YELLOW KNIGHT (1928)

YOUNG (1921)